Sustainable School Transformation

ALSO AVAILABLE FROM BLOOMSBURY

Learn to Transform: Developing a 21st Century Approach to Sustainable School Transformation, David Crossley and Graham Corbyn
Tweak to Transform: Improving Teaching - A Practical Handbook for School Leaders, Mike Hughes
Rethinking Educational Leadership: From Improvement to Transformation, John West-Burnham

Sustainable School Transformation

An inside-out school led approach

DAVID CROSSLEY

B L O O M S B U R Y

LONDON · NEW DELHI · NEW YORK · SYDNEY

Bloomsbury Academic

An imprint of Bloomsbury Publishing Plc

50 Bedford Square	1385 Broadway
London	New York
WC1B 3DP	NY 10018
UK	USA

www.bloomsbury.com

Bloomsbury is a registered trade mark of Bloomsbury Publishing PLC

First published 2013

British Library Cataloguing-in-Publication Data
A catalogue record for this book is available from the British Library.

ISBN:	HB:	978-1-7809-3675-8
	PB:	978-1-7809-3817-2
	ePub:	978-1-7809-3783-0
	ePDF:	978-1-7809-3791-5

Library of Congress Cataloging-in-Publication Data
Crossley, David, 1956
Sustainable school transformation : an inside-out school led approach / David Crossley.
pages cm
Includes bibliographical references and index.
ISBN 978-1-78093-675-8 (hardback) – ISBN 978-1-78093-817-2 (pbk.) –
978-1-78093-791-5 (epdf) – ISBN 978-1-78093-783-0 (epub) 1. School improvement programs–United States. 2. School improvement programs–Great Britain. I. Title.
LB2822.82.C794 2013
371.2′07–dc23
2013017198

Typeset by Newgen Knowledge Works (P) Ltd., Chennai, India
Printed and bound in Great Britain

Contents

Acknowledgements

First, I want to thank all the system leaders, school leaders and other educators who have either directly contributed to this work or have contributed to the thinking that inspired me to embark on it.

Secondly, I want to particularly thank my wife Ione for her practical support in proofing the final manuscript, for her tolerance of the demands the development and, particularly, the completion of the book in December and early January 2013 put on family life and also for her role as a sounding board drawing on her professional experience as an educator too.

I want to thank all those who by their efforts and actions clearly model and demonstrate that answers to real school and system improvement lie within schools and the system itself. Further I want to pay particular attention to all those who have a leadership role at whatever level in the system who understand that the very greatest things are achieved when the relationships are right and when they play their part in fostering and unleashing the creativity of both their colleagues and the students in their care.

Finally, I hope that in some small way this book will give you the confidence to seize the agenda as you play your part in enabling every student to achieve their potential.

David Crossley
February 2013

Notes on contributors

David Carter is Executive Principal of the Cabot Learning Federation. The federation consists of ten Academies in East Bristol, including the John Cabot Academy where David was Principal from 2003–7. David joined the Department for Children, Schools and Families (DCSF), UK, to lead the National Remodeling Team, supporting primary, special and secondary schools to introduce the workforce remodeling programme.

Pat Collarbone taught for 28 years in inner-city London and established a reputation for innovation and achievement during her headship at Haggerston School in Hackney. In 1996 she established the London Leadership Centre at the Institute of Education, University of London, UK. In September 2002 she was seconded from the Institute of Education as Director of Leadership Development Programmes to the National College for School Leadership (NCSL), UK, a post she held until December 2004. Recently she has been involved in the design and development of online material for the National Professional Qualification for Headship (NPQH), UK, Headstart, UK and the Accelerate to Headship programme, UK, as well as the National Standard for School Principals in Australia.

Jonathan Crossley-Holland was Director of Children's Services for Sheffield City Council, UK, for 12 years. Sheffield became in this period one of the best-run cities as judged by external inspection and had the mostly highly rated childrens' services of any major city. He joined Tribal PLC as Director of Strategy for Children's Services in 2008 and is now an independent education consultant and is one of two Education Advisers to the School Teacher Review Body.

Jonathan De Sausmarez is Executive Headteacher of Romsey School in Hampshire, UK. He previously taught at an outstanding school in Winchester and currently supports the Academies and Enterprise Trust academy chain, UK.

John Dunford, a former teacher and Headteacher, was General Secretary of the Association of School and College Leaders (ASCL) from 1998–2010 and is currently an independent Education Consultant. He also chairs: Worldwide

Volunteering, Whole Education and the Chartered Institute of Educational Assessors.

Simon Edkins has worked as an organizational consultant for nearly 30 years with clients drawn from both the private and public sectors including media, health, IT, telecommunications, banking, insurance, logistics and utilities. For the past six years he has worked with Dame Pat leading change programmes in schools, further and higher education.

Karine George is a very experienced headteacher working in a large junior school in Hampshire, classified as Outstanding by Ofsted in September 2011. As an active research practitioner Karine is an ardent advocator of technology to support twenty-first-century learning. As a result her school has won a number of awards including Leadership and Vision for the development of ICT, Third Millenium Learning and Parental Engagement. Karine has contributed to a number of articles on a range of educational issues and has spoken for a number of organizations on how technology is changing the learning landscape.

Mark Grundy is Executive Headteacher of Shireland Collegiate academy in the West Midlands, UK. He developed Shireland Learning and is one of the leading proponents of Learning Gateways and use of ICT in education.

Marc Hill was hired as the first Chief Education Officer for the Nashville Area Chamber of Commerce, USA, in 2007, reshaping the organization's work to improve public K-12 education in Nashville, USA. He currently serves as Chief Policy Officer, leading the Nashville Chamber's advocacy efforts at the state and local level to create an environment in which businesses can prosper. His work in education policy includes roles with the Nashville Mayor's Office and the Tennessee state legislature.

Chris Holmwood is Senior Deputy Headteacher at Shenley Brook End School in Milton Keynes, UK, and is Principal of the school's Leadership and Training Centre. The Leadership and Training Centre aims to grow the skills and confidence of those who work in school communities in order to develop their leadership potential and contribute to the creation of an educational climate that makes it possible for young people to do the same.

Jeff Hale is a former teacher, deputy head and school adviser for assessment who is now a qualified school inspector and regularly quality assures reports for Ofsted.

David Jackson was a headteacher for 14 years and is an expert on education, leadership, organization and system change. He is a Partner at the UK's Innovation Unit, a consultant to the Global Education Leaders Programme

(GELP) and has supported New York City's iZone initiative since 2010. Between 2000 and 2006 he was also a director at the National College for School Leadership, UK.

Judith Judd was formerly Editor and Editor at Large of the Times Educational Supplement and Education Editor of the Independent, UK.

James Park is a writer and organizational consultant. He was the founder-director of Antidote: Campaign for Emotional Literacy, which developed the PROGRESS Programme, a process that involves everyone in making their school great. The Programme is now delivered to schools by Human Scale Education, UK. Recent publications include *The Emotional Literacy Handbook* and *The Emotional Literacy Pocketbook*.

Jay Steele is Chief Academic Officer and also the Chief Officer for Secondary Education at Metro Nashville Public Schools in Nashville, USA. Prior to that he was Director for Career Education for the St. Johns County School District in St. Augustine, Florida, USA. His academy work in St. Johns County has become a national model.

Kirsty Tonks is e-Learning Director at The Collegiate Academy Trust, Shireland Learning Manager at The Collegiate Academy Trust, UK.

Michelle Wilcox is Lead Principal responsible for High School in the Metro Nashville Public Schools District in Tennessee, USA.

Alan Yellup is the Executive Head of Wakefield City Academy, UK, Head of the Wakefield Regional Teaching School Alliance, UK and Chief Executive Officer of the Wakefield City Academies Trust, UK. Alan and his team have provided extensive support for other schools in his roles which include RATL coordinator, School Improvement Partner, National Challenge Adviser, National Leader of Education and Consultant Head with the Specialist Schools and Academies Trust, UK (serving on the Leading Edge steering group) and Whole Education, UK.

Introduction

David Crossley

Achievement is addictive

The late American management guru Peter Drucker, in a powerful chapter called The Accountable School in his book *Post Capitalist Society*[1] said 'achievement is addictive'. He was talking about students. He argued those identifying students' strengths and building on them not only motivate, but also encourage them to build on things they are less good at too. This book is based on the premise that this notion of addictive achievement applies to staff and schools too and if we are to build a truly world-class system it will only be achieved through the motivation, engagement, buy-in and resultant efforts of all those in our schools. In the opening chapter of this book I draw on some influential international studies and reflect on their conclusions to guide us. I then explore an alternative approach that combines the rigour of traditionally top-down accountability models with the engagement and buy-in of school- and educator-led or 'inside-out' approaches. McKinsey and Company[2] in their book *How the World's Most Improved Systems Keep Getting Better* suggest an evaluation of 20 school systems, 'The journey from great to excellent systems focuses on creating an environment that will unleash the creativity and innovation of its educators'. Professors Andrew Hargreaves and Dennis Shirley argue in their book *The Fourth Way: The Inspiring Future for Educational Change*, 'the inspiring future of school improvement lies in the fear factor giving way to the peer factor'.[3] All this seems a long way away from top-down dictats, a focus on floor targets and harsh top-down, done to accountability regimes.

Inspired by the approach to delivering the Olympics in the United Kingdom in 2012 and the positive culture that was created, we explore lessons that we can learn and apply, not just about what we should do but how best to inspire and motivate educators and the students in our care. We pose the question of what could be achieved if we approach our schools and school systems in the same positive way. The book seeks to determine how we can best build a sustainable and truly world-class education system. There are many examples of world-class state schools and many examples of world-leading practices in both inner cities and more leafy suburbs. Yes we can, should and must improve further and few would deny that there is too much variation and that every child has a right to go to a good school. However, the important question is how can our systems best move forward?

The theme – *there is another away* – will be a common strand of each chapter as it explores ways, thoughts and reflections on both current practice and how every one of us can contribute to enabling every young person in our care to achieve. The book begins by exploring what world-class currently looks like, the increasing consensus about the future direction of travel and the suggested way for systems like our own to move forward. It progresses to explore what we can learn from the experiences of a range of contributors of current innovative approaches to teaching and learning in both the United Kingdom and the United States. It then explores what we can learn from them, how they were implemented and whether there is another way which will both deliver a sustainable world-class education system in our countries and more specifically how to develop schools and schools systems so they will really meet the needs of twenty-first-century learners and their communities.

The book will use the framework in Hargreaves and Shirley's *The Fourth Way*[4] – an inspiring future for educational change – to provide criteria to test how far the examples we include illustrate the characteristics they think we need to focus on. In addition, as few expect increased resources in the period ahead, one of the focuses in terms of sustainability will be on how schools can benefit from stopping doing things that are not making a difference. We will explore what could be abandoned and how existing resources might be re-deployed or improved.

In terms of what we can learn and do the lessons are all already out there and to me one of the best ways we can move forward and also influence policy within our countries is to learn from them and apply them in practice. This is something that we have more freedom in than we often think we do. The book seeks to give teachers, current and future school and system leaders the confidence to make a difference and to recognize that it is usually the sum of the parts that make the whole.

It offers a manifesto for change which includes:

1 making the most of the teachers we have and unleashing their creativity;

2 offering a curriculum that really meets the needs of twenty-first-century learners;

3 embedding effective collaboration within schools, between schools and between systems;

4 developing a smarter approach to accountability and use of data;

5 making the most of the choices we have.

By demonstrating what works, being bold and showing that more innovative approaches do not just develop wider skills but also deliver in conventional ways too is surely the best way forward.

This is not really about new money; it is about abandoning things and redeploying the resources we already have. It is about giving us the confidence to do something different in the knowledge that we are not alone and that there is a world of lessons to draw on to inform and help us assure we do the very best for all the young people in our care. As Henry Ford once remarked, 'if you believe you can or can't you are right!'

Notes

1 Drucker p. 184 ff.; Butterworth Heinemann 1993.
2 McKinsey and Company 2010.
3 Hargreaves and Shirley 2009.
4 Hargreaves and Shirley (2009).

PART ONE

Becoming World Class

1

From Theory to Practice

David Crossley

An inside out approach

This book is based on the premise that if we are to build a truly world-class system it will only be achieved through the motivation, buy-in and resultant efforts of all those in our schools. The major focus of the book is *how* this can best be achieved. We explore an alternative approach that combines the engagement and buy in of school- and educator-led or inside-out approaches with the rigour of traditionally top-down accountability models and offer another way as Figure 1.1 illustrates.[1]

Figure 1.1 illustrates and compares a system level outside-in and inside-out approach to change. An outside-in or top-down approach illustrated on the left-hand side of the diagram both determines and manages the implementation of policy. It creates and adds cost through complex and often ever-growing armies of people outside schools, some who support implementation and others who check on compliance. At a system level an inside-out approach, as illustrated on the right-hand side of the diagram suggests that it is perfectly acceptable and appropriate for governments to determine what they want from a school's system and for educators to advise, inform and seek to influence that. Their obligation is to generate a

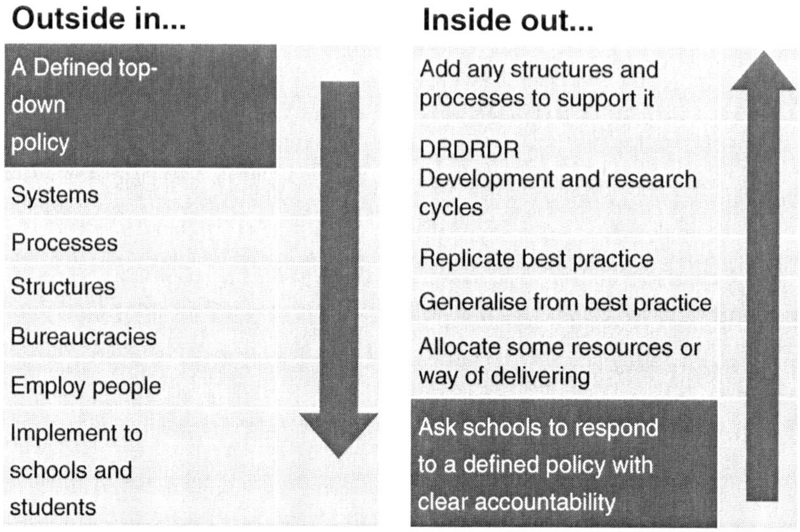

Outside in...

A Defined top-down policy

Systems

Processes

Structures

Bureaucracies

Employ people

Implement to schools and students

Inside out...

Add any structures and processes to support it

DRDRDR
Development and research cycles

Replicate best practice

Generalise from best practice

Allocate some resources or way of delivering

Ask schools to respond to a defined policy with clear accountability

FIGURE 1.1 *An inside-out approach*

buy-in and broad acceptance of those goals and aspirations among educators and the wider community. This is less difficult than it can be made to be with appropriate give and take, as its foundation is a core moral purpose for a society and for educators: to enable all young people to achieve their potential. What is less acceptable and usually far less effective in the long term is for governments to seek to prescribe how these goals are achieved. Traditional outside-in approaches often create both a culture of fear and a pressure for quick fixes rather than longer-term sustainable solutions. Study of business and other organizations reveals that you have to get the culture right if you are to achieve real change. The concern is that top-down solutions rarely generate a positive culture but at the same time there is a fear that unless hard accountability exists schools, public education systems will simply not move forward. While not rejecting accountability strategies, this book explores and questions why so much resource is invested in what is in effect quality control when far better value could be achieved from investing the same resources in getting things right in the first place and working with rather than in some ways against schools.

The benefits of inside-out approaches apply at a locality and school level too

The danger of outside-in approaches is that they can end up being replicated throughout the system at a locality and school level too. An inside-out approach is important within localities and schools as Figure 1.2 below illustrates. The problem here is that the traditional model of school leadership is based on executive authority and under outside-in pressure a top-down, 'done to' approach can be endemic within localities and schools too.

An irony of the English system with almost total devolution of economic resources to the school level is that engagement with important debates about how resources are used stops at the school leader's office door. Team leaders in schools become animated by the amount spent or not spent on curriculum resource, yet this is at most 5 per cent of the cost of operating their team. Staff are not only the most important but they are the most expensive resource and there are choices that can be made at this level too. This is not to say there is never a case for a top-down approach. As we will see in the next part of this chapter this can be effective in the early stages of improving very weak schools systems but it is certainly not the way the best systems have achieved their success and keep improving. A top-down

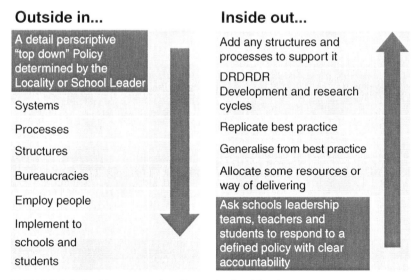

Outside in...

A detail perscriptive "top down" Policy determined by the Locality or School Leader

Systems

Processes

Structures

Bureaucracies

Employ people

Implement to schools and students

Inside out...

Add any structures and processes to support it

DRDRDR
Development and research cycles

Replicate best practice

Generalise from best practice

Allocate some resources or way of delivering

Ask schools leadership teams, teachers and students to respond to a defined policy with clear accountability

FIGURE 1.2 *Inside-out at a locality and school level*

approach can be an effective initial catalyst for change but unless it moves on, distributes leadership and develops real buy-in and engagement its success will be limited and arguably unsustainable. In many situations it may not even be the best way of improving failing systems or schools. Provided a community and its educators are prepared to get on the bus, what better way of creating long-term, sustainable change than generating engagement, buy-in and responsibility from the beginning of the journey?

> The inspiring future of school improvement lies in the fear factor giving way to the peer factor. (Hargreaves and Shirley 2009)

There is another way: to build in a positive journey from where systems, localities, schools and teachers are. This is motivating and builds on the fact that no educator came into this job to help students do worse at school. Professors Andrew Hargreaves and Dennis Shirley argue in their book *The Fourth Way – The Inspiring Future for Educational Change*, 'the inspiring future of school improvement lies in the fear factor giving way to the peer factor.'[2] All this seems a long way away from top-down dictats, a focus on floor targets and harsh top-down, done to accountability regimes. We are all prisoners of our background and products of our past. This is of course true of all those at a leadership level in our school systems and our schools. The past impacts on what we do in the present and can guide us about both what to do and not to do in the future. There are lessons to learn, but what are the right ones? When we consider emerging or future practice that will yield world-class systems the danger is that we will simply feel it is not how you do things. Yet outside education many of the now most successful companies have often emerged very quickly and certainly have done things very differently than their equivalents would have done before.

This first chapter will begin by drawing on international lessons we can learn from and apply whether it is as teacher or team within a school, a school as whole, for groups of schools when they collaborate together or at a system level. It seeks to offer guidance for school and systems leaders at all levels about the roles they can play and to give them the confidence to stay true to core principles and an all-pervading moral purpose to do the very best for all students in their care. It will draw on major research studies and practical examples from successful countries and jurisdictions.

The chapter will also describe and then use the framework in Hargreaves and Shirley's *The Fourth Way*,[3] to provide criteria to test how far the examples we include in later chapters illustrate the characteristics they think we need to focus on. In addition, as few expect new resources or a growth of resources in the period ahead, one of the focuses in terms of sustainability will be on how schools make the most of the choices they have by stopping doing things that are not making a difference by exploring what they are abandoning or could abandon, and how they redeploy or make better use of existing resources. This can be seen as something negative but in reality if approached in the right spirit it can be seen as empowering and something that helps us all recognize and make the most of choices we have.

It is the sum of the parts that make the whole.

In terms of what we can learn and do, the lessons are all already out there and to me one of the best ways we can move forward and also influence policy within our countries is to understand them and apply them in practice. This is something that we have more freedom over than we often think we do; thus we can learn from studies of the world's best performing systems and the growing consensus about what systems need to do at different stages of their improvement journey. Above all else the book seeks to give teachers and current and future school and system leaders the confidence to make a difference and to recognize that it is usually the sum of the parts that make the whole.

International lessons – theories behind the practice

The first McKinsey report – How the world's best performing school systems come out on top

McKinsey and company have published two influential reports on global education systems. *How the world's best performing school systems come out on top*,[4] first published in 2007, came to the relatively simple conclusion that if a system can attract the best people to become teachers then it will be successful. They cited countries like Finland where teaching was described as a highly attractive profession to join and was highly regarded by wider society. This was contrasted with countries like the United States where in general students with lower grade degrees tended to become teachers and this led to a plethora of strategies to attract the most able into teaching with Teach for America,[5] Teach First[6] and Future Leaders[7] in the United Kingdom being three important and successful schemes. At a system level the problem is that attracting more high calibre candidates into teaching is a very slow burning solution and it raises the question for the immediate term of whether it is possible to do much more than tinker at the edges with the quality of those who choose to be teachers. The report also led to a strong focus on best practice and how we can replicate it. Teachers attended professional development sessions where outstanding practitioners and other experts demonstrated excellence and they went back to the schools thinking, 'I can't do that here'. In England the National Curriculum and National Strategies[8] included attempts to pre-plan exactly how teachers should teach and deliver lessons. This in effect accepted the variability in the quality of teachers as unsolvable but by treating teachers as technicians sought to ensure a guaranteed minimum quality for every lesson. It was largely successful as studies of the UK National Curriculum between 1997 and 2003 show but then it tailed off. It seemed to be able to lift a system from satisfactory to good but it fell short of being able to deliver something world-class and in the twenty-first century's fast-changing world this simply is not good enough.

The second report – How the world's most improved systems keep getting better

In 2010 McKinsey and company published their second, and to me far more significant, study – *How the world's most improved systems keep getting better.*[9] They sought to answer two key questions:

1   How does a system with modest performance become great?

2   Which aspects of a school system reform journey are universal and which are context-specific?

They studied 20 different school systems and gathered and studied the experiences of nearly 575 reform interventions, based on interviews with more than 200 system leaders and their staff, supplemented by visits to view all 20 systems in action. They codified their research and they created a four-stage performance spectrum:

1   From poor to fair;

2   From fair to good;

3   From good to great;

4   From great to excellent.

In their research they only classified one system, Finland, as excellent and their group of 20 included 'sustained improvers', Singapore, Ontario and

Poland and a second set, 'promising starts' too. From this they observed dominant clusters of interventions that all improving systems carried out at each journey stage on the long path from poor to excellent. They found six interventions occurred with equal frequency across all journeys.[10]

Six common interventions

1 Building the instructional skills of teachers;
2 Improving the management skills of principals;
3 Assessing students, improving data systems;
4 Facilitating improvement through the introduction of policy documents and education laws;
5 Revising standards and curriculum;
6 Ensuring an appropriate reward and remuneration structure for teachers and principals.

McKinsey 2010

There are two key conclusions that arise from this. First systems should learn most from systems that are at a similar or the next stage in the journey to their own system and second, a system will not continue to improve, in their own words, 'by simply doing more of what brought them past success'. The first conclusion could also be applied to developing teachers where an undue focus on attempting to learn from the very best may well not be the best way to help a teacher improve from being satisfactory to good. The latter conclusion was a lesson that the UK system failed to learn after the initial successes in the late 1990s. In addition the difference in how certain interventions are implemented at different performance stages revealed a particularly important element of their study – *how was often more important than what* so that how you implemented an intervention at particular stages of an improvement journey is more important than the intervention itself. Further, their interviews with system leaders suggest that one of the most important implementation decisions is the emphasis a system places on *mandating* versus *persuading*[11] stakeholders to comply with reforms.

> The journey from great to excellent systems focuses on creating an environment that will unleash the creativity and innovation of its educators.[12]

A further important lesson is that the good to great and great to excellent stages involve greater degrees of informed professionalism. Good and improving systems like the United States and United Kingdom have found this change in method a hard one to make. This could explain why both systems seem to have plateaued and why despite growing levels of expenditure they have not kept improving at the same rate as the best systems. The McKinsey study provides a detailed analysis of what the world's best systems have done and are doing at different stages in their improvement journey.[13] In summary:

- Poor to fair systems – focus on literacy and numeracy and a common menu of central interventions;

- Fair to good systems – focus on consolidation, embedding systems and a greater focus on student skills;

- Good to great – focus on shaping the teaching profession and its professionalization;

- Great to excellent – focus on improving through peer-led support and teaching innovation.

The lessons that can be drawn from each stage are instructive too. Fair to good systems recognize that most initiatives failed because of the quality of implementation not the concept or idea. In my view this is not usually the focus of educators and school systems tend not to be leading edge on quality systems and quality of implementation. Secondly, the 'great to excellent' journey in what McKinsey terms as the final frontier of school improvement focuses on creating an environment that will unleash the creativity and innovation of its educators and other stakeholder groups. The interventions used for the journey *from great to excellent* serve further to enhance the educators' responsibility for looking after each other's development; the systems give their teachers the time, resources and flexibility to reflect upon and try out new ideas to better support student learning.

There were some further concluding observations in their work including one that challenges orthodox thinking about *the importance of context*. They did not say that context is not important, but that it is secondary to getting the fundamentals right. Context is something schools and systems often hide behind when challenged, versions of 'you don't understand my . . . class, school, village or town or even system' are common excuses given by educators but this study in part challenges that as they see context as being more about how you do things in that context rather than what you do. They also expressed their view about *how long it takes for a system to change significantly* and viewed that systems at all performance levels can improve outcomes substantially in as short a time as six years. There are key lessons here for system leaders when planning school improvement programmes. When did we last hear politicians talk of a six-year journey? Six years is both a very short and a long period of time. In political terms it is beyond the term of office of many elected national or state governments. However an inevitable and undue focus on just the immediate can clearly detract from longer-term improvement and is something to be guarded against. A political reality and a moral purpose for students currently in our schools is likely to require immediate gains but the lesson to me here is that these gains need to be integrated into and be part of a longer-term plan. Finally, their report also shows that *a school system can improve from any starting point.* Further I would argue that by concentrating on schools as a whole rather than parts of schools, significant capacity for system change can be lost by failing to unleash the creativity in the pockets of greatness that exist within most schools, not just the schools that are the best overall. To me building from where schools are and moving forward in a positive way is surely far more likely to motivate and lead to sustainable long-term improvement.

The Fourth Way

This provides a useful link to our next key text that we draw lessons from, Hargreaves and Shirley's *The Fourth Way*[14] which looks at and categorizes trends in school improvement over the last three decades. Their greatest unease is over the prescription for all the systems that are less than good and I suspect they have concerns over judging and responding to systems as a whole and are therefore in some ways critical of the McKinsey reports. In their words, 'The Fourth Way is based upon substantial first hand assessments of high performing systems and promising practices from around the world'.[15] These include Finland, Singapore, the Canadian state of Alberta, an American district, a London borough and a national raising achievement network RATL[16] that I had the privilege to lead and learn from between 2004 and 2008.

The first part of their book reflects on the past and categorizes four time-specific stages of school improvement.

Four ways of educational change

- 1950s–1980s – A First Way of state support and professional freedom; of innovation but also of inconsistency;
- 1990s onwards – A Second Way of market competition and educational standardization in which professional autonomy is lost;
- 2000 onwards – A Third Way – *the both and way* – that tries to navigate between and beyond the market and the state, and balance professional autonomy with accountability;
- The Fourth Way – an inspiring future for Educational Change.

Hargreaves and Shirley 2009

TABLE 1.1 What to retain and what to abandon from the first three ways

	Retain	Abandon
FIRST WAY	Inspiration, innovation and autonomy	Inconsistency and professional license
INTERREGNUM	Broad standards with devolved interpretation	Weak development of teachers, leaders and communities
SECOND WAY	Urgency, consistency and all-inclusive equity	Exhaustive prescription and standardization
THIRD WAY	Balance and inclusiveness; professional networks; public involvement; financial reinvestment	Persistent autocracy; imposed targets; overreliance on measurable data

In my view, as we will see in the section that follows, the authors would describe the first two and even much of the third stage of the McKinsey model as Second and Third Way approaches but I also think there is a clear link between their Fourth Way and the McKinsey good to excellent stage.

They urge that we should not reject the past but sort out which aspects should be rekindled and which ones left behind. They progress to both identify and explore the legacies each 'Way' has left us and distinguish what we should keep or retrieve, and what we should abandon. Their summary of things to retain and abandon from the first three ways is shown in Table 1.1.

Why the Third Way failed

While sympathetic to the aims of the Third Way – in their words '*both/and* thinking is plain commonsense for most teachers' – they then argue that its great promise has not been fulfilled because 'paths of distraction' have diverted us from it.

In their view many Third Way policies have drifted from the Way's original ideals – alienating students, corrupting classrooms, manipulating educators and deceiving the public. This statement could be seen as a proxy for the reasons why the current approaches to school improvement in both the United States and United Kingdom are not delivering and why there is a need to learn from and apply the real lessons from the best systems. In their words, 'the elephant in the room of the Third Way was an excess of government control.

It is time now to forge a Fourth Way that will create more room inside the government elephant'.[17] They identify the distractions as *autocratic imposition* of targets and testing, *technocratic obsessions* with data and spreadsheets and *effervescent enthusiasm* of teachers in securing quick lifts in test gains. The first two distractions are key tools and accountability measures used by both the UK and US governments and the third is a problem that arises not just from external pressures but also from within the profession itself. Educators rush around, energetically and enthusiastically delivering the government's narrowly defined targets and purposes, rather than also developing and realizing inspiring purposes of their own. Schools in their words become addictive organizations, obsessed with meeting targets, raising performance standards and adjusting strategies right down to intervening with every individual child: 'Each jump in scores gives educators another fix to exchange and apply more of the same short-term strategies, focused on measurable results.'[18] This addiction to the immediate in their view derives not just from politicians and system leaders but can also come from teachers themselves. Faced with 30 demanding young people in a classroom immediate answers are appealing but they can provide a trap or a hamster wheel that is impossible to escape from. Worse still this urgency addiction to the immediate does not produce world-class schools or outcomes.

The Fourth Way framework

- An inclusive vision with school, communities and partnerships working together;
- Learning that is creative engaging and demanding;
- Prudent accountability;
- Shared ambitious improvement targets;
- Strong schools helping their weaker peers;
- An evidence informed rather than data driven profession;
- Sustainable leadership that spreads and lasts.

Hargreaves and Shirley 2009

The authors progress to argue that we are entering an age of post-standardization in education. In their words 'It may not look, smell or feel like it, but the augers of the new age have already arrived'. They argue,

It's time for a change that is disruptive not incremental. It is time to bring the magic and wonder back into teaching. It is time to recover the missionary spirit and deep moral purpose of inspiring all students. It is time to put down the spreadsheets and look to each other and elsewhere for how to get beyond the present turning point so we can transform our society and schools.[19]

Hargreaves and Shirley offer a framework which we will use to both reflect on the examples in the book and also to test them against their characteristics.

Abandonment and redeployment of existing resources – a key lever for sustainable school transformation

The one thing that is clear in discussion with school and system leaders is that few expect the level of resources to increase in the period ahead. If sustainable and real transformation is the goal this must not be an inhibitor to change. There is a lesson for many schools and school systems here. Schools and schools systems tend to incrementally add to what they do already all the time. Traditionally a new initiative usually comes with the carrot of some new resources, and often this is not quite enough. This tends to result in a shift of emphasis and in doing things we do already less well, and not doing the new things as well as they could be done. It some ways this avoids hard choices but also tends to contribute to overloading schools and school systems. This is certainly unsustainable and is why we argue throughout this book that abandonment, stopping doing some of the things we do now and redeployment or using the capacity and resources released, is a key lever for sustainable school transformation.

Origins

Abandonment's origins are explored in Schumpeter's book *Capitalism, Socialism and Democracy* and the economic concept of Creative Destruction[20] – an inspiring phrase that is a good fit with our wider objectives of sustainable transformation of schools. It is also, going back to its origins, highly appealing in times of recession in terms of how to get more for money already invested rather than the negative and destructive notion of simply how to cut costs.

At first sight it is initially very appealing to schools as staff often feel overloaded. Abandonment offers an opportunity to create capacity by abandoning some of what you do now, concentrates on core purpose and makes a difference. If you ask a group of teachers if there are things they would like to abandon they are very enthusiastic. However as the main resource in schools is staff, abandonment very quickly enters the territory of people's roles, responsibilities and status: at that point people can become defensive. This is a key point and a challenge to leaders at all levels; and this is a time for a key decision on whether your approach is as a destroyer or builder. To me this is directly linked to one of the key ideas of this book that moves beyond simply attracting the best people into teaching, rather making the most of teachers we have at different points in their careers. I draw on two examples from my own career. When I was taking on responsibility for a failing school in England I met a 58-year-old head of languages. Hers was not an easy job. She was clearly a good teacher but was frustrated as students were not really motivated and did not want to study her subjects. Some days after a somewhat frank exchange of views I persuaded her to take responsibility for the schools' new learning centre that was to be open both before and after school. Within a few months she had enlisted and was supported by an army of undergraduates and postgraduates from the local university and was like a new person – she arrived before most others every day and left after them. She describes her first 18 months in the regenerated school as among the best in her career. My second example was in a large high school in the United States where a veteran teacher said to me that perhaps he should give up and leave it to the young guys like the one he was sitting next to. I said to them both that 'perhaps he can manage and relate to young people better than you'. The young teacher smiled and nodded in agreement. Two months later I revisited the school and they were working together delivering what by any standards was an energizing example of project-based learning. This is what is involved in creative destruction and redeployment of existing resources: identifying people's strengths and aspirations, thinking creatively, unleashing creativity and making the most of the talent we have. As was remarked at the beginning of this chapter, achievement is addictive! It is not always easy, and sometimes some, but in reality very few, will need to get off the bus. It can take time and trust needs to be built but the rewards for all involved are great. How can we as educators justify letting so much potential go untapped?

Abandonment is a concept that works at all levels. For a teacher it raises questions of how you can create time by doing things differently in your classroom, engaging students more and giving them more responsibility. For teams within schools and for a school as a whole it poses questions of how we can work together to save time rather than add more work. For school systems it can raise questions of the numbers involved who work outside schools and their roles. These ideas are summarized in Figure 1.3. In countries like England it has led to a focus on school improvement being led by those within schools rather than outside. For the government it involves questions of how much money is invested in quality control as opposed to quality assurance.

1 Abandonment at an individual level – what can I abandon, how do I employ myself and use my time? How can I make best use of the resource I have?

2 Abandonment at a team level – what can we as a team abandon, how do we re-deploy ourselves? How can we make best use of the resources; books, equipment, IT we have?

3 Abandonment at a school level – what can we as a school abandon, how can we re-deploy: the staff, other resources, time and spaces we have?

4 Abandonment at a middle or mediating tier level – linked to redefining the role, relationships, sharing responsibilities and use of staff and other resources

FIGURE 1.3 *Elements of abandonment*

So abandonment and redeployment of existing resources responds to the key questions and challenges posed in this chapter including:

- How do the world's most improved school systems keep getting better?
- How do we help more young people to achieve their potential?
- How do we enable a greater degree of informed professionalism to drive the next stage in school improvement?
- How do we make sure less can be more? – You can do anything but not everything.
- How do we sustain what we achieve?
- How can we help raise the ceiling as well as the floor?

Used in the right ways it empowers educators and reduces the dependency culture which can often suit governments and systems. It gives choices to staff at all levels and avoids them always having to ask for more. The solutions it generates are usually practical and practice driven. It can go further and be a cost effective way of linking best practice to next practice. It can create a 'can do' culture but benefits depend on how it is approached and what it is used for, that is linked to the most important thing of all: how can we create and foster a positive culture?

A greater focus on implementation

This is all linked to putting a greater focus on implementation and the key reasons why most things succeed or fail. In my work in supporting school improvement I tend to find schools know what they want to do but have often paid little attention or inadequate attention to the how's. The best schools have effective systems and processes – the way they do things – but they are often in people's heads and transferred by word of mouth. This is great as an embedded process but that is an end game not a first step. Abandonment tackles the issue of creating sustainable systems too. It engages with efficiency, effectiveness and sustainable quality. Educators are often perfectionists and in my experience if you ask any group of educators to set up a system it will probably be unsustainable. So the question to ask at the beginning is not whether it will work at the start of the new school year but whether it will work mid-November or February. Another important lesson in creating sustainable systems is to always move a stage beyond writing policies – rather than write a policy, describe the practice and the process. I remember vividly my own first school inspection when a formidable inspector said to me 'Mr Crossley you have no policies in this school' – he paused for what seemed a very long period of time and then said, 'what you have is very clear simple descriptions of what you do and how you do things and that is good enough for me!'

Effective implementation of current systems and ways of doing things are something separate but linked to wider transformation and change. They are in effect stages in development of abandonment; see Table 1.2. The first stage is to make the practice efficient and effective and possible to be complied with.

Refining and making existing systems sustainable

1 Write down the process, *carry out an initial check / consider / ask yourself if it is sustainable*;
2 Test the process and find out why it is or is not complied with. *In a school ask teachers and students as customers too*;
3 Refine, confirm and communicate the process;
4 Add simple ongoing quality assurance processes to ensure you sustain an embedded process.

The second stage involves re-imagining the practice. This approach can be applied to major, system-wide initiatives or day-to-day realities in school like the homework schedule. Ask the question: are they complied with? Then either make the expectations realistic and sustainable or rethink or re-envisage what you are seeking to achieve.

Always ask the question 'how far will any activity, function or initiative raise achievement and impact positively on students?'

TABLE 1.2 Stages of abandonment

Stage 1 Abandonment	Stage 2 Abandonment
First Stage is about efficiency and effectiveness of what we do now. It is about creating capacity. Most schools are doing many of the things that make a difference. If you 'optimize' what you are doing already it will often transform a school?	Second stage is about doing something radical; abandoning the way we do things and dramatically changing what we do and how we do things. However, one thing leads to another which in combination harmonizes and builds a sustainable journey to transformation

So, abandonment in my view is about, and is linked to, the fundamental questions and core purpose of schools of enabling every student to achieve their potential and the challenge to any school or district of how far the focus, efforts and expenditure of time is on learning and achievement. A good test is always to question how far any activity, function or initiative will raise achievement and positively impact on students. If not, abandon it. At a wider system level as Hargreaves and Shirley showed in *The Fourth Way* the lessons of almost four decades of educational change show us that we should *abandon* as much as we should *retain*. How do we avoid unacceptable inconsistencies in professional competence and quality? How do we evade the dead hand of standardization?

Autonomy

McKinsey and the Organisation for Economic Co-operation and Development (OECD) both identify greater autonomy as a key element of the best systems. This is linked to where in a system the right to make choices, including what to abandon and how to deploy resources, lies. It has been argued already that even in a centrally controlled system teachers and schools have more choices than they often think. However, there is a dichotomy in England where there is one of the world's greatest devolution of resources and decision making to the school level. England perhaps gave the wrong sort of autonomy or perhaps limited its potential in two ways. Financial autonomy was accompanied by exceptionally high levels of accountability and thereby enforcement of prescribed curricula which in turn limited creativity. In addition 'Second Way' thinking led to tracts of government initiatives attracting additional external funding for schools to implement these central policies so schools never took real responsibility for their teachers' development. Instead most did what they were told and the most autonomous system in the world gave relatively little autonomy to those who deliver in the classrooms. As a caricature there was autonomy to decide who to buy a photocopier from and who to employ but not on the core purpose of what they teach and how they teach it. In Finland maybe they made sure autonomy was in the right place.

How far can you replicate what is successful elsewhere?

There is one other question we need to reflect on to close this chapter and consider the range of inspiring examples that are explored in this book: how far can you replicate what is successful elsewhere? McKinsey argued that context is less important than we have often thought but that it is also about the hows of implementations rather than what you do. In *The Fourth Way* Hargreaves and Shirley express more concerns stressing that whether you are learning from a country or a state, from a network, community or district, it is important to approach this learning in the right spirit as it is not feasible to import change off-the-shelf either. The conclusions from Hargreaves and Shirley are instructive at a wider level. In their words

> When we combine what we can learn . . . we start to see the emergence of powerful new principles of improvement. These new principles start to delineate a Fourth Way of Transformation that will bring together an energised profession with an engaged public and a guiding but not controlling government, in an interactive partnership of equals dedicated to serving and improving the public and educational common good.[21]

The question that remains: is this too idealistic or is it something we can see, foster, develop and apply in practice? What is clear to me is that it is the responsibility of all of us in whatever role we play in the system to try to model Fourth Way practices. In the first part of the next chapter we explore examples that show elements of this way and assess how far this sort of approach has been the cornerstone of their success.

Notes

1 Crossley and Corbyn 2010, 140.
2 Hargreaves and Shirley 2009.
3 Hargreaves and Shirley 2009.

  4 McKinsey and Company 2007.
  5 www.teachforamerica.org/
  6 www.teachfirst.org.uk
  7 www.future-leaders.org.uk/
  8 National Strategies were first introduced in 1998 and until 2011 provided the teaching and learning strategies to deliver the English National Curriculum.
  9 McKinsey and Company 2010.
 10 McKinsey and Company 2010, 50.
 11 McKinsey and Company 2010, 58.
 12 McKinsey and Company 2010, 38.
 13 McKinsey and Company 2010, 17.
 14 Hargreaves and Shirley 2009.
 15 Hargreaves and Shirley 2009, xii.
 16 Raising Achievement Transforming Learning (RATL) – an English Department For Education funded programme that supported 700 schools between 2004 and 2008.
 17 Hargreaves and Shirley 2009, 45.
 18 Hargreaves and Shirley 2009, 42.
 19 Hargreaves and Shirley 2009, 45.
 20 Schumpeter 1942.
 21 Hargreaves and Shirley 2009, 68–9.

References and further reading

Drucker, P. *Post Capitalist Society* (Oxford, England: Butterworth Heinemann, 1993), 184 ff.

Crossley, D. and Corbyn, G. *Learn to Transform* (London: Continuum, 2010).

Hargreaves, A. and Shirley. D. *The Fourth Way* (California and London: Corwin, 2009).

McKinsey and Company, *How theWorld's Best Performing Schools Systems Come Out on Top* (London: McKinsey & Company, 2007).

Schumpeter, Joseph. *Capitalism, Socialism and Democracy* (New York and London: Routledge, 1942).

2

Leadership and Collaboration

David Crossley

Being world-class requires both leadership and collaboration that is effective and fit for purpose in a different context than we have been used to and what went before. Through theory, research and examples drawn from practice this chapter seeks to explore the key characteristics of leadership and collaboration that will contribute to sustainable school transformation. The first section focuses on leadership. It will argue that the essential leadership characteristics apply in all these quite different contexts but also that what is fostered from above often ends up being modelled below.

Leadership as a catalyst for improvement

Leadership or a change in leadership often acts as a key catalyst for improvement and change, but what sort of leadership is most likely to lead to sustainable change in good to great and great to excellent systems? To me these approaches require what Jim Collins[1] describes as Level 5 leadership – combining personal humility with professional will and drawing power from inclusion, language, persuasion, influence and shared interests rather than the more traditional Level 4 leadership of concentrated executive power. In addition it requires an approach to leadership that fosters and embeds a longer-term vision and clearly integrates this with the response to more immediate challenges. It also requires strategies and approaches to accountability that promote confidence rather than fear and that genuinely make the most of the workforce we have. This extends to avoiding a reliance on top-down one-size-fits-all solutions and above all else a positivity that seeks to build on success rather than obsess over failures. This does not just apply to system leaders, it applies equally to the approach to leadership within a school or team too; although it starts from the top and what is modelled from the top often ends up being modelled within the wider system too. It is interesting that the McKinsey study[2] identifies the debate over persuasion or mandating as a key one.

> Using persuasion, support and influence with those whose schools and teachers are struggling can be as important as the notion of earned autonomy that is offered to the more successful.

I would argue that using persuasion, support and influence with those whose schools and teachers are struggling can be as important as the notion of earned autonomy that is offered to the more successful, especially as the weakest may simply be a product of the fact that they work with more challenging or less advantaged students. Further closer analysis of schools reveals that there are pockets of greatness in most schools and that many students are succeeding in schools deemed as satisfactory or failing. My premise is that if you take the view that it is not the right time to trust educators it will never be the right time, and this in turn dramatically limits system-wide improvement creating a culture of adequacy at best rather than excellence. A further and more practical problem is that the first two McKinsey stages are simple to understand, relatively easy to implement and can be closely managed and run from the centre. The next are more challenging as they involve 'letting go' and implementing new forms of power and control. We have found and include an impressive example of letting go in a school district / local authority area in Chapter 8. Of course politicians and system leaders are under immense pressure to deliver in a short timescale too and this tends to lead to the more directive style and approach to leadership in Level 4.

> The best systems rely on peer to peer support as the source of innovation and deep improvement.

A significant conclusion from the McKinsey study[3] was that the best systems rely on peer to peer support as the source of innovation and deep improvement. Here I would want to stress their conclusions about what systems like the United States and United Kingdom particularly need to focus on as they move from good to great and what the best systems routinely are doing, that is a greater focus on informed professionalism and collaboration.

Collective endeavour is also cited as a key feature of the approach in Finland. There is a clear logic that team working will be able to have more impact than the individual teacher within a school or the individual school in a system. Linked to this is a recognition that the real expertise lies within schools and the real learning comes from practitioners. School to school support is both good value for money and effective. England is focusing on what I describe as school-led system leadership as the key lever for improvement. Further, the ultimate badge of the best leaders of school in England, National Leaders of Education, is awarded for and in expectation of an ongoing commitment to supporting schools other than their own. In addition the Organisation for Economic Co-operation and Development (OECD)[4] recently highly praised the leadership in English schools as one of the key strengths of its system. The report, 'Preparing Teachers and Developing School Leaders for the 21st Century', put UK heads at the top of an index that showed they were more involved with the details of education and teaching than their counterparts in any other industrialized country. OECD sees this concentration on what happens in the classroom as key to improving standards. The organization ranked school heads from 33 of its 34 industrialized member countries according to how likely they were to carry out 14 potential areas of their job related to pedagogy, pupil progress, the curriculum and behaviour. The United Kingdom finished top overall in the 'leadership index' yet in a seeming anomaly, the Programme for International Student Assessment (PISA)[5] high performers Finland and South Korea finished near the bottom of the school leadership index. An OECD spokesman said: 'There, it is the high quality of teachers that makes a difference, because every teacher there is a leader . . . so they focus less on the post of school principals. But for other countries, improving school leadership is important. And the UK has invested a lot in this area and this shows in the results.' Their spokesman said Finland was now looking at the role of principals and that the United Kingdom was a model for other countries, but developing and empowering leadership at all levels is clearly a next step for the UK system. The missing trick could be that autonomy has worked but has to an extent stopped with the headteacher. Finland's bottom-up approach may have had more impact on day-to-day teaching.

So, what are we learning about that makes leadership and peer collaboration effective? The key word is of course 'informed' but it is also the way of maximizing the yield, motivation and contribution of teachers. I argue that this sort of approach also provides the best way of ensuring sustainability by creating capacity, exploring capability and assuring commitment. In terms of leadership this requires a set of key behaviours and a leadership style that empowers and moves beyond the traditional exercise of or reliance on executive power. It is also a leadership style that fosters effective collaboration. This chapter continues by focusing on two countries. First, Finland topped the international PISA rankings three times and was the only system described as excellent in the McKinsey study. For the second, Canada, we focus on two high-performing jurisdictions: Ontario and Alberta. The focus is on their approach to leadership and collaboration and how they have achieved their success.

Another way – can we learn from Finland's approach?

It is in Finland[6] and jurisdictions like Alberta in Canada[7] that we see our current best examples of Third Way and emerging Four Way practice. Finland is at first an unexpected enigma. It came to the fore in the first PISA tests in 2000 as well as in both the McKinsey studies. It avoids standardized tests altogether and reaches high levels of achievement by attracting highly qualified teachers with supportive working conditions, strong degrees of professional trust and an inspiring mission of inclusion and creativity. In some ways it was harder for countries like the United States and United Kingdom to dismiss as the cultural differences are less marked than those in other high-performing and fast-improving countries like South Korea in the Far East. However, some argued that it was also difficult to compare as a result of the view that if you attract the best people into teaching you will have the best performing system, something that was viewed as less easy for countries like our own to do. So, it was a cultural thing after all! The reality is more complex than that and more revealing.

True, the Finnish system attracts high-quality teachers, who all possess Masters Degrees. Although teachers are paid only at the OECD average, high school graduates rank teaching as their most desired occupation. Because of the social mission and resulting status of teaching, Finns are able to make entry into the highly competitive profession, with applicants to teacher education programmes having only a 10 per cent chance of acceptance. This led to the simple and unsurprising conclusion in the first McKinsey[8] report that if you attract the best to be teachers you get the best performing system. Their approach to curriculum is however of more significance. Here in Hargreaves and Shirley's words, 'the state *steers* but does not *prescribe*' in detail the national curriculum. Practical rather than deep philosophical differences may be of great significance too. Teachers teach fewer hours, have more time to prepare and work with *small classes* of no more than 24 students, smaller than the US or UK average. They are not distracted by having to respond to endless initiatives and targeted interventions. This enables them to know their children well. This seems to me to have a created a practical action-centred rather than data-driven every child matters policy that really does seem to ensure no child is left behind! Even more interestingly, Finland has *no system of standardized testing* except for confidential samples for monitoring purposes. There is also *no indigenous Finnish term for 'accountability'*; instead public education is seen as a collective social and *professional responsibility.* In addition the principals recognize they are not just responsible for children in their own school, but jointly responsible for all the children of the area. Hargreaves and Shirley's opine that Finland contains essential lessons for knowledge societies that seek to better educate all their students and become world-class systems.

What then of an insider's view? Pasi Sahlberg is Director General of Centre for International Mobility and Cooperation (CIMO) at the Finnish Ministry of Education and Culture. In his book *Finnish Lessons*[9] he gives a first-hand account of how Finland built its system and its success over the last three decades. And he argues that there is another way to improve education systems. In his words, 'This includes improving the teaching force, limiting student testing to a necessary minimum, placing responsibility and trust before accountability and handing over school and district level leadership to education professionals.'[10] Finland moved to a comprehensive system in the 1970s and stuck with it. It did face ongoing challenges and in reality it took PISA in 2001 to finally fully validate it. Prior to that time some feared they would be left behind but they were not and went ahead!

Lessons for politicians

A key area and focus for Sahlberg's work is teachers and teacher education in Finland. He examines the key role that teachers play. In top-down approaches and in focusing on structures this could be the trick that countries like our own have missed. It affirms the view we will explore later that focusing on things that politicians can control – structures, testing and accountability – may have distracted systems like our own from something they cannot control as directly – but something that really matters – teaching, learning and pedagogy.

Less is more

Less is more is a mantra of the Finnish system too at a number of levels from the age students begin schooling, to the mantra test less to learn more, to teach less as referring to the amount teachers teach. According to OECD Finnish teachers teach on average 600 hours annually compared to 1,000 hours in the United States and 900 hours in Canada. Less teaching means more time to prepare and could directly correlate with better teaching. The final interesting aspect of the book is the impact of the success on what they are doing now as they plan for the future. It may be here that there is most to learn? Finland certainly has not become complacent, is now far more outward looking than before and is already preparing to take its next steps.

Is the future Finnish – what can other systems learn?[11]

So what do they regard as the Finnish prescription?

1   Equal opportunities and good public education for all – a moral purpose;

2   Strengthen professionalism and trust in teachers creating an inspiring profession – in other words get the culture right;

3   High status and good working conditions for teachers with small classes and good support;

4   Smart Accountability – steer educational change (steer is an interesting word here) through enriched information about the process of schooling and smart assessment policies so people trust schools;

5   Facilitate network-based school improvement collaboration between schools and non-governmental associations and groups;

6   Create sustainable leadership and political stability.

It is hard to say what could not be applied elsewhere – as ever in my view perhaps the answer lies in the quality of implementation or the existence of distractors that undermine those very same initiatives in other countries. Old style accountability may be the villain here. Sahlberg quotes O'Neill's[12] words 'Although the pursuit of transparency and accountability provides parents and politicians with more information it also builds suspicion, low morale and professional cynicism'.[13] As anyone who has ever worked in a bad school knows, the damage professional cynicism can cause probably exceeds the benefits factors that cause or validate it bring. The political stability factor, also a feature of the world's best systems, is also significant as Finland has not experienced the plethora of external reforms and laws which inevitably lead to a focus on their implementation and cause frustration and a resistance to change from within schools.

So is it replicable?

Much to me is simply a choice, and much of what is different in the United Kingdom and United States are relatively recent phenomena. It is interesting to contrast the application of similar aspirations in the United States 'no child left behind' and its data-driven inflexible approach and its consequences and the previous English government's similar approach in 'Every Child Matters' with the Finnish success for all. It does raise the question, why did it work better in Finland? While we may reflect that it is due to the greater diversity it is worth reflecting on the view that it was due in part to relatively small schools and good leaders especially within schools – this resonates with the range of effort in the United States to create smaller schools within larger schools and the efforts of organizations like Human Scale Education[14] in the United Kingdom.

In terms of teaching and learning perhaps the most important aspects, Pasi Sahlberg sees the future requiring are the development of a personal road map for learning; less classroom-based teaching; greater emphasis on the development of interpersonal skills and problem solving; and engagement and creativity as positive indicators of success. His reflections on accountability and the fact that the word accountability cannot be found in Finnish Educational discourse are something we should reflect more on and is to me aligned with change in the most successful businesses. Some have said to me that the public sector cannot handle accountability in the same way as successful modern companies – Finland shows that perhaps they can. Instead the focus in the public sector is on developing professional responsibility by educators and encouraging learning among teachers and schools rather than by applying bureaucratic accountability policies.

If you get the culture right anything is possible.

Some would argue that it could not be done in countries like the United Kingdom as it is a product of their culture, but is it? You only need to look at the opening ceremony of the Olympic Games to see what is possible when there is a clear vision that people trust and it is interesting that many commentators saw it as representing what Britain is now. Whatever, it showed how we as a nation could unite around something inclusive and what is more inclusive than collective aspirations for all our young people? This is not far off the common shared view that I developed and explored in my own book;[15] if you get the culture right anything is possible, and if you do not you will limit what is achieved however much you spend. Interestingly the United States and United Kingdom spend more than the OECD average but have delivered at best around the average; perhaps this is why. So the Finnish way could save money especially as top-down accountability adds costs too.

Canada – Ontario and Alberta

Ontario

The Deputy Minister for the province and academic Ben Levin (2009) helps guide us on what to avoid, what is likely to lead to success and why the approach is more likely to lead to sustainable transformation. His book *How to change 5000 schools*[16] offers an approach that is designed to win the hearts of teachers but its real strength is in its subtleties. His approach to school improvement has enjoyed proven success in Canadian Ontario, where it was taken to scale and designed in a way that won it the support of school leaders and teachers. It is underpinned by a clear moral purpose and from this all else follows. In his words, 'There are good grounds for thinking that we are underestimating the potential of many students, even entire groups and communities'. There are many similarities in approach to the programme I led in England. These include the recognition that simple things make a difference. For Levin, these include preparation time in primary schools, a recognition of the lack of meaningful use of data and the chance for schools initially to volunteer rather than be told to take part. He clearly recognizes the importance of winning hearts and minds but also the importance of challenge too. Levin's moral purpose is not enough on its own. I would suggest his approach is both realistic and pragmatic. He has applied what we have learned through approaches to change in schools in a number of countries in the recent past. He stresses that accountability matters and in his reform efforts guiding the Ministry of Education in Ontario found ways of linking the benefits of genuine accountability without the loss of buy-in that results from conventional top-down approaches. We all know that if there is real buy-in success is much more likely to follow and be sustained.

Here, to me, two aspects reflect the strength of his approach beyond its essential optimism and stand out. First, he is realistic: 'yes it is necessary to focus on teaching and learning but the building has to be run as well.'[17] Second, he provides a real prospect for sustainability in his approach by engaging with the challenge of taking improvement to scale by focusing on what ordinary people rather than superheroes can achieve and sustain. In management theory terms this owes something to the thinking embodied in Total Quality Management and approaches to sustainable quality in other organizations.

Alberta

The second example from Canada focuses on a long–running, state-funded school improvement initiative that is in part match funded by the districts. The province of Alberta has an impressive record of student performance as measured by provincial and international achievement tests. It is also a state where 98 per cent choose to stay in public schools. Unusually school leaders and teachers are in the same union and it appears to be a system that is well positioned to manage the challenges and opportunities of their future. Further, its approach to curriculum is forward-looking and learner-centred. An innovative and impressive feature of the state's provision is the Alberta Initiative for School Improvement (AISI), a bold approach to improving student learning by encouraging teachers, parents and the community to work collaboratively to introduce innovative projects that address local needs. Initiated in 1999 by the Alberta Government and its partners, AISI provides targeted funding to school authorities to improve student learning and enhance student engagement and performance. To date, AISI has inspired almost 2,000 projects. In October 2008, AISI held a province-wide colloquium to take stock of the progress of the initiative and to help set directions for the future. AISI invited to the colloquium several researchers who acted as critical friends. The team was invited to undertake deeper research on the design, impact and future of AISI, including its sustainability. The results were published in 2009.[18] AISI is viewed by Finland's Pasi Sahlberg, one of the researchers, as 'a shining star in the sky of global large-scale school improvement'. The team in their summary report stated that AISI constitutes a world-class and world-leading example of a system-wide educational strategy that inspires teachers and administrators; enhances their professional growth and enthusiasm; seeds new, research-informed practices within local communities then spreads them across districts and schools and diffuses existing knowledge as well as creating new knowledge. They praised it for avoiding the excesses of unregulated chaos and permissiveness of unco-ordinated innovation on the one hand (a First Way approach), and of hierarchical and inflexibly linear systems of top-down or layered implementation on the other (Second Way approach). In conclusion they viewed that AISI had created a culture of inquiry, openness, reflection and adaptation that is rare among government-sponsored innovations.

Developing a better relationship between politicians and educators

At the heart of this issue is the relationship between politicians, system leaders and educators in schools – they all have key roles to play if this is to be productive. We see a productive and positive relationship as a key facet of the Finnish success and see simple characteristics exhibited in Ontario and Alberta too. In the United Kingdom and United States there seems less willingness to trust educators and to me this is undermining the potential of the system to really improve. Politicians need to recognize that there is not one best way of achieving things but we as educators need to recognize that we should compare what we do with the best and ensure what we do is both evidence-informed and evidence-based. However, given what we now know about what systems that move from good to great need to do why is a focus not on informed professionalism where our systems energy and emphasis lies? Governments around the world lean heavily on structural or legislative solutions because it is what they can do and do best. They attempt to 'blanket wash' the whole system with one-size-fits-all solutions. These seem to be successful at raising the floor as the McKinsey analysis suggests and they always look neat on paper but are shrouded in variations of implementation and often do not 'fit all'. It is clear this is not the way to raise the ceiling. Two politically competing approaches that extend beyond education emerge here too. Politicians to the left of the system focus on equity – a focus on the rights or entitlement of every student in every school, though of course the reality on the ground can often be very different. This reinforces structural system-wide solutions. Those towards the right have engaged with more market-orientated solutions but seem always to temper these with accountabilities and controls. Arguably we end with the best of neither world. Estelle Morris, a former English Secretary of State for Education, reflected on the relationship between educators and politician in a key note speech at the National College for School Leadership conference in 2011.[19] In her words, 'Politics changes the pieces. Education changes lives. But you have to have both doing it'. She stated that before politics really got involved in education lots of kids did not get an opportunity but that it is essential that politicians and educators get their relationship right.

She commented that we all now want something more from our education systems. In her view the politicians who have been most successful are the ones who find the most effective levers. Governments seem to have coalesced around four key areas: changing the structure; allowing the market to improve things; having accountability mechanisms and changing them; or dealing with pedagogy. Clearly politicians find the first three structural levers easier to implement but they are the furthest removed from practice. She views that there needs to be an honest conversation and a real partnership between educators and politicians and that educators are best qualified to focus on pedagogy which is of course what is most likely to make the most difference to a young person's learning.

England

The English system was probably an early global leader in promoting school to school collaboration but most of the endeavours were focused on ameliorating failure and operated within increasingly punitive accountability regimes. First,

I draw on the writings of a leading UK academic Professor David Hargreaves who once led the Inner London Educational Authority and has made a major contribution to thinking on school to school collaboration in his recent writings for England's National College for School Leadership. He was also a key guide on the side and participant in the initial delivery of the programme I led (see below). An early pamphlet produced in 2003 for Demos[20] is particularly insightful and still provides very useful guidance and an antidote to those who struggle to let go. There are three key points I would draw from his work. First the notion of disciplined innovation; second the value of lateral (i.e. interest group, less locality-based or formal networks), in his words, 'soft strong networks' and third the limited impact of traditional ways of sharing good practice and conventional professional development programmes. His more recent work for the National College for School Leadership (2011 and 2012)[21] on what effective partnership working offers is of particular relevance. He provides a focus on the lessons that educators might learn from partnerships and alliances in the business world and offers what he describes as a maturity model consisting of three dimensions, each with four strands.

David Hargreaves' three dimensions of a maturity model

The *professional development* dimension and its strands:

- joint practice development;
- talent identification and development through distributed leadership;
- mentoring and coaching;
- distributed staff information.

The *partnership competence* dimension and its strands:

- high social capital;
- fit governance;
- evaluation and challenge;
- distributed system leadership.

The *collaborative capital dimension* and its strands:

- analytical investigation;
- creative entrepreneurship;

- alliance architecture;
- disciplined innovation.

Raising Achievement Transforming Learning

My next example is a personal one that was featured as one of the Four Exemplars of Hope in the Fourth Way.[22] Raising Achievement Transforming Learning (RATL) was an English national government-funded programme I designed and led on behalf of a not-for-profit organization the Specialist Schools and Academies Trust (SSAT) from 2004–8. It involved some 700 underperforming English Secondary Schools. The programme was focused on the least worst schools just about the then floor target outcomes at age 16 and up to the national average. All were in the bottom 25 per cent in terms of their value added scores. These represent the rump of any school system; they are sometimes described as coasting schools. In reality they are key to the success of any school system and, as a statistical truism based on numbers of schools, in combination more students underperform in these schools than in failing schools. In England they are also schools with two main types of school leaders. First, they are often schools where new head teachers find their first post and second, they are often schools where head teachers have become 'stuck in post' for more than 5 years. Unusually the Department for Education allowed considerable freedom in the design of the programme. They did what the government can do best: set out its aspirations and expectations of improvement in test result at age 16 but left those to whom it was entrusted to develop the programme and design it. The first thing I did was name it with a positive name that linked the immediate with the longer term – rather than the 'underperforming schools programme'. The second was picked up in the evaluation – we invited participation. This was a risk but changed and set the tone for the relationship which one head teacher described as 'Raising Achievement with Dignity'. In the end all but one or two agreed to take part. The other then relatively unusual feature of the programme was that all the support came not from consultants but from school leaders and their schools who were chosen because they were all in the top 25 per cent of value added performance measures. It was one of the first to scale examples of school-led system leadership. Many of the current leaders of academy chains did their first school support work for this programme. Workshops, conferences and school to school visits acted as a key catalyst. Assigning or offering school leaders as mentors/coaches offered practical solutions and the support of staff in their schools to help schools on the programme apply and implement similar approaches. In addition the support of leading academics provided research-informed experience particularly in the area of use of data but also in terms of leadership and networking. Of particular significance is the way the impact of a modest level of resource that is not linked to formal structures and cost bases can lead to a high level of buy-in and release/create far more capacity than would usually be expected.

The evaluation of the programme was carried out by a US team led by Professors Andy Hargreaves and Dennis Shirley and the team from Boston College, Mass in 2006 and a summary of their research is also included in the recent book by Professors Hargreaves and Fullan – Professional Capital.[23] This book also relates their conclusions to a wider context.

Sequence, harmonize and integrate the short, medium and long term.

The research team from the United States, led by Professors Hargreaves and Shirley, noted that the model was 'practically based in experience yet also intelligently informed by evidence. It values inside-outside engagement of development and research undertaken by, with and for schools in energetic, peer-driven networks (rather than top-down impositions) focused on student learning.' RATL in their view,

> combined a sense of urgency and a push for success with a culture of optimism and inspiration which leads educators to understand and appreciate that, with some outside assistance, the solutions to raising achievement lie within their own professional hands. It replaced the fear factor with the peer factor as the prime instigator and motivator of change.

In addition, a concluding comment from the research 'sequence, harmonize and integrate the short, medium and long term' provides a very powerful design model and the case for integrating short, medium and longer-term objectives from the beginning. A focus on implementation and capturing implementation strategies was my own major learning; this informs all I do now and links to adding the concept of abandonment and the question of what you can stop doing to enable whatever change needs to happen.

London Challenge

London Challenge has continued to improve outcomes for pupils in London's primary and secondary schools at a faster rate than nationally. London's secondary schools continue to perform better than those in the rest of England and if it was reported separately would arguably stand out as an impressive jurisdiction in international studies. Programmes of support for schools are planned with experienced and credible London Challenge advisers using a shared and accurate audit of need. 'Excellent system leadership and pan-London networks of schools allow effective partnerships to be established between schools, enabling needs to be tackled quickly and progress to be accelerated.'[24]

The London Challenge school improvement programme was established in 2003 to improve outcomes in low-performing secondary schools in the capital. Primary schools were included in the scheme from 2008. The programme uses independent, experienced education experts, known as London Challenge advisers, to identify need and broker support for underperforming schools. Many of these advisers were also school principals.

What made it successful? What follows is a summary taken from the Office for Standards in Education, Children's Services and Skills (Ofsted) report on the London Challenge published in 2010.[25]

1   From the beginning of London Challenge, London schools have received *clear, consistent leadership* from the team leaders. Their message has been the pressing need to improve educational standards and the sense of *professional duty incumbent on teachers* to do this for London children.

2   Over time, that message of commitment and encouragement has been repeated consistently by the London Challenge leadership team. These endeavours have reinforced a clear sense of *moral purpose* among teachers and school leaders to close attainment gaps between London and the rest of the country. The staff in almost every school that contributed expressed their commitment to London children, not simply to those in their own school.

3   Once the actual needs of a school have been identified and support for the leadership has been set up, the main work of helping to improve the quality of teaching and learning in the school begins. This may be through local authority advisory staff or externally brokered consultants. Recently, however, *substantial improvements have been achieved through effective partnerships with so-called teaching schools*. Teaching schools are successful schools relative to their entry that provide extended coaching and practical activities on their own site to groups of teachers from several schools that need support and are within easy travelling distance.

4   *Using data to evaluate the effectiveness of school provision* and particular programmes of intervention has become embedded in these improving schools.

A *self-improving system*

This notion was given real impetus by the National College for School Leadership (NCSL) through a range of initiatives from 2006, the most important of which has been the development of system leaders through the National Leaders in Education (NLEs). This ultimate badge for the leaders of outstanding schools in England is awarded for and expects an ongoing commitment to supporting schools other than their own. This has now extended to the creation of Local Leaders in Education (LLEs), and also Subject Leaders in Education (SLEs). This emphasis on school to school support was confirmed in the English coalition government's White Paper in 2010[26] which commented, 'The primary responsibility for improvement rests with schools . . . Our aim should be to create a school system which is self-improving . . . We know that teachers learn best from other professionals . . . We will make sure that schools are in control of their own improvement and make it easier for them to learn from one another.' Their proposals included setting up National Teaching School Alliances (with over 200 in operation and a further 150 approved in April 2013 rising to 500 by 2015) each allied to up to 40 schools. The Teaching Schools initiative put the prime responsibility for professional development and teacher training in successful schools that form teaching school alliances. Fullan and Hargreaves express concern,

> The displacement of the original purposes and successes of British school networks and federations by markets and mandates means that the results are now a very mixed bag. Indeed Chris Chapman's research[27] on effectiveness of different types of networks shows that only those who have designs similar to the original architecture in RATL actually yield positive results.[28]

This really leads me into the areas of what makes any organization successful and wider guidance on what makes any network work. The Teaching Schools initiative led and co-ordinated by the English, National College for Teaching and Leadership is only in its second year and it is as yet difficult to draw many conclusions. The risk is that it is seen as a system-wide answer rather than part of a complementary range or diversity of provision. I was fortunate enough to undertake a strategic role in guiding the first iteration of this new approach with the development of the Middle Leadership Development Programme (MDLP) that replaced what had been a previously provider-led response. Its aim was to increase the numbers involved without increasing costs but also to have a greater focus on the job development. The rationale for the change was twofold and it applied to the wider development of Teaching Schools. The first reason is financial: that it saves money and enables a greater reach. The second is that many view it as better and more focused on students and their outcomes.

This programme was originally piloted by 39 clusters that were given a small amount of funding to deliver it. The key role of the college was to design the programme, offer high quality resource and, of particular importance, train the programme facilitators. After the initial success of the pilot the programme has grown to involve over 1,800 school-led clusters of primary, secondary and special schools; funding is virtually non-existent; schools charge a nominal fee to provide for others; the training of facilitators has remained as has the design of the course which interestingly encourages school-based research and a focus on student outcome. The simple provision of an assessment rubric for the end of programme leadership challenge has proved to be an effective form of quality assurance. In addition far greater numbers of middle leaders have been trained than before and the expectation that they present their outcomes to head teachers of their cluster has proved a great success, and is yet another indicator of what led to the positive assessment of English school leaders by OECD.

Teaching Schools

Teaching Schools have a wider brief but if they begin to replicate the success across their areas of focus they will certainly exceed expectations. As ever the success lies in the attention to detail and the quality of implementation. As well as offering training within their alliances the will identify and coordinate expertise focusing on six distinct areas including training new entrants, leadership development, support for other schools, designating and brokering Specialist Leaders of Education and engaging in research and development.[29]

This is a major shift from what was the norm before, yet this has not been supported by significant additional government funding. Alliances will in the end have to make their school improvement business work for them. Teaching School Alliances are a key element in the five local authority areas that are reflected on in Chapter 11.

An assessment of current developments in England

The desire to be world-class dominated the English 2010 schools white paper *The Importance of Teaching*[30] produced following the election of the coalition government in May 2010, which set out a radical reform programme for the English schools system. In the words of Secretary of State for Education Michael Gove, 'Other regions and nations have succeeded in closing this gap and in raising attainment for all students at the same time. . . . These regions and nations – from Alberta to Singapore, Finland to Hong Kong, Harlem to South Korea – have been our inspiration.' Yet while there are some similarities of approach there are probably far greater differences and as ever the devil can lie in the detail and in how a system chooses to deliver the desired and widely shared aims and goals. Few could argue with the aspirations but the problems emerge in debates about what sort of curriculum is deemed to be modern, the form that accountability takes and what performance data is relied on. In their later work Hargreaves and Fullan[31] reflect on the innovative energy and improved learning and achievement that RATL and other related programmes like the London Challenge unleashed. The danger came, in their view, when government sought to legislate, universalize or in their words to 'hook it up to' purposes other than those for which it was originally designed.

Lessons to learn and apply

In the English context of devolved resource to schools a self-improving system is sustainable; it can encourage research by teachers and reduce government control but only if government has the confidence to let go. There are risks, especially as schools despite the devolved funding have not been used to resource professional development and teachers have been used to being told what to do. There is also a further danger that balancing this by ever-increasing accountability will detract from its potential and limit creativity. The cost benefits are clear and it does focus resource in schools. However, there is a wider question of whether schools can take responsibility for everything – what will they need to help them succeed and what sorts of smart accountability will help them flourish?

Christine Gilbert the former Her Majesty's Chief Inspector (HMCI) and leader of local authorities who has also chaired a major independent commission on the academization for the English system[32] examining the implications of this 'education revolution' argues that the job of school improvement should be left to schools themselves: 'What I am seeing at the moment is schools that are really upbeat and positive about the agenda for a self-improving system and for collaboration across schools. Local authorities have a role particularly in making sure that vulnerable children are well served but I see the energy in the system coming from schools.' Schools in her view relish working together and taking, 'a moral and professional accountability for pupils in other schools'.[33] The commission she led stressed the vital importance of collaboration in an autonomous school system stating that, 'It is best seen as a community of schools, each independent but working best if connected to the rest of the system. These schools would work with one another to accelerate school improvement, in particular the quality of teaching and its impact on learning and the achievements of children and young people.'[34]

National government in addition to setting its goals and assuring the accountability for the system and the expenditure of public money could move to focusing more on the gaps than the provision of the whole. That is possibly a more realistic and sustainable role. Other systems like the United States could benefit significantly by transferring greater roles, resource and responsibilities to schools themselves. What is clear is that the English system is now an outlier in terms of school financial autonomy, devolving responsibility for schools but also the degree of accountability it demands. Its challenge is to find its own equivalent of the Finnish way or to go on improving at a slower rate than the best systems.

Notes

1 Collins 2005.
2 McKinsey and Company 2010.
3 McKinsey and Company, *How the World's Best Performing Schools Systems Come Out on Top* (McKinsey & Company, 2007).
4 OECD 2012.
5 PISA is a worldwide study by OECD in member and non-member nations of 15-year-old school pupils' performance in mathematics, science and reading. It was first performed in 2000 and then repeated every three years.
6 Hargreaves and Shirley 2009, p. 52–5.
7 For a full evaluation of the work in Alberta see Hargreaves et al. 2009.
8 McKinsey and Company 2007.
9 Sahlberg 2011.
10 Sahlberg 2011, 5.
11 Sahlberg 2011, p126.
12 O' Neil 2002.
13 Sahlberg 2011.
14 Human Scale Education – www.hse.org.uk
15 Crossley and Corbyn 2010.
16 Levin 2009.
17 Levin 2009, 5.
18 Hargreaves et al. 2009.
19 Estelle Morris 2011.
20 Hargreaves 2003.
21 Hargreaves 2010, 2011, 2012.
22 Hargreaves and Shirley 2009.
23 Hargreaves and Fullan 2012.
24 Ofsted 2010.

25 www.ofsted.gov.uk/resources/london-challenge – December 2010.

26 DFE 2010.

27 Lindsay et al.

28 Chapman, Mujis and MacAllister 2011.

29 From a presentation at the Training Session for the first cohort of Teaching Schools in 2010 and the National Teaching Schools Handbook National College 2010.

30 DFE 2010.

31 Hargreaves and Fullan 2012.

32 Gilbert 2013.

33 TES May 4, 2012 – It is hard to see that there can be any turning back.

34 Gilbert 2013.

References and further reading

Chapman, C., Mujis, D. and MacAllister, J., 'A study of the impact of school federation on student outcomes', National College, August 2011.

Collins, Jim, *Good to Great in the Social Sectors* (London: Random House, 2005).

Crossley, D. and Corbyn, G., *Learn to Transform* (London: Continuum, 2010).

DFE, 'The Importance of Teaching', *The Schools White Paper*, 2010.

Gilbert, C., 'Unleashing Greatness', Report of the academies commission (Pearson RSA, 2013).

Hargreaves A., Crocker, R., Davis, B., McEwen, L., Sahlberg, P., Shirley, D., Sumara, D. with Hughes, M. et al. *The Learning Mosaic: A multiple perspectives review of the Alberta Initiative for School Improvement* (AISI) (Alberta, 2009) http://education.alberta.ca/aisi; copyright crown in right of Alberta.

Hargreaves, A. and Shirley, D., *The Fourth Way*, (Thousand oaks, CA: Corwin, 2009), 52–5.

Hargreaves, D., *Creating a Self-improving System* (England: National College, 2010).

— *Education Epidemic* (London: Demos, 2003).

— *Leading a Self-improving System* (England: National College, 2011).

— *Leading a Self-improving System in an International Context* (England: National College, 2012).

Hargreaves, D., and Fullan, *Professional Capital* (London: Teachers Press, 2012).

Levin, B., *How to Change 5000 Schools* (Canada: Harvard Education Press, 2009), 5.

McKinsey and Company, 'How the World's best performing schools systems come out on top', London, 2007.

Morris, E., *National College Seizing Success* (Annual Leadership Conference, 2011).

O'Neill, O., *A question of Trust* (Cambridge, England: Cambridge University Press, Reith Lectures 2002)

OECD, 'Preparing teachers and Developing School Leaders for the 21st Century,' Paris, 2012.

Ofsted Report on the London Challenge, London, 2010.

Sahlberg, P., *Finnish Lessons* (New York and London: Teachers College Press, 2011).

3

What should a world-class curriculum look like?

David Crossley

So far much of this book has focused on how three examples of the world's best systems not only improve but also sustain improvement. We have not yet explored the growing international consensus about what schools and systems should offer in terms of their approach to curriculum, teaching and learning. This is a major focus of the section that immediately follows this chapter. So what is this consensus suggesting? Peter Drucker as early as 1993[1] presented a specification that included universal literacy of a high order well beyond what literacy means today and a system which imbues students on all levels and ages with a motivation to learn and keep learning. He also argued that technology while important is only important because in his words, 'it should force us to do new things rather than because it will enable us to do old things better'. Sir Ken Robinson in his Royal Society for the Encouragement of Arts, Manufactures and Commerce (RSA) Animation Changing Education Paradigms[2] – which has been downloaded some 9 million times points out that the problem is, 'that people are trying to meet the future by doing what they did in the past and along the way are alienating millions of kids'. He goes on to state that by and large schools are organized along factory lines with the most important determination of how you are taught being how old you are and your date of manufacture. He argues that if you are interested in a model of learning you do not start from a production line mentality. He also stresses that great learning happens in groups – collaboration is the stuff of growth and we once and for all need to do away with the academic and vocational divide. In an earlier Technology, Entertainment, Design (TED) Lecture in 2006[3] he challenged the way we are educating our children. He champions a radical rethink of our school systems to cultivate creativity and acknowledge multiple types of intelligence.

Oceans of Innovation – unleashing untapped potential from families, schools and workplaces

Michael Barber and colleagues take up the question of what is needed for the future in their pamphlet Oceans of Innovation published by the London based Institute for Public Policy Research (IPPR).[4] In the main body of the report they comment on the importance of innovation stating,

> what's required now is an entrepreneurial mindset.. . . whether you work for a ten-person company, a giant multinational corporation, a not-for-profit, a government agency, or any type of organisation in between – if you want to seize the new opportunities and meet the challenges of today's fractured career landscapes, you need to think and act like you're running a start-up.

They progress to focus on education's contribution questioning how families, schools and workplaces can unleash their all-too-often untapped potential. They quote Sir Ken Robinson[5] who says the challenge is to combine people's talent with their passion. They also confirm the importance of collaboration as increasingly scientific and technological breakthroughs are being made by teams not individuals. While they view mastering the basics is important they state that being good at securing high standards in reading, writing and arithmetic alone does not guarantee high performance across a broad, rich curriculum.

Their proposal encompasses much of what sometimes goes under the heading of 'twenty-first-century skills' – the ability to communicate, work collaboratively in teams, stand up for a point of view, see another's point of view and make decisions. They also take up the argument of measuring what we value too and the whole question of data that we will explore in Chapter 10 by suggesting that schools should keep records of students' progress not just in the subjects, as they do routinely, but also in the development of these other, broader qualities. The intention of the Organisation for Economic Co-operation and Development (OECD) Programme for International Student Assessment (PISA) to test collaborative problem-solving in 2015 is one indication of the future direction.

C21st exams need to reflect the knowledge and skills that matter for the future of our students – not just those that parents remember from their own schooling or those that are easy to measure.[6]

Andrew Schleicher from OECD also shared these views arguing that, 'Today schooling now needs to be much more about ways of thinking, involving creativity, critical thinking, problem-solving and decision-making'. He progressed to express a view on assessment stating: 'C21st exams need to reflect the knowledge and skills that matter for the future of our students – not just those that parents remember from their own schooling or those that are easy to measure.' This seems far removed from the English government's current proposals for an English Baccalaureate (EBacc) comprising a limited range of traditional subjects assessed by three-hour terminal examinations. John Cridland, the Director General of the Confederation of British Industry (CBI) in England, supported this at their annual conference in 2012 by stating, 'Employers sought school leavers who did not just possess a clutch of examination passes but were rounded and grounded. Emphasis on exams and league tables has produced a conveyor belt rather than what I would want education to be an escalator.'[7] In Singapore education system's new strategy it wants to move beyond just focusing on content as it aims to prepare its students for the demands of the next 20 years. Their focus is now on an approach that cultivates creativity and what they term as 'holistic education'. Minister for Education, Heng Swee Keat, speaking in May 2012[8] said this is 'less about content knowledge' but 'more about how to process information'. He describes this challenge to innovate as being able to 'discern truths from untruths, connect seemingly disparate dots, and create knowledge even as the context changes'. Singapore also now emphasizes 'Teach Less, Learn More' and mandates 10 per cent 'white space' for teachers to bring individual initiative and creativity into their teaching.

In San Diego the highly regarded High Tech High (HTH)[9] which consists of 11 schools (five high schools, four middle schools and two elementary schools) serving approximately 4,500 students has a mission to develop and support innovative public schools where all students develop the academic, workplace and citizenship skills for post-secondary success. With an all-pervading focus on project-based learning they argue that change in schooling happens, not incrementally by adding programmes, but by generating holistic designs that enable new ways of teaching and learning.

Simple principles beget complex behaviours

High Tech High (HTH), in contrast to what the name suggests, is not very high tech. In fact the school ethos is based around a small number of simple principles that inform everything that goes on throughout the HTH schools. Larry Rosenstock the principal of HTH in San Diego, California, says that 'Simple principles beget complex behaviours'.

The principles that drive everything at HTH schools are as follows:

- Project-based learning – students engage in learning through well-designed projects which set learning in an authentic and real-world context. Projects are usually designed by two teachers from different subjects working together so, for example, a project may be arts/science or humanities/language based project. Projects are designed around the '6As' (see HTH website).Typically students will have two project teachers who they will see every day and will engage in semester-long projects. Mathematics is however taught as a separate subject.

- High degree of personalization – there are no more than 550 students in each of the HTH schools and relationships and knowing students well is at the heart of each school. Teachers operate in grade teams so if you are a grade seven teacher then you only teach grade seven students. This means that teachers see fewer students overall and see these students more often. In fact because of the way the curriculum is designed teachers see the same group of students every day. Compare this to UK teachers who may well take up to 10 classes each week.

- Teachers are seen as designers of the learning experience – all teachers are on one year tenure and are responsible for designing high-quality projects. Typically teachers will design a project, then engage in 'project tuning' with other teachers/students where projects are fine-tuned and the detail is worked out, and will also do the project themselves before giving it to their students to work out any 'bugs'.

- All learning is publicly exhibited (authentic destination) – At HTH teachers are surprised that in UK schools, students complete work in exercise books that by mutual agreement between teachers and students inevitably end up in cupboards before being finally thrown away. All learning at HTH is publicly exhibited and each term parents are invited into the school to view student learning.

These are big events and a lot of time and effort goes into high-quality display of student work. Around the school site every space is literally crammed with student learning which helps to create a culture of high expectation and 'beautiful' work. On my tour of HTH I asked the grade 12 student who was escorting me if I could see his work. He replied that some of it was on the walls of San Diego airport, other pieces were in the museum at Bilbao, and he thought that a primary school teacher was using resources he had created in her science class. Students also regularly publish books online which are available to the general public, and an enterprise project cycle hire scheme set up by HTH students is still running in a town in Mexico. Authentic destination!

It is also worth noting that teachers, especially in the lower grades (grade 6/7), spend a lot of time teaching students the skills and behaviours needed to manage their own learning. Teachers will spend a lot of time building a 'community' of learners and will frequently throw the problem or challenge over to students saying, for example 'how do you want to go about tackling this?' or 'how will you solve this problem?'. Students are often allowed to fail with an emphasis then on debriefing the process along the lines of what did you do well, what do you not do so well and what will you do differently next time. This kind of debrief is a regular feature of classroom practice. Another firmly established classroom protocol is critique – students regularly critique each other's work The protocol is deceptively simple – be kind to the person, be tough on the work, be specific and useful with the feedback; all students' work (and even staff projects) goes through this kind of process so there is always an emphasis on high-quality work.

Lighthouse projects like HTH provide inspiration for the wider system and show what is possible. It is often easier just to screw down the lid on the pressure cooker by doing what schools have always done and focus on short-term gains but that is all they are, and the short-term gains often are not sustainable. I would argue that as long as more radical change does not make things worse in the short term in the way students are currently judged there is a moral obligation to do something different. Two US examples show that it is possible to be bold in very challenging circumstances as they attempt system-wide change. The New York iZone[10] described and assessed in detail in Chapter 5, is a Development and Research (D & R) hub for New York City (NYC) schools which aims to create a community of NYC schools committed to personalizing learning to the needs, motivations and strengths of individual students on behalf of the wider system. The mission for the transformation of the Nashville High schools in Tennessee (Chapter 6)[11] is that all high school students will belong to a personalized smaller learning community engaged around interests where relationships are valued. Instruction will be project-based, applied and integrated, where meaningful business engagement is evident and post-secondary institutions are involved.

Wider replicability of a HTH or other innovative approach?

To those who say but we could not do it the instructive reflections of Mark Lovatt from Cramlington Learning Village in North East England, that features as a case study in the next chapter, is one of the most sustainable examples of an innovative school. Being innovative does not mean you cannot deliver in conventional ways; in the words of their late Head Teacher Derek Wise it is being a pragmatopian that brings them both together. Cramlington separates out the urgent from the important by having an operational management team and a strategic one. This separates the urgent from the important even if the people involved have overlap. The two groups have different functions and meet separately, the strategic team take an 18–24 month view, the operational team focus on the day-to-day.

They also take a 3D approach to planning requiring plans to focus on three things: (1) Engagement, (2) Progress and Achievement and (3) Developing Independence.

In Mark's view finding ways of layering in habits for effective learning is just good teaching and learning. The key question for Mark and arguably our school inspectors is whether students are making progress in their learning. For this to happen students need to be engaged. It is important to note that Mark views that engagement is not enough on its own but in his words, 'whilst you can have engagement without progress but you probably can't get progress without engagement'.

Innovative practice need not be the preserve of only the very best teachers

Another key question is whether innovative practice such as this is the preserve of the very best teachers. Mark and I share the view that it is not. The biggest thing is having a framework for learning and a template for planning that gives a clarity about the ingredients for successful learning as the 3D planning process illustrates. This of course is linked to ensuring the teacher is not an island and has the necessary usually in-house practice-based training and support. Finally in terms of implementation the advice is to begin small. Cramlington offers a three-stage process:

1   Pilot – with a few key individuals in one year / grade or team to build confidence and learn lessons;

2   Embed – within that team;

3   Scale – then take to scale across the school or wider team.

Schools can do anything but not everything

We often take for granted the way schools teach; it is just how things are and was the way things were when we were at school, so it is how things should be. It is a sort of comfort blanket in an age of change. But the world has changed and schools need to as well. They simply cannot do what is now expected of them by doing things the way they always have or by adding to what they already do. Schools can do anything but not everything and will only be able to do things really well if they stop doing some of the things they did in the past. I close this chapter by offering five almost illogical features of the present system and ask whether they are really fit for purpose and is there not another way. . . .

Is the secondary or high school model really fit for purpose?

Our predominant model for teaching with one teacher in a classroom with up to 30 students was designed for a different way of learning in a very different age. Either it or its associated pedagogy is the very best way of teaching and learning or it is time to explore something different. Today we expect a teacher to do far more than simply lecture from the front of class. We expect them to meet the needs of every student in their care. Society expects a much more personalized approach and differentiation is the current byword but described as a weakness in so many classrooms.

Is it really appropriate for students to only be taught in set times and set places?

Schools are dominated by schedules. Mathematics is often taught for limited periods at set times perhaps three times a week and within minutes students are expected to move on to something completely different, often taught in different ways. Is this really the best way to develop learning and understanding? It is a way of dealing with managing students and avoiding them becoming bored by work that is not interesting enough. Yet it is quite simply not how we now live life or work. We expect things to be on demand anytime, anywhere. We press the red button on the remote control, open an app on our smart phone or tablet, we search for what we want to know when we want to know it, we work on projects and we work in teams. We expect services to be available when we need them, we do not expect them to be closed for more hours than they are open. Why can a teacher not be routinely available on demand to support a student doing homework in the evening? Why can there not be more choice about when learning is scheduled? Technology enables us to do things in different ways; it has changed many aspects of our lives but has changed schools and schooling least of all.

We know teachers work and develop better if they work in teams yet they spend most of the day working on their own

Yet is it realistic for a teacher to be able to meet all of these individual needs every day in every lesson? The primary / elementary school model is better suited because at least the teacher is with the same students most of the time but is the secondary or high school model where teachers often teach as many as 300 students in a week in lessons as short as 50 minutes at a time really fit for purpose? We know teachers work and develop better if they work in teams yet they spend most of the day working on their own.

Why do we expect young people at the time of their lives when they have most energy to spend most of their days sitting at desks?

At the end of a school day or even half way through it teachers are often exhausted while their students are full of energy. In part this is because we expect too little of students. Being passive learners is not that demanding and if we do not focus their energy on learning they find other distractions to occupy their minds. Our young people combine the desire to be an adult with the imagination of a child. We should utilize that energy, imagination and enthusiasm to the full. Learner voice and learner engagement is an immensely powerful force and students when challenged usually not only meet but exceed our expectations. This is what we need to challenge when we talk of offering a curriculum that is real, relevant, demanding and engaging.

Schools cannot be all the things they were supposed to be in the past and all the things they need to be in the future too

Schools cannot be all the things they were supposed to be in the past and all the things they need to be in the future too. Something has to give. Our best schools, especially those that succeed against the odds, require almost superhuman efforts. That is quite simply not sustainable. It is time to recognize what schools do really well in ways that cannot be replicated but also to abandon things that could be done better in other ways. The sense of community, of being part of something, of being together is precious but are classes of 30 in a group of up to 2,000 in one place at set times the only way to achieve these things just because it is what we know best and how we have always done it? Schools are in some ways the last factories, but they need not be like that and some are already showing us that there is another way and it works!

Achievement is addictive

When Peter Drucker commented that achievement is addictive,[12] the phrase I used to open the book and reapplied to staff and schools, he was talking about students and the fact that they spend too much time in too many schools getting marginally less bad at something they are not very good at. How motivating is that? Is it any wonder that students become disengaged? I would argue if we focus on students' strengths, validate and build on them, they will be more rather than less likely to persevere with and find success in the things that they find more difficult too. This is something that will often be enhanced when they find they need these things to help them progress further in their areas of strength.

Interestingly, Drucker argued that effective learning is not just about enjoyment alone as real success at something involves discipline and dedication that only comes from real motivation. This is how students not only meet but exceed the expectations we have of them. We see it in sport, in music and when students teach themselves how to progress to the highest levels of a computer game! When did routine work in school ever inspire that level of motivation?

> A one-size-fits-all education system modelled on a factory production line really has had its day.

To me a twenty-first-century curriculum is about being more personalized, recognizing the different aptitudes, skills and talents students have and building on their strengths – not just focusing on their weaknesses. This is more likely to motivate, inspire, foster the creativity and flexibility our societies need if they are to thrive and prosper. A one-size-fits-all education system modelled on a factory production line really has had its day. It was never a really good fit anyway as inside the classroom the teacher operated an individual craft model of delivery arguably resulting in a worst rather than best of both worlds, or at least something somewhat incongruous. Drucker argued that we should return to the original purpose of schooling and schools[13] and I would stress this time for all not just some. Creative thinking should never just be the preserve of the most academically successful, it is something education should foster and encourage for all students. It may be even something that can be taught and learned! He cited the need for schooling to impart knowledge as both substance and process and for schooling no longer to be the monopoly of schools rather something that in his words, 'has to permeate the entire society with schools increasingly working in partnerships with employers and employing organisations. . .'.

> A twenty-first-century curriculum needs to recognise students are not all the same, are not identical widgets that have to be passed along a production line.

Beyond perhaps a focus on literacy and numeracy (and that can be overplayed as it can and should be developed in many different situations and contexts), a twenty-first-century curriculum needs to recognize students are not all the same, are not identical widgets that have to be passed along a production line. In life most people work in teams, teams seek to utilize and maximize the contribution and the particular skills of each individual. Schools need to learn how to work in these ways more and some already are.

Exploring examples of what schools and systems are doing

In the next part of the book we explore examples of what schools and systems are doing in terms of the principles and approaches to teaching and learning we have explored in this chapter. The first chapter focuses on powerful examples from a range of quite different schools in England, the second on the impact and potential of technology and the following two on system-wide approaches to change in two large challenging urban districts in the United States. In each case they have had the confidence to do what they believe in and offer something more than what is required by a conventional curriculum. They have found that what they are doing has not detracted from how they are judged in more conventional ways. This could be for two reasons, one quite simply because if students are engaged and enthused they go the extra mile and really do achieve more than we might expect or it could be because these schools make sure that they are very good at everything they do. In either case it does pose the question of what they and others could achieve if we stopped tying their hands behind their backs and focused their energies and the energy of others on becoming world-class.. . .

Notes

1 Drucker 1993, p. 180.

2 Robinson 2010.

3 Robinson 2006a.

4 Barber et al. 2012.

5 Robinson 2006b.

6 Schleicher 2012.

7 Cridland (Director General CBI) 2012.

8 Singapore Minister for Education, Heng Swee Keat speaking at the sixth teacher's conference, May 2012.

9 www.hightechhigh.org

10 New York Izone, http://schools.nyc.gov/community/innovation/izone/default. htm

11 Nashville Academies, www.mnps.org/Page68146

12 Drucker 1993, Chapter 11, p. 184.

13 Drucker 1993, Chapter 11, p. 182.

References and further reading

Barber, M., Donnelly, K. and Rizvi, S. et al., *Oceans of Innovation* (London: Institute for Public Policy Research, 2012).

Cridland, J., CBI Annual Conference, November 2012.

Drucker, P., *Post Capitalist Society* (Oxford: Butterworth Heinnemann, 1993), 180.

High Tech High, www.hightechhigh.org/

Robinson, K., 'Schools Kill Creativity', www.ted.com/talks/ken_robinson_says_schools_kill_creativity.html, February (2006a).

— 'Bring on the Learning Revolution', TED (2006b); www.ted.com/talks/sir_ken_robinson_bring_on_the_revolution.html.

— *RSA Animate – Changing Paradigms in Education* (2010); www.thersa.org/events/rsaanimate/animate/rsa-animate-changing-paradigms.

Schleicher, A. 'OECD', TES, 16 November 2012.

PART TWO

Ideas into Action

4

Innovative Examples from English Schools: Whose Curriculum Is It Anyway?

Judith Judd with John Dunford

Are English school leaders and teachers trammelled by the diktats of politicians or are they free to innovate and shape what happens in their classrooms?

In 2009, Julian Chapman, a teacher at Bournside School, Cheltenham, and president of one of the largest teacher unions,[1] received enthusiastic applause when he told its annual conference that teachers were under so much pressure to follow every twist and turn of the national curriculum that they could no longer respond to what their pupils really needed. The curriculum, with Whitehall's accountability measures, had crippled their creativity. A year earlier, a report from the Organisation for Economic Co-operation and Development (OECD) had described the English schools system with its well-established local management of resources as the 'second most devolved in the world'. Who is right? Are English heads and teachers trammelled by the diktats of politicians or are they free to innovate and shape what happens in their classrooms? This chapter looks at the tension between the proven benefits of professional freedom to tailor the curriculum to individual pupils and the need for governments to secure accountability. To use Hargreaves and Shirley's formulation, how do we keep the inspiration and autonomy of the First Way while casting off the persistent autocracy and imposed targets of the Third Way? How much scope do teachers already have to change the curriculum in schools and how many are using their opportunities?

It is easy to see why many teachers share Julian Chapman's feelings of helplessness. In the past quarter of a century, a new public awareness of the importance of education has pushed Conservative and Labour governments into attempts to control the curriculum. In 1988, Kennneth Baker, the Conservative secretary of state for education, introduced the national curriculum and a series of working parties wrangled for months about whether pupils should learn long division and the date at which school history should finish. The 1997 Labour government went further. The literacy and numeracy strategies outlined in detail what primary teachers should teach and, for the first time, how they should teach it. The late Ted Wragg, professor of education and a columnist, called them 'weapons of mass instruction'.[2] Yet most of those involved in these attempts to dictate the curriculum from Whitehall came to see the limit of their influence. Gillian Shephard, Conservative education secretary 1994–7, interviewed in 2009 said: 'You go round the track you make these announcements, you can't deliver them, none of them can because the only person who can deliver is the teacher in the classroom.'[3] Sir Michael Barber, adviser to the Blair government and head of the Downing Street delivery unit, was arguing by 2002[4] 'for an era of informed professional judgement – give education back to the teachers but with the requirement to be informed'.

In 2010, the coalition government appeared to accept the view that the heavy-handed intervention of its predecessors would never achieve the school improvement it wanted. It promised a new era of freedom, basing its argument on the evidence from around the world that countries with the most successful schools were moving towards more 'informed professionalism'. The foreword to that year's White Paper the Importance of Teaching[5] by Prime Minister David Cameron and his deputy, Nick Clegg, said:

> The second lesson of world class education systems is that they devolve as much power as possible to the front line, while retaining high levels of accountability. The OECD has shown that countries which give the most autonomy to head teachers and teachers are the ones that do best. Finland and South Korea – the highest performing countries in PISA (Programme for International Student Assessment) have clearly defined universal standards, along with individual school autonomy.

Greater Freedom and Proper Accountability for schools do not necessarily conflict but the history of politicians' attempts to reform education shows that they often do.

England's coalition government has not always followed its own theory of the importance of professional freedom. In June 2012, a review of the primary curriculum[6] recommended a curriculum as detailed as anything proposed by the labyrinthine Baker working parties. It outlined what pupils in each year group should know. For example, in maths pupils were to add nine and nine and subtract seven from 16 by the age of seven. Michael Rosen, the author, said that to describe the plans for English as 'anal' was 'unfair to backsides'.

Indeed, two consecutive sentences in the 2010 coalition agreement, the working handbook of the new government, show that Messrs Cameron and Clegg have grappled with the same tensions as their predecessors. First, it promises that all schools will have 'greater freedom over the curriculum'. Then it says that all schools will be held 'properly accountable'. The two do not necessarily conflict but the history of politicians' attempts to reform education shows that they often do.

Yet this time, the backdrop is different. The introduction by the Blair government of academies, publicly funded schools that are independent of the local education authority, and the coalition government's determination that most schools should convert to academy status is the biggest shift in the educational landscape since the 1944 Education Act. Academies' freedom is not just from local authorities. It also extends to the curriculum. While they must teach a broad and balanced curriculum, including English and maths, they may also develop the curriculum in response to local circumstances and tailor it to students' individual needs. They may put greater emphasis on vocational courses, literacy and numeracy and teach a wider range of subjects.

Under Michael Gove, secretary of state for education since 2010, schools have begun to convert to academies at a startling speed. In September 2012 the Department for Education in England, said that 2,309 schools were academies, including 1,484 secondaries, 769 primaries and 56 special schools, 300 were approved in that month and applications by 295 secondaries and 483 primaries were being processed. Almost half of secondaries (and counting) were academies and they employed 120,000 teachers. In addition, there were more than 70 free schools with a further 114 expected to open in 2013. These, too, have freedom over the school day and term, the curriculum and how they spend their money. Gove is also backing new studio schools, free schools and University Technical Colleges,[7] all with similar independence.

In his memoirs, Tony Blair, proponent of state-imposed targets and strategies, wrote: 'Freed from the extraordinarily debilitating and often in the worse sense politically correct interference from state or municipality, academies have just one thing in mind, something shaped not by political prejudice but by common sense: what will make the school excellent.'[8] In a speech at Haberdashers Aske's Hatcham college in January 2012, Michael Gove cited evidence of the effectiveness of autonomy: 'Research from the OECD and others has shown that more autonomy for individual schools helps raise standards. In its most recent international survey of education, the OECD found that "in countries where schools have greater autonomy over what is taught and how students are assessed, students tend to perform better."' Schools must, of course, be accountable, he said but the advantages of freedom were clear. The temptation for governments to meddle remains but the direction of the political wind is plain.

The research evidence quoted by Cameron, Clegg and Gove in support of Hargreaves and Shirley's inspirational autonomy is growing. A 2010 report from global consultants McKinsey, co-written by Sir Michael Barber, looking at schools in 20 countries, including England, said teachers should be given more freedom to be creative if schools were to move from 'good' to 'great'. It found that English schools had plateaued at 'good'. Singapore, which in 1997 'required schools to be given much greater flexibility and responsibility for how they should teach and manage their students' was now classified as great. Teachers were also given greater freedom in classroom practice. A report from McKinsey in 2007 had already pointed to teacher quality as the key ingredient of successful schools.

Are heads and teachers ready to take advantage of these changes? Many teachers would identify with the fears and frustration described in Mr Chapman's presidential address. After years of top-down reform and a blitz of Whitehall initiatives, reformers worry about the mindset of a profession that is used to keeping its head down and doing as it is told. When the Labour government took the first tentative steps towards freeing the key stage 3 curriculum in 2008, school leaders feared that teachers had been disempowered for so long that they would lack the will to start devising their own curriculum. John Dunford, the secondary heads' leader, said: 'Let us have the professional courage to do what is right for children.'

A common reaction from teachers was that they liked the ideas but dare not change without permission from Ofsted inspectors.

The independent Cambridge primary review that reported in 2009 was the most thorough investigation of primary education since Plowden in the 1960s. The Labour government, which had its own review, brushed it aside but the review began its own grassroots movement based on the belief that reform should start with teachers and held a series of events throughout the country. According to the review team, a common reaction from teachers was that they liked the ideas but dare not change without permission from Office for Standards in Education, Children's Services and Skills (Ofsted) inspectors.

In March 2012, a survey by the think-tank Reform[9] found that relatively few academies had used the power to create their own curriculum or vary the school day. Yet, times are changing. Teachers may doubt that politicians really mean it when they speak of professional autonomy but they know that the nature of the debate has changed. Governments acknowledge that anyone marking schools' performance after the central prescription of the past 25 years would say 'not good enough'. In particular, the curriculum has failed to motivate the least able pupils. Around 13,000 pupils leave schools each year without a single qualification and a further 13,000 simply disappear from the system and never sit an exam. Academies and the other new types of schools give teachers a real opportunity to show that they can give pupils a better deal through their own creative efforts. The idea that the strong should help the weak (present in *The Fourth Way*), for instance, through teaching schools, is another powerful force.

Growing number of schools are already developing new types of curriculum

Despite, or perhaps because of the pressure mentioned by Julian Chapman, a growing number of schools are already developing new types of curriculum. They are addressing the issue often raised by employers of teaching skills that will prepare students for life and work alongside knowledge in a world where they will need to update their skills many times. As Caroline Waters, head of people and policy at British Telecommunications (BT) put it:

> One of the most important skills is being able to discern from all the information racing towards me the things that are relevant to me and, most importantly how to apply it. If you have grown up in an environment where you don't have to think, how does that prepare you for a world based on change?[10]

The skills and qualities that interest employers according to a recent Confederation of British Industry (CBI) survey of skills of young people leaving school and college are problem-solving, self-management (accepting responsibility and being ready to improve), team work and a positive attitude to work.

The Opening Minds project run by the Royal Society for the encouragement of Arts, Manufactures and Commerce (RSA)[11] was developed in response to a similar survey published by the CBI in April, 2006. The aim was a curriculum that better matched employers' needs and prepared students better for life. The project set about encouraging teachers to introduce innovative and integrated ways of thinking about education and its content. It proposed that they should design and develop a curriculum suited to their own schools based on competencies.

The five competencies proposed by the RSA were citizenship, learning, managing information, relating to people and managing situations. In practice, schools have varied the competencies to suit their own circumstances but the key idea has remained the same: skills should be an integral part of every student's education. More than 200 schools have joined this project and the skills they emphasize include self-reliance, creativity, communication, relating to people, coping with change and risk taking.

Case study – St John's school, Marlborough

St John's Marlborough in Wiltshire is an 11–18 comprehensive and a specialist college for technology and languages. More than a decade ago, the school decided that the national curriculum was damaging pupils' progress. Dr Patrick Hazelwood, the head, threw it out and embarked on an innovative and individual journey. In Years 7 and 8, the school introduced themes based on five Opening Minds 'competencies': learning to learn, managing information, managing situations, relating to people and global citizenship. 'The curriculum was written from the perspective of learners,' says Dr Hazelwood. Teachers planned the timetable so that the 'competencies' were integrated across different subjects. That means that themes continue from lesson to lesson with students going from a statistics lesson in maths to the application of statistics in geography and then to using statistics in science practicals.

An Ofsted report in 2009 praised 'the innovative curriculum in Years 7 and 8' which focused 'on developing students' generic skills for learning as well as their subject knowledge. The strategies that teachers use in lessons are very effective because they allow students to be actively engaged in their learning.'

The next stage, after a highly successful pilot, was to apply the strategies across the school – one of Ofsted's recommendations. The school had strong support from the community for its plans.

'We had parents clamouring for their children to be part of it,' says Dr Hazelwood.

Ofsted also commented on the school's improving exam results and the very good progress made by pupils with learning difficulties and disabilities. Dr Hazelwood has no doubt that the changes have brought academic dividends. The pilot group comfortably outperformed the control group when they reached General Certificate of Secondary Education (GCSE). And the effect continued after they left school when they proved to be confident, independent learners. The group recently graduated and at least 20 of the 27 who have contacted the school achieved first-class degrees.

Meanwhile, results have continued to improve and staff have refined and developed the curriculum, though the five competencies remain at the core.

Dozens of schools have visited St John's and taken inspiration from its work. Dr Hazelwood says that every school will adapt Opening Minds to suit its needs. It could look different in every single school but the philosophy remains the same. 'What we have tried to do with Opening Minds is to make sure they really are lifelong learners. They see the power of learning and, more important, they have joy in learning.'

The Opening Minds programme emphasizes that learning how to learn is as important as what students learn. Researchers such as Professor Guy Claxton, co-director of the Centre for Real World Learning at Winchester University, have given that idea fresh impetus by the practical work they are doing with schools. They are trying to work out what schools would look like if they were apprenticeships for life. Professor Claxton's building learning power programme, already adopted by hundreds of schools, aims to foster those life skills. He talks about curiosity, independence, reflection, resilience, courage and collaboration. It is not just a question of fostering skills, he argues. Schools also need to change pupils' attitudes and values, their disposition. 'Learning capacity is as much a matter of character as it is of skill. It's no use being a skilful questioner if you lack the courage to ask the questions,' he says.

Moreover, teaching skills helps to promote high academic attainment, his work suggests. The experience of primary schools that introduce programmes based on skills bolster his case.

Case study – Westfields junior school, Yateley, Hants

Karine George, Westfields' head, asked a group of senior teachers to rethink the curriculum from scratch. They started by asking what the ideal learner should look like and went on to research different curriculum approaches. They read much of Guy Claxton's work and some of the writing of Professor Michael Fullan, the Canadian authority on education reform. They looked at the research on learning skills and picked four that were appropriate for their pupils: team work, creativity, reflecting on learning and stickability. They mapped out the curriculum so that each year group learned a different skill during each half term with Year 4 building on Year 3.

The backdrop to that – or the big picture as Karine George calls it – is the need to prepare our children for the wider world, for changes in technology, the climate, international competition for jobs and even wars. 'You have to have a real context for learning,' she says. 'We use a huge amount of technology that brings children to the world'.

The school uses a series of challenges to help pupils acquire the skills and knowledge it hopes they will acquire to prepare them for this world. Teachers act as guides to help them through but the onus is on the pupils to find the answers to the questions that they themselves have posed. In one, the puzzle of the pyramids, they turn the hall into a museum, gather information, work out how best to display it, assign roles, use Information and Communication Technology (ICT) and make artefact replicas. They reflect on everything they do: what have they achieved, how have they done it.

The school encourages them to use the expertise of the community so they e-mail questions to the Yateley history society. The school radio station was set up with help from Eagle Radio, the local station, and after talking to other schools about their experience of radio. Karine George says they really do listen to children. They scrapped a plan for adults to read bedtime stories on the radio when children said they did not want adults involved.

How does Westfields' philosophy fit with the need to satisfy Ofsted and the Key Stage 2 tests? Very well, according to Ofsted, which in 2011 judged the school outstanding. Ruth Davey, the deputy head says: 'We make sure they are prepared for the test and that they know what a test is. It's not the majority of the curriculum.' Yet much of the skills training is relevant to testing, she says. The toolkit for stickability, for instance, provides ways of helping pupils through unfamiliar questions.

But Karine George accepts that keeping faith with their beliefs and meeting government demands can be tricky. The grammar test, due to start in 2013, is a problem. 'We are building in time to look for opportunities in the curriculum to highlight, for example, how you explain an embedded clause. One possibility is a caption share screen cast.'

She says that schools can build a risk-taking culture if they have the right relationships between all those involved. 'We all want the accolade of Ofsted but we know it's a narrow output. You have to have a moral purpose'.

A growing number of schools share Westfields' recognition of the importance of learning how to learn through the skills that underpin its curriculum. Research evidence for the effectiveness of this approach is mounting.

Chris Watkins of London University's institute of education studied how pupils learn in 12 Leeds primary schools. He found that students whose teachers concentrated on improving their learning obtained better results than those who concentrated on improving their performance. The average point score of pupils in the first groups doubled.

Some secondary schools also provide evidence of the benefits of learning how to learn. Few schools know more about it than Cramlington learning village in Northumberland.

Case study – Cramlington learning village, Northumberland

Cramlington is an 11–18 college with around 2,300 pupils. Its journey began when Alistair Smith, the trainer and author who devised the Accelerated Learning Model, visited the school in 1997. His work about how the brain learns led to a review of teaching and learning in the school's science department. This soon spread to other departments and eventually the whole school.

Students learn the five Rs – respect, responsibility, reflection, reasoning and resourcefulness – by developing skills of communication, thinking and collaboration.

Teachers write all these into their schemes of work and lesson plans and students are graded one to five against the five. The grades are reported to parents. The school also gives grades for academic work but it does not give grades for behaviour or effort.

Thorough Continuing Professional Development (CPD) is an essential ingredient of the programme's success. Cramlington's lessons finish at 2.15 pm every Wednesday so that staff can take part in CPD. From the moment a new teacher arrives, they become part of a four-year CPD programme.

Teachers plan all lessons around a six-part cycle based on evidence about effective learning. For example, all new learning is built on what a student already knows and understands.

The idea that students should take an active part in learning underpins the cycle. They pursue enquiries into questions or problems with the help of ICT: they set up e-portfolios, blogs and wikis.

They learn how to describe and reflect on their thinking. Through Assessment for Learning, they set their own goals and judge how successful they are.

The school believes learning to learn is a vital skill. Mark Lovatt, deputy head in charge of teaching and learning at Cramlington learning village in Northumberland says; 'We spend a lot of time selling to students the idea that if you can learn how to learn you can go on learning all your life. The idea is that they should join in learning. It isn't something that the teacher does to them.'

In Year 7 all students have three 75-minute lessons a fortnight on learning how to learn. During this course, they are asked to think about what great learning looks like and to consider that there are many different ways of learning. They will reflect on how they learnt to swim and to talk and how their brain helps them to learn. Teachers ask them to think about a lesson they had earlier in the week and to see if they can plan a better one. In Year 8 they take an inquiry-based course on how to research topics and a Year 9 course builds on the earlier work.

None of this has jeopardized exam results. Around 65 per cent of students get five or more A*–C grades including English and maths and 95 per cent get five A*–Cs. The school has been judged outstanding in its last three Ofsted inspections, most recently in 2009. Mark Lovatt says: 'Why would teaching someone to be a better learner not help them to pass exams? People seem to perceive that you can either teach skills or knowledge. You can do both.'

Listening to students and shaping the curriculum with them rather than for them is an essential ingredient of the Cramlington experience.

If you move towards a more learning-centred culture with students reviewing how they learn, behaviour gets better, relationships get better and performance gets better.

Chris Watkins says: 'In the past 20 years classrooms have been pushed into being very teacher-centred and students' performance has not improved. If you move towards a more learning-centred culture with students reviewing how they learn, behaviour gets better, relationships get better and performance gets better.'

The search for a culture that puts students at the heart of learning is not confined to secondary schools. Primary schools are pioneering partnerships where even the youngest children and their parents have a say in what is taught. Despite complaints that the Key Stage 2 tests stifle teachers' creativity, the experience of some shows that schools that listen to pupils do not have to sacrifice standards. Equally, schools that refuse to teach to the test or to restrict teaching to the test subjects still achieve excellent results.

Case study – The Wroxham school, Potters Bar, Hertfordshire

Wroxham's head, Alison Peacock, says that its philosophy can be summed up in a single phrase: 'the school that listens.' The one-form entry primary is an academy and, since September 2011, a Teaching School with around 40 partners, that include an Isle of Wight primary in special measures. When Alison Peacock became head it was in special measures. In 2009 Ofsted judged it outstanding.

Yet the school's curriculum and pedagogy are among the most radical in the United Kingdom. Her recipe for success is 'to listen to children and the community and that leads to a dialogue where everybody is trusted'. From Year 1, children are asked to express their views and listen to their peers. By Year 6, they are expected to give a presentation of their work, their challenges and their successes, including several PowerPoint slides to their parents, teacher and the head. They sit in the head's swivel chair in her study and join in a conversation with the adults about their progress. It is an important aspect of the school's work to involve the community. Alison Peacock says: 'The parents don't turn up to receive a judgement about their child. The child leads the conversation.'

Critics who think that giving pupils a say in their learning leads to a free-for-all misunderstand what is happening. It is the teacher who decides they will study the Vikings and who outlines a framework before offering the class a list of options for further study.

Wroxham's approach to assessment is also distinctive. The school's rejection of the view that a child's ability is fixed is based on research done by Alison Peacock and others in the Learning without Limits project. There is no setting by ability except when children first start guided reading sessions and they are told their grades only after the Key Stage 1 and 2 tests. Teachers and children alike should be free to take risks. 'The cool thing to do here is to challenge yourself but it is also perfectly acceptable to try something and find it's too difficult to do today,' says Alison Peacock who is also a network leader of the Cambridge Primary Review.

The curriculum stems from the belief that broad and balanced fare leads to better results. A drumming session in the morning pays dividends in a mental arithmetic lesson later in the day. Pupils enjoy 'forest school' throughout their time at Wroxham and Year 6 spend a week in September on a school journey that aims to improve team-building. The starting point is always the national curriculum. In 2012, Wroxham introduced a curriculum based on the domains of the Cambridge Primary Review but this still tracks back to the national curriculum. Alison Peacock is confident that she can navigate her way through the proposals in the Gove primary curriculum review. She says that some schools have allowed Key Stage 2 tests to constrain them.

But the government's standards agenda and a broad, creative curriculum go hand in hand. 'It isn't an either or. All the evidence is that a rich curriculum with a diverse set of experiences, taught well, means that children attain more highly in the basics'.

She is enthusiastic about Teaching Schools partly because they have freedom to choose their priorities: in Wroxham's case professional education. Teachers in the Wroxham alliance visit each others' classrooms not to criticize the teaching but to observe whether children are learning. 'Did you notice that Robert found it really hard to pile up bricks beyond six?' they might ask. Teaching Schools can also connect schools and give them confidence to do things in their own way.

She talks about 'fear in the system' that stops teachers taking their children out to see a rainbow that someone has spotted out of the window. But her experience shows that rainbow-spotting and meeting the government's accountability demands can go hand in hand.

Many of Wroxham's pupils come from comparatively comfortable backgrounds but Alison Peacock is confident that its approach to parents would work just as well in a deprived area. She says:'Very few parents don't want to listen to what their child has to say.' Hartsholme Academy, a Lincoln primary with nearly 300 pupils, proves her right.

Case study – Hartsholme Academy, Lincoln

Three years ago, Hartsholme was in special measures and threatened with closure by the local authority. Last year it received an outstanding accolade from Ofsted, a record turnaround, inspectors say. The school sits in the middle of three council estates and Carl Jarvis, who has been its head since 2009, says getting parents involved has been difficult: 'A lot of people in the area are very sceptical about all public services.' But the school is making headway. It bases its curriculum on a two-year cycle of themes decided at an In-service training day that children, parents and teachers attend. One of the present themes – children in the second world war – arose from such a day.

The starting point for the approach was not parents but children. Mr Jarvis decided 'to wipe the slate clean'. He wanted to stop pupils switching off from education by involving them. The result is a Key Stage 2 class where the air raid siren goes off, an unexploded bomb has landed and the children, sheltering under their desks, have to work out the route to the code that will defuse the bomb. While they are studying this theme, the classrooms are set up as second world war living rooms. Mr Jarvis says this type of 'immersive learning' is based on research carried out for the past 12 years.

Teaching and assessment methods pay scant regard to tradition. Not all the classrooms have desks because the school believes some children learn better without them and it has substituted a 'learning journal' for traditional marking. The teacher spends ten minutes with each child every week discussing their progress and recording what they have achieved and what they need to work on. 'The feedback from these sessions is much more powerful. The only reason teachers do formal marking is for Ofsted,' says Mr Jarvis.

Every Friday afternoon, children get a glimpse of the world of work. They bake cakes in the bakery that supplies a café that sells them to parents. There are strong links with business and public services. Hard-to-reach boys, for instance, spend time at Royal Air Force (RAF) Waddington where their mentors talk to them about working towards a career.

Teachers exploit technology to the full. Children take home an iPad that introduces them to a topic for the following day. They view a video clip explaining a process and then practise the skill. They e-mail the result immediately to their teacher. If they get stuck, the teacher can take control of the iPad to go through the process again.

Mr Jarvis rejects the idea that any of these ideas are extreme. 'The notion of sitting on the carpet being talked to doesn't work. All we have done is consider kids.'

It is notable that the ideas adopted by all these successful schools have not been plucked from thin air. Nor are they the whim of a single head. They are the result of a careful study of research about what works, often over many years. For some, the search for evidence to support new developments never ends. Staff at Fallibroome academy carry out small-scale research projects on each new idea before they introduce it across the school.

Case study – Fallibroome Academy, Macclesfield

Fallibroome is a 1,500 strong 11–19 converter Academy and National Teaching School serving North West Macclesfield. The school has a reputation for innovation in teacher training and system leadership. Principal Peter Rubery outlines the principles of evidence based practice and 'Whole Education' that underpin the school's ambition to become 'world-class'.

As the Ebacc and Tech Bacc vie for political favour it is worth asking the simple question: which educational theories are supported by evidence of impact? At Fallibroome we have pursued the principle of Development and Research in order to inform decision-making before transferring innovation into policy.

This model: small-scale pilot projects, framed by rigorous, peer-assessed research and supported by student and parent surveys, has served us well in our pursuit of continuous improvement. Our ambition, to move 'From Frist-Class to World-Class' requires a commitment to searching out sources of evidence-based practice from around the world. For instance we discovered Spencer Kagan's Co-operative Group-work at the Learning Brain Expo in the United States; our commitment to a 'Wild Tasks' curriculum grew from exposure to the model of project-based learning developed by the High Tech High group of schools in the Napa Valley, combined with the 'Rich Tasks' curriculum we saw in Victorian schools in Australia. Closer to home our transformation of assessment practice is rooted in Black and Wiliam's model of assessment for learning that was first promoted in the Inside the Black Box series.

Evidence of impact, however, could be contextual, hence our desire to test these theories in situ. Reassurance was also gained from the guidance of Newcastle University and The Campaign for Learning which brought consistency to the enquiry model.

We have maintained this commitment to small-scale innovation as a precursor to policy change and currently have 11 staff working on 'Innovations Projects', supported by our research partners Futurelab whose seven-stage action research model brings validity and reliability to project findings. Several current projects are linked to our proposed investment in mobile technology for all Year 7 students – a development with huge potential for transformation but, as yet, only assumed benefits for learning. It is only by following the model described above that we will gain the assurances required to progress.

Major policy initiatives can only be truly effective if classroom practice changes and that can only be achieved by high-quality training. To this end we remodelled the school day to create bimonthly 1.5 hour training sessions for staff and create a training programme that serves both the school's strategic aims and student and teacher needs. Our commitment to sharing our findings is demonstrated by regular 'Visitor Days' designed to showcase practice, and the organization of the bi-annual Learning Brain Europe Conference. Our recent designation as a National Teaching School provides further opportunities to influence practice on a system leadership scale.

The Ebacc and Tech Bacc appear be construed by political whim. We prefer evidence-based practice and can point to the best A Level results in the county; top rank GCSE results (at least until the 2012 fiasco!); significantly positive values added measures and a full set of grade 1 judgements at inspection as proof of impact.

None of this would mean anything without an equal commitment to shared values, grounded in Noval & Purkey's Invitational Framework and a commitment to creating the conditions for personal growth and self-worth to flourish. Our overarching aim is to prepare students to make an active contribution to a complex world; we intend to achieve this aim by providing a 'Whole Education' but make decisions on the basis of evidence rather than whim.

Whole Education

The schools included in this chapter are remarkable for their individual achievements and also for their links with and influence over others. They exemplify the co-operation and trust that Hargreaves and Shirley place at the heart of the Fourth Way. They show that schools can achieve far more together than they can in isolation.

> Schools need the encouragement of others to make the changes that they know will benefit their students.

That is partly because change against a backdrop of government edicts, league tables and inspection requires courage. Many schools are still in the grip of the fear that Julian Chapman and Alison Peacock describe. They need the encouragement of others to make the changes that they know will benefit their students. There is safety in numbers. Whole Education (WE) is a partnership of like-minded schools and organizations that believe that all young people should have a fully rounded education, developing the knowledge, skills and qualities needed to help them thrive in life and work. Education should be much more than examination syllabuses, national tests or the national curriculum so WE encourages everyone involved in education to look outside the narrow confines of these externally imposed constraints. It is working with over 500 schools and colleges including over 50 Pathfinder schools that recognize the need for a network of schools to help heads and teachers to seize the initiative to improve education. It wants to help schools, employers and the whole community to find new ways of involving students in their own education, engaging disillusioned teenagers, creating independent learners and promoting the most effective teaching skills. A huge variety of schools have joined. Some have transformed themselves. Others have made small changes.

The WE network acts as a 'community of practice' where schools and partner organizations that have signed up to a statement of common beliefs can collaborate, share knowledge and support each other. WE believes that teachers can integrate knowledge and skills in their lessons. It wants to develop ways of mapping different skills across the curriculum in primary and secondary schools. For example, pupils in Year 5 can develop team working and problem solving as part of their normal curriculum. At secondary level, the geography department could, for example, be charged with improving research skills in Year 9 and the English department could be asked to ensure that all students develop presentation skills in Years 7 and 8. In this way, a school can build a matrix of knowledge and skills. The network is also enthusiastic about the Fourth Way's insistence on the importance of the community in raising aspirations, particularly in deprived areas, so that students can make connections between education and the world outside their school. Network partners such as National Literacy Trust's work in engaging local communities and RSA through their Area Based Curriculum in Peterborough are bringing together young people with others in their community from many different walks of life. In 2003, the government's paper on Excellence and Enjoyment, found that in the best primary schools children learned in many ways: outdoors, through music, art and sport. All these activities, WE says, are part of a whole education.

> Large scale changes that have great impact do not originate in plans or strategies from on high. Instead they begin as small local actions.

The impetus behind its work is clear. As the figures at the beginning of this chapter show, more than 30 years of top-down reform, driven by politicians and civil servants, has produced only modest results for most young people. For those at the bottom of the educational heap, the effect has been, at best, negligible. WE looks to teachers to improve schools because it believes that change happens in a different way. It supports the view of Margaret Wheatley, co-founder of the Berkana institute in America, that

> Large scale changes that have great impact do not originate in plans or strategies from on high. Instead they begin as small local actions. While they remain separate and apart, they have no influence beyond their locale. However, if they become connected, exchanging information and learning, their separate efforts can suddenly emerge as very powerful changes, able to influence a large system.

Communities of practice are common in American education. They connect teachers, administrators, professionals who are trying to solve specific problems such as improving reading or developing new types of CPD.

WE offers the space to explore where schools are and where they might go next. It is not just about exceptional pioneers but about any school that wants to make progress towards the goals that so many teachers share. By bringing schools together, it hopes to take the risk out of innovation and to give them confidence to follow their instincts.

Common threads

Some schools have been doing this for many years regardless of the political climate. Cramlington's journey began in 1997 and St John's a few years later. Neither was reacting to government proclamations. At both, teachers looked at their pupils and decided that the lesson content and teaching methods needed to change if their pupils were to make faster progress and to leave school with the skills they needed for life. Theirs was not a short-lived sprint of improvement that petered out after a burst of enthusiasm. Their school-led approach to curriculum planning and pedagogy continues to pay dividends. Whatever edicts streamed out of Whitehall, they remained on their chosen path and they will continue to do so. At Wroxham, Alison Peacock had no fears about the new primary curriculum proposed by Michael Gove and the coalition government. The school would stick to its principles: there would be no drilling in grammar but teachers would be looking for ways to improve it. She pointed out that the new national curriculum was not meant to take up the whole week and offered plenty of opportunities for creative teachers. Like Wroxham, all the schools work within the framework of externally imposed constraints: Ofsted, public examinations and league tables. Their pupils do well in exams and win plaudits from inspectors. Asked how he had broken free of these constraints, Peter Rubery, Fallibroome's head said that he had not. The school had been able to shape its own destiny because its innovations had been coupled with success in examinations and with Ofsted.

> They share a set of values and a belief that education is not just about getting through exams. They look beyond school and encourage knowledge and skills that students will use throughout their lives.

What do these schools have in common? It is no accident that most are members of the WE network. They share a set of values and a belief that education is not just about getting through exams. They look beyond school and encourage knowledge and skills that students will use throughout their lives. They are all outward-looking and enlist the help of individuals and groups with a stake in education. In particular, they value links with other schools. They give and take. They have new ideas about what their students should learn but also pay close attention to how they learn it. Ofsted sees St John's 'generic skills for learning' and Cramlington's learning how to learn lessons as fundamental to their success. Reflection on learning is an essential component in Westfields' success. All listen to their students. They find out what motivates and interests them and they expect them to take an active part in learning. They are constantly looking for links with the world outside school. Hartsholme's Friday afternoon work sessions and use of its RAF connections ensures that even young children have to think about life after school.

Improving teaching is at the heart of everything they do. They take seriously the findings of the 2007 McKinsey report that good teaching is the most important ingredient in school improvement. Hence, Cramlington's decision to clear Wednesday afternoons for professional development and Fallibroome's adoption of Kagan co-operative learning. They base their curricula and pedagogy on research: at Wroxham, the learning without limits research underpins everything the school does. Fallibroome's groundbreaking Learning Brain Europe conference links teachers with the latest thinking in neuroscience. Westfields' journey began with a study of the work of Claxton and Fullan. Their improvement does not depend on exceptional resources though their heads are always alert to opportunities to attract funding through good relationships with the community. Hartsholme has used the pupil premium to help fund iPads. It means tests parents and those who can afford to lease them do so. Westfields uses a young apprentice as a technician for the radio station and pupils raised £3,500 by car and shoe polishing and selling hot drinks.

But if these schools share some general principles, they are also distinctive. Each has looked at its own students and chosen different ways of helping them progress. They believe in the importance of good teaching, for instance, but promote it in their own way. They take seriously research literature but adapt it to their own circumstances. They do not see themselves as special. They have persisted in trying new things regardless of outside pressures.

Risk-taking works if teachers are confident that they will not be blamed if it goes wrong.

To heads who say 'It's all very well for you, you have an outstanding Ofsted', Karine George replies that she was experimenting for years before she received the Ofsted accolade. What counts, she says, is culture. The message from the schools described here is that staff must be behind the changes if they are to endure. Risk-taking works if teachers are confident that they will not be blamed if it goes wrong. The benefits of co-operation are equally clear. Changes that might seem daunting for a single school are manageable with the support of others. Teachers achieve more by linking with others, by learning from them and by joining networks such as WE. They share new ideas but, most importantly, they share confidence.

REFLECTION

Five steps to building a whole education curriculum

JOHN DUNFORD

In spite of the narrowness of the accountability regime in England, many primary and secondary schools are looking for ways to enrich the curriculum. Most schools are wary of straying too far from the requirements of the Department for Education and Ofsted, as they perceive them to be from the school performance measures and the Ofsted inspection framework. Indeed, it would be both unwise and unfair to the young people to pretend that these did not exist and that a school could create a curriculum that did not prepare young people to achieve useful qualifications, taught well and learned thoroughly.

Giving all young people a whole education does not mean ignoring the knowledge that the government believes that pupils and students should acquire; it does mean, however, looking at the curriculum in a new light and finding ways in which young people can learn more than the state requires them to do. Curriculum development is a process and the following five steps ensure that this is done thoroughly and well.

Recognize that education is the development of knowledge, skills and personal qualities

The school curriculum in England has always been largely knowledge-focused. In an attempt to catch up with the world's best-performing education jurisdictions – Finland and the Far East – most of the discussion in England is about the knowledge curriculum and the pedagogical approach to transmitting that knowledge to young people. Yet, even as we try to catch them up, the top-performing countries are moving on, recognizing that they may be top of the wrong league table and that young people in the twenty-first century need much more than success in knowledge-based tests and examinations.

A good definition of the curriculum is 'all the learning that takes place in school' – which is much wider than simply what happens in lessons. Schools in England already do much more than teach knowledge. Overtly or accidentally, young people acquire a wide range of knowledge, skills and personal qualities during their schooling. It is the contention of WE that not only should skills and personal qualities be identified as part of the curriculum, but that young people's development in these areas is as important as the development of their store of knowledge.

Primary and secondary schools that build the development of skills and personal qualities into the curriculum are finding that students achieve more with their knowledge too.

Recognize that the statutory national curriculum is only a small part of the school curriculum

The government is encouraging schools to think that they have greater autonomy. Those that are academies are not restricted by the national curriculum, but by the testing and accountability regime. Whether a school feels confident or constrained in the wake of the wider national education policy agenda, it should be remembered that curriculum autonomy is not just for academies. All schools have masses of opportunity to think creatively about the curriculum, and still do well for their pupils in external tests and examinations. In Figure 4.1, the national curriculum forms only a small proportion of the school curriculum and the government in England has said that it intends to reduce the core further.

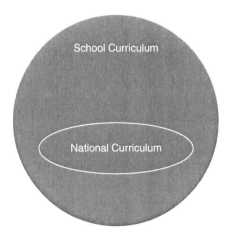

FIGURE 4.1 *The relationship between the national curriulum and the whole curriculum*

By 2013, all teachers under the age of about 45 have spent their whole career under a prescriptive government-directed curriculum and one of the biggest challenges for school leaders is to create the culture change that is necessary for teachers – and senior and middle leaders in particular – to recognize that they have great opportunity at the present time to innovate, planning and building a curriculum that is right for the pupils in their school and combining national imperatives with local priorities.

Plan a curriculum that develops skills and personal qualities at the same time as knowledge, not as separate entities

The debate about the teaching of knowledge and skills often seems to assume that they are different entities, wholly divorced from each other. Nothing could be further from the truth. Knowledge cannot be taught effectively without developing skills too; and skills cannot be taught in a knowledge-free vacuum. Curriculum planning should not put skills into a box marked 'personal and social education' or any other title that implies that that is where young people learn skills.

The most efficient and effective way to provide a whole education, fully developing knowledge, skills and personal qualities, is to think of the curriculum as warp and weft. In Figure 4.2, knowledge is the warp, developing progressively, while the weft of skills and personal qualities is developed at the same time.

For example, primary and secondary schools – working in conjunction with parents and pupils – can set out a list of skills and personal qualities that they wish to see developed in all young people. Then they can allocate specific elements to particular stages of primary and secondary schooling. Primary schools can allocate aspects of skills to each year group. For secondary schools, subject departments can be given responsibility for the development

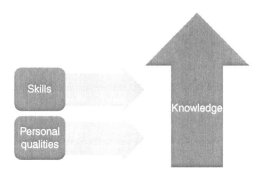

FIGURE 4.2 *The relationship between skills, qualities and knowledge*

of particular skills. So, for example, working in teams can become the responsibility of the science teachers, presentation skills of English teachers and so on.

To ensure universal coverage during the secondary school years, it is important to plan skills development at Key Stage 3 or in the core subjects at Key Stage 4, not in Key Stage 4 options where some will miss out if they are not studying subjects in which certain skills are being exclusively developed.

Enrich the curriculum by looking out for inspiration – locally, regionally, nationally, internationally – and not looking up to the government to be told what to teach

Schools that are developing a WE approach to the curriculum are not reinventing the wheel. Instead, they are looking outwards to find examples of excellence in curriculum development in other schools. There is no shortage of examples from which to draw inspiration and ideas to adapt to a school's own context. Internationally, schools like High Tech High in San Deigo provide lessons that can be applied to schools in England. Ofsted reports, such as *Twenty outstanding primary schools* (2009) and *Twelve outstanding secondary schools* (2008) contain many transferable ideas that have proved successful in challenging conditions.

Because recent governments in England have put their trust in school-to-school support as the means to school improvement, school leaders have been encouraged to look elsewhere for proven ideas and strategies. The WE network is a good place to start.

Networks are important, both for schools and for individual teachers. Using these professional networks as the basis for professional development and leadership development, the transfer of expertise and experience can be maximized. New ways of creating a learning community and providing professional development may be just one of the beneficial side effects of implementing a WE curriculum.

Teach all elements of the curriculum as rigorously as the content that will be examined externally

In some schools, the curriculum outside the test and examination subjects is regarded as of lesser importance than the subjects that contribute directly to the school's results. Talk to any teacher for more than five minutes, however, and s/he will be stressing the importance of developing in young people skills and qualities that contribute as much to their lives as to their learning. So will parents. So will employers. Indeed, the CBI produced a report, *First steps: a new approach for our schools* (Cridland 2012), that called for 'a shift away from exam league tables to new Ofsted reports which assess academic rigour and the broader behaviours and attitudes that young people need to get on in life', with 'a new commitment from business and community organisations to support schools by providing role models, advice and experience.' The CBI is adding its voice to those calling for a WE.

If these things are as important as the development of knowledge, schools need to find ways of ensuring that they are taught and learned with the same degree of rigour. That means developing an approach to assessment that meets future needs, but without being over-complex, as attempts in England at the assessment of key skills have been in the past.

A wider range of outcomes needs to be assessed by a wider range of assessment tools, evaluating what students can do in ways that are appropriate to the aspect being tested. Reliance on written terminal examinations just will not do. Assessment for learning has a role to play here, but so has more imaginative summative assessment, using modern technology to assess progress made by students.

And, when it comes to the final assessment of a young person's full-time education, we need to look at something more comprehensive than GCSEs and A-levels, or single vocational qualifications, although these may well be part of a final overarching qualification, as they are in Wales. A baccalaureate for England that reflected a WE would include much more than knowledge acquired, and it would be at 18, not 16, so that the qualification at the end of full-time education encourages schools and colleges, young people and their parents, to value the development of all those aspects that will make the students life-ready, work-ready and ready for further learning.

Notes

1 Julian Chapman, President of NASUWT, 2009 speech reported in the Guardian on April 13, 2009.

2 Wragg 2004.

3 Gillian Shepherd, Secretary of State for Education 1994–7, in an unpublished interview with the author in 2009.

4 Barber 2002.

5 DFE 2010.

6 DFE 2011.

7 Free schools, UTCs, Studio Schools.

8 Tony Blair.

9 Reform.

10   Caroline Waters BT speaking at Whole Education Conference Dinner November 2012.
11   RSA Opening Minds.

References and further reading

Claxton G., Chambers, M., Powell, G. and Lucas, B., *Building Learning Power: Helping Young People Become Better Learners* (London: TLO, 2002).
— *The Learning Powered School: Pioneering 21st Century Education* (London: TLO, 2011).
Cridland, John, CBI annual conference, 19 November 2012.
DFE, 'The Importance of Teaching', White Paper, 2010.
— 'A Framework for the National Curriculum', A report by the Expert Panel, December 2011.
RSA Opening Minds, www.rsaopeningminds.org.uk.
Smith, A., Lovatt, M., and Wise, D., *Accelerated Learning: A User's Guide* (London: Network, 2003).
Wragg, T., TES, February 2004.

5

Technology and Change

Mark Grundy, Kirsty Tonks and Karine George

In terms of transforming learning and schools technology has often punched below its weight. It can be regarded as having had less impact in schools and schooling than it has on almost every other aspect of our lives. In my last book, I argued it was in part because those who lead schools are of a generation that thinks that is not the way we should do things. Zealots have not always helped either and sometimes expenditure on technology has not proved to be good value for money, yet use of technology is and will be a key feature of all our young people's lives; digital literacy and programming skills are felt by some to be almost as important as more conventional basic skills. Further, technology can enable students to learn anytime, anywhere and enable educators to really personalize learning. This chapter consists of two reflection pieces from two schools that are real advocates, with proven practice and expertise that illustrates the potential technology has to truly transform learning. Both in their own way, through their experience grounded in practice, contribute to our learning and understanding. The first from Karine George of Westfields Junior School in Hampshire, UK, poses the question why we should bother embedding technology and then describes how it is an almost seamless part of learning in every classroom every day in her school. The second is from Sir Mark Grundy and Kirsty Tonks of the Shireland Academy, a large and very successful secondary school in a challenging area and one of the United Kingdom's leading schools in the use and development of the use of technology. They give an unusual perspective seeing technology as a great leveller, explore the importance of their learning platform and progress to describe the potential of flipped classrooms.

REFLECTION

Why bother embedding technology?

KARINE GEORGE

The importance of technology

As teachers, we come into the profession to make a difference. In fact, during my 30 years in the profession, I have never met a single person who has said differently!

In front of each and every teacher around the world sits the future. There they are – 'Hope' and 'Possibility' and our job, lest we forget, is to give this future the best chances possible, for them to grow and learn and make a valuable contribution to society. Why? Well you need only to turn on your television, or watch or listen to one of your portable devices to hear the news, to know that around the world a myriad of problems exist – global climate change, disasters, wars and infectious diseases, to name but a few – and all of these caused by our generation and those of our forefathers!

If you really came into the profession to make a difference then you need to make sure that you prepare the 'Hopes and Possibilities' well enough so that they can make the valuable contributions to society that we will all depend on if our world is to survive some of the biggest problems that it faces. This means our children in school will need a purposeful, creative, engaging and challenge-based curriculum, where they can contribute to their learning. No longer can they be passive in the education process. Instead we need to radically rethink the way children learn, particularly if we want people who come from very different cultural backgrounds to unite and collaborate across the globe to solve these major world issues. More importantly, we need to give all children the best tools to allow them to develop the skills to do just that! However, many schools lag behind in this respect and surprisingly very little comment is made. For example, we would never dream of taking our car to the local garage where they had the building with the sign and the mechanics, but not the tools of the trade to do the very best job. So why do we allow our children to attend schools where many of the key technological resources are missing, resources that could prove to be the key to our children's future life chances?

Technology now pervades every aspect of our daily lives and if we as teachers really claim to want to make the difference to children's life chances then we need to reflect the resources that are used in everyday life. We need our schools to provide our children with the relevant technology and the skills to use it and that is the scary part, particularly if we as the professionals are not confident users of the resources ourselves.

What technology should you use?

Stop worrying about what technology you should use or should buy! Having a clear vision not only for learning but for the technology that you want children to use is more important. This will act as the directional compass needed to help prioritize and thus make the right purchasing decisions.

At Westfields Junior School, we have spent a great deal of time discussing our vision for learning and our role as professionals within that. We have also underpinned our vision by clarifying the role that technology should play through the following simple statements:

1 Revolutionizing learning, teaching and communication for the third millennium through the use of cutting edge technology.

2 Enabling 'anytime anywhere' access for all stakeholders (teachers, support staff, governors, children, parents and community users) to resources and information, including those which promote social networking, collaboration and engagement within and beyond the confines of the classroom, safely.

This vision is not static, it is continually being reviewed, refined and updated and when we purchase any resources for the school these are some of the criteria that we use in our evaluation process. As a result technology is seamlessly woven into the very fabric of our school.

Like building blocks, technology has transformed even the simplest of procedures and given a level of independence to our children not evident previously. For example, trained radio leaders signal the start of the day with their radio show. By playing Young Person's Guide to the Orchestra by Benjamin Britten they signal a ten-minute warning to children who can choose to come directly into school or stay out on the playground and continue with their games. However, as the music changes in tempo the children know they need to enter school, self-register and be prepared to begin the first lesson. Radio leaders give notices to the whole school from teachers and digital leaders organize technical resources and calibrate white boards ready for the start of lessons. All designed to teach our children to take responsibility and demonstrate a level of independence. Real skills for life.

Through social media tools such as Skype our children have connected with people all over the world that they may not otherwise have had the opportunity to meet. Questioning a Muslim lady from Qatar about her Quaran and her beliefs or discussing cultural differences in schools and home lives with children in Holland, for example, are just some of the ways we are able to break down the barriers that may exist, while building tolerance and an understanding of cultural diversity.

Mobile technology such as the iPads has allowed our children to extend their learning beyond the classroom and collaborate from home or send reports from school visits and trips. The use of Iris Connect technology has allowed our teachers to become active research practitioners by analysing the strategies they employ to support and extend children's learning.

The children's parents are used to a level of technology which supports their children and their everyday working lives from simply being able to book an online parental appointment to following a school event or visit on twitter. Parents are able to see screen casts of mathematical concepts to support them in working with their children at home or receive a text from school which acknowledges their child demonstrating one of the schools' key skills or values.

So technology has to be used where it is fit for purpose, not bought by the Information and Communication Technology (ICT) manager or department and used in isolation, only to be abandoned when that person leaves the school. It is always important to remember that it is not the technology alone that will secure the improvement, but the pedagogical reason and subsequent planning for doing it!

Take the purchase of our radio station as a key example; this was bought as a result of a developing trend observed through children's writing over several years, which showed their inability to express themselves in different written forms, fluently and with ease, to different audiences. We know, as professionals, that written language has its foundation in oral skills and that to improve children's responses in writing we needed them to be able to express their ideas clearly in spoken language using appropriate vocabulary and grammar first. We believed that the more we could provide our children with opportunities to develop their speaking skills, the more we would provide the firm foundations from which to build and support their written language skills.

We knew that the purchase of the radio station would engage and motivate the children and provide them with a real context for learning. However, to have any sort of real impact on learning, it is the thinking and planning behind the initiative that secures the improvement. This involved us thinking about some key areas, as shown in Figure 5.1.

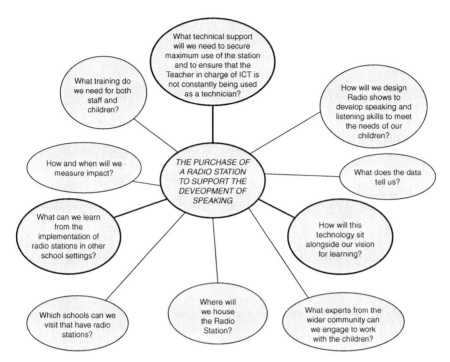

FIGURE 5.1 *Purchase of a radio station – spider diagram*

Through our initial starting point (messy thinking), we were able to plan a long-term strategy for the development of this initiative, which included visits to other schools so that we could learn from other colleagues. We developed a plan that engaged all staff, listening to their ideas, views and concerns. Everyone, including the children, was involved in the design of the radio station and great care was taken to plan for the training needs of staff and children alike. We ensured that regular evaluative meetings were programmed in, so that our ultimate goal of developing children's oral skills was met. In short, when we introduce anything at Westfields, we always start with small steps, but with an end goal and a realistic timeframe. Knowing what we are aiming for is key.

Through powerful, easy-to-use tools, such as the radio station, green screen, blogs and screencasts, our children are contributing content to their own learning in more engaging, real and relevant ways.

How do we persuade staff to use technology?

So if our schools are going to keep in sync with the pace of change, how do we persuade staff, who are feeling overwhelmed with their current workload, to see the value of technology in supporting learning? How do we build confidence in our colleagues?

For me it ends where we began. You have to win hearts and minds. You have to have buy-in. As a leader, whatever your role, you need your directional compass, your vision! To understand leadership you must have an understanding about why people will follow. I believe that success comes from the inside out, by developing leaders within. So for my school I began by developing a vision and sharing that with all my staff, who were able to question and share their views. All I asked was for them to discuss, read and come on a fact-finding mission with me. I visited many schools and I took different staff with me each time. Slowly, the discussions grew, as did our vision. Different staff tried different strategies and gradually interest grew. It is worth noting here that when I talk about staff I mean everyone who works in our school in whatever capacity. By tapping into their thoughts and ideas you often unearth a wealth of unexpected expertise!

We ensured that time was given to follow up on each area of development; that there were regular reviews with a timing structure for staff to try things out and bring back their thoughts, both positive and negative. In this way, different staff claimed ownership of the idea and took the lead.

Our job as leaders is more like shepherds to guide and keep people together on the same path. You have to find a way through every obstacle if you believe what you are doing is important. The *key* to any new development is to not have a piecemeal strategy, but to have a vision to work together with your team and let people share their ideas, concerns and questions. After all, it is not about what each of us does or says individually but what we all do and say together that will have real impact.

Nevertheless, even with a vision, there still remain two main obstacles to negotiate for many staff, which arise in any discussion on technology. Obstacles born out of fear and anxiety:

- That learning time will be wasted when the technology does not work.

- That the technology needed to deliver the innovative types of learning that they would like to create, would be beyond them.

So with each new development it is important to plan who will be the 'lead', the person responsible, and to identify what form the technical support should be. It is also essential that the training for staff needed to support each new strategy is identified and that time is built in to give it justice. In short, small, well-planned steps with support and training was our recipe for success!

What have we learned?

Four top tips that we have learned along the way are:

- Do not buy technology for technology's sake; buy it because you have a strategic intent.

- Minimize the risks by visiting colleagues and schools that have already trodden the path that you are thinking of embarking upon. Always go armed with your questions and someone whose job will be affected by any new initiative. If they are convinced they will champion the cause and move things on more quickly.

- Consider the technological support that may be needed particularly if you want to ensure that the Information Technology (IT) Manager is not being pulled out of his/her class constantly.

- Plan for the training needs of all staff in order to get maximum use.

Technology is integrated into the strategic day-to-day running of my school now. It supports learning, engages parents and has a positive impact on workload and, in turn, staff wellbeing!

The future

While schools generally have moved slowly, there has been a revolution happening in front of us, with learners spending far more time working with different forms of technologies away from the learning environment than inside it. Even preschool children can be seen using mobile phones and iPads, for example, while waiting in doctor's surgeries. These young people are using technology in a way most schools would be envious of, because it is real, relevant and motivating. Leaders of education can no longer afford to ignore the transformational affect that technology has on our everyday lives. We need to act now and harness this motivation to develop children's learning and support them in developing their digital skills. Why?
Because:

- Third millennium learners need to be digitally fluent. This generation has access to massive amounts of information. Anyone can publish anything. We need to teach children how to examine the information so they can evaluate what that they find.

- Technology offers engaged learning, that is, activities that involve active cognitive processes such as creating, problem-solving, reasoning, decision-making and evaluation. All skills valued by employers. Real-world skills.

- Technology has the ability to meld learning episodes together.

- Technology has the ability to record learner achievements in new and exciting ways, for review and refinement

- Technology will help children to break out from the confines of the classroom, to connect with others locally, nationally and globally. A sharing of our collective learning can only serve to help us solve more of the world's problems creatively.

Evidence of impact

And if you want evidence of impact, look no further. This blog represents the thoughts of a 16-year-old boy who found his voice through his blogs and Twitter feeds. In his blog (part of which can be seen below) he refers to of our old whole school vision strapline `confidence to achieve' and the affect it had on him . . . If only we could have a school measure for this!

> You can spend the rest of your life forgetting or pursuing a minute of your childhood.
>
> . . . If you've seen the first post I made here, you will find that the reason I pursue a career in computer science is because of two reasons that relate to my childhood. First being Cliff Huizenga, or 'cliffpro'. . . . the second reason – I was told that I was good by people and the primary school I went to.
>
> Actually, it wasn't just being told that I'm good. It was everything that came with it that really fuelled the *confidence to achieve* and become what I am now. From a nine year-old impressing teachers by saving *.jpg format images – up to having three programming languages on my back and getting into networking applications. My school had a reputation for being somewhat slightly more 'technologically advanced' than many other schools at the time. I think so anyway, we won awards for it.
>
> But my childhood did have highly defining moments in it that link in to me actually doing this project today. An amazing moment of my childhood was when I was given the opportunity to talk to some visitors to the

school that later awarded the school the 'BECTA Awards', an award that is now extinct. . . . It really did please me, I was being recognised for my passion. . . . The point I'm making, recognise the potential and talents in someone. Not just a child, but anyone. When you do so, go ahead and garner it. It'll probably make someones day – and life.

REFLECTION

Technology as an enabler

MARK GRUNDY AND KIRSTY TONKS

Technology as a leveller

One of the primary reasons for our developed use of technology to support school improvement has been the enormous leveller that technology can be in school. Technology does not judge; it is always there as a safety net and provides the sort of consistency needed when trying to implement whole school changes or targeted interventions.

> The essence of our success with technology is based around our clear belief that the technology must serve the school and not vice versa

At Shireland we were an early adopter of our Learning Platform and as such did not have to follow other's suggestions as to how best to use one. We shaped and moulded it to our own needs and over the years it grew and changed as the school did, as we moved from specialist school to academy and now towards Teaching School. The essence of our success with technology is based around our clear belief that the technology must serve the school and not vice versa.

Our Learning Gateway quickly became the skeleton upon which we hung almost everything. It became the key driver of solutions and the virtual personification of the school itself. Each year the Gateway changed as the school changed direction and this adaptability made it the success it is rather than the sluggish monolithic structure that many schools were provided with.

One of the keys to using technology in education successfully is the ability to change path quickly when things arise. This was never as apparent as when Shireland found itself in Special Measures in 2009. One of the reasons was the move away from using the Learning Platform and associated technologies and back towards more traditional methods. The leadership teams within the school recognized this as an attributing factor and were swift to look at redressing this. An audit of key processes began and we looked at how technology could once again move us forward and underpin these processes. The solutions we generated were very targeted and implemented with purpose and clear direction.

Getting the technology to deliver solutions when and where they are needed

We have been able to use the Learning Gateway to provide students with the sort of resources they require to achieve (both commercial and home produced). In the challenging area that our schools serve our students rarely possess at home the resources required to study and revise so we have developed Resource Sites that they access via the Gateway and we have stored all of the key learning resources here. We have identified a number of commercial solutions such as 'Mathletics' and 'Little Bridge' that we have funded both in our Academy and our cluster Primary schools. We want to provide environments for our family of schools that allow students to make accelerated progress because the activities and resources that they need are delivered to them. This is the second key feature of Outstanding use of technology: getting the technology to deliver solutions when and where they are needed.

The Learning Gateway provides a unique 'safety net' for achievement that is absent in the homes of many of our students and we think that this potential solution and its replicability is the reason why Learning Platforms should have prospered but for this to happen schools needed to look beyond the school gates if they were to see the potential.

The bespoke school learning environments that can be created for schools will allow technology to support the students in a far more personalized way. The main reason that technology fails to deliver in many schools is that the environment that schools 'settle for' is not their own. Their Learning Gateway should reflect their school, their students and their families. It should not reflect the emphases of a vendor!

The ICT test bed project

In the period between 2002 and 2006 Shireland and its family of primary schools was involved in the DfES ICT Test Bed Project that was initiated to explore how ICT can be used to support the government's wider agenda for education reform. The project took a holistic approach to ICT implementation in three areas of relative socio-economic deprivation.

The key identified benefits of the ICT Test Bed Project[1] were as follows:

- ICT creates a new and increased culture of sharing of materials and resources between teachers, through shared server areas or online learning environments at all schools levels. In primary schools, sharing of resources happens within year groups and in secondary schools within departments.

- When the planning and presentation is accomplished in advance, the teacher can concentrate in the lesson on the pupils and their responses, creating an easier forum for discussion and interaction with the pupils. The ease of adapting, adding and saving interactive whiteboard pages leads to more teacher-student interaction in developing conceptual statements and greater coherence and consistency in these descriptors over time.

- 'Ownership' of resources – that is, teachers having a close understanding of, and sympathy with, what the programme contains and is trying to achieve – is a critical issue for teachers and hence content development needs to be tailored to individual and local needs.

Evaluation of the ICT Test bed project
final report june 2007

Our e-learning Test Bed exemplified how powerful e-learning could be in raising standards. We know from leading on the ICT Test Bed at Shireland and our experience of hosting 130 schools nationally that e-learning based solutions well integrated in a personalized manner make a significant difference. The project acted as the catalyst for many of the key practices and processes that have taken Shireland to Outstanding but more importantly these processes are now helping to move staff to Outstanding and delivering the systemic improvements that our schools so desperately require. For the last three years we have delivered our Key Stage 3 curriculum through the Learning Gateway with students using their own netbook in class and either their own home computer or one co-provided by ourselves and the E-learning Foundation. The key indicators for the current Year 9 are the highest in the school's history.

> The last two years have seen an explosion in the number of resources created by students for others

The resources that we have produced are easily transferable to other classrooms and this has been a continual driver for us in embedding technology but more importantly in our personalization of learning. Our staff have for some time developed resources which our e-learning team have 'polished' into key prompts to support learning. In the last few years we have increasingly developed resources which could be used by others. Recent years have seen an explosion in the number of resources created by students for others with the Young People's e-learning Network (YPEN) and our Furtheryourmaths.co.uk sites just two examples.

Advantages

The ability of a Learning Gateway to act as the 'glue' for school improvement has the potential to be highly cost effective. The Sharepoint base of the Learning Gateway saves hours and thousands of pounds in document storage but more importantly improves data presentation to all of the key stakeholder groups: to staff, to students, but just as importantly to families.

The 'flipped classroom'

The most significant recent development in school has been around the use of the 'flipped classroom' methodology. Staff provide students with a stimulus or catalyst for their learning prior to the lesson and students then identify what they need to learn. The flipped classroom methodology changes the whole dynamic of the lesson and makes the learner the primary questioner not the dumb recipient. But this will require a level of resourcing to be provided that currently does not exist in some schools.

Students have traditionally received generalized instruction delivered by teachers in class, which normally has been via presentation and explanation interwoven in the better classrooms with Assessment for Learning (AfL) strategies. In some schools the traditional diet has been enhanced with a number of online activities. In flipped classrooms students receive a stimulus and then dictate the agenda. I have never really understood how we manage to convince ourselves that homework really works! The idea of giving the learner a series of questions about something that they may not be sure of to establish that they do not fully understand it seems somewhat flawed. The idea of providing learners with a stimulus of a video which explains a concept and then asking them to compile a list of questions or issues that cover the areas that they are unsure of seems far more valuable.

Our use of formative assessment can be maximized in a flipped environment and the benefits of online resources are obvious to all. If we could provide a library of stimulus material that could be used to prompt this methodology we could make such a difference to our learners and staff time can be used for richer interactive learning and reinforcement activities in which students apply what they have learnt outside the classroom on a deeper level than ever before. The teaching can be more personalized as students understand their own strengths and weaknesses and the feedback delay that 'kills' many homework activities is rectified.

The challenge for staff is to locate, select and make the best use of online resources which will act as the catalyst for a different form of learning dialogue and then fully utilize face to face time for group work, collaboration, creativity and engaging purposefully with real problems. This can only be facilitated via technology.

The development of student-for-student-authored resources is growing hugely based on work that one of the 2012 Year 11 students who developed a site called furtheryourmaths.co.uk, produced with other students, where resources were collected and developed to explain key mathematical concepts to other students.

The group who were working on English have just created their equivalent site – Furtheryourenglish.co.uk. This co-creation of resources by students however needs a home and this is where our Learning Gateway comes into its own. We should also be looking at sites such as O2Learn and Khan Academy and reconfiguring them to support this methodology. We need guidance for Senior Leaders, classroom teachers and support staff but most importantly for our students and their families if we are to maximize this lesson changing opportunity.

Technology as a key lever for change

Many of the detractors of the benefits of technology will cite that this can only happen in 'new builds in nice areas'. But we know that this is simply not true. Shireland Collegiate Academy is situated in Sandwell, one of the most deprived boroughs in the country, and serves three of the most deprived wards in the country with high levels of unemployment, significant health-related problems and a history of underachievement at all age levels despite the outstanding efforts of a number of local schools. In the last decade Shireland has changed from a modest comprehensive to a specialist school taking a key role in the use of new technology and the teaching of Languages, and finally to a partner Academy in the Collegiate Academy Trust. In the last 11 years we have radically changed our school structures, our curriculum and probably most significantly our use of new technologies. In 1997 attainment at Shireland was low and teachers were finding it very difficult to engage with families. We all knew that it would be necessary to make some big changes in order to persuade parents and the local community to get involved with the school, and to raise levels of attainment as a result.

Right from the start we tried to use technology as a medium to join people together; we are acutely aware that we cannot maximize individual's talents on our own. Technology can be a wonderful leveller, but for it to be used effectively it is vital that all learners have access to it, both in the classroom and beyond the school gates.

Bridging the digital divide

In order to bridge the digital divide that existed at the school, we arranged for Personal Computers (PCs) to be set up in 2,000 pupils' homes, along with broadband connections for those without it. Every family attended a training session to deal with any problems if they arose. We also established clusters of PCs in local community venues attended by our students and their families. We encouraged the venues to set up homework clubs and to allocate weekly time slots where the PCs could be used for learning and communication with the school.

Suddenly all of our learners were able to work with appropriate technology in a time and place that suited them. Sandwell is one of the most deprived boroughs nationally, but our scheme gave each of our pupils an equal opportunity to take full advantage of the technology on offer. Providing computers and internet access for our pupils and community venues was a huge step, but new pieces of technology are not enough on their own – you need a context.

Our pupils really value their 'Student Portal' on the Gateway, which currently gets two million hits each term. We try to mirror the look and feel of sites that pupils use in their free time, such as Facebook and Bebo, so that the personalized spaces which we provide are engaging to use. Being able to log on anytime and anyplace means our students are in control of their learning. Gone are the days when pupils could only learn during the school day. Pupils who miss classes can also log on to pick up homework assignments.

Technology can support our pupils' learning without embarrassing them

One of the reasons we are so keen on technology at Shireland is that it does not judge – it can support our pupils' learning without embarrassing them. Pupils feel less apprehensive about being tested on the Learning Gateway because the assessment methods are less formal. They can succeed or fail in private, which makes them more willing to take part. Technology of this kind engages pupils and builds their confidence.

The Learning Gateway has had a major impact on communication with parents, who can also log on at any time and find out about their child's target grades, punctuality and merits. It is not just about telling parents where their children could do better – pupils often keep achievements to themselves, so it is a great way of making sure parents know when their children are doing well. Online learning resources for families are vital in raising engagement and attainment at the school. Increasing literacy and numeracy among parents has meant that they, in turn, can help their children to learn. Families can also receive their own learning units from the Shireland Gateway – mostly aimed at improving adult literacy and numeracy – along with additional services such as health advice and even job opportunities in their local community.

Technology is a hugely powerful tool which can transform teaching and learning when deployed in a context. All too often we superimpose conflicting contexts on top of technological tools and wonder why learners do not succeed, and staff freeze!

Young people today have grown up with computers, the internet, mobile phones and MP3 players, and we need to harness their enthusiasm for technology and use it to engage them in learning. When pupil motivation and parental engagement are low in a school, it is often because teachers do not have enough time to talk to pupils and their families. Giving pupils and their families access to the internet and, in particular, to the resources available on the Learning Gateway, has been absolutely crucial in ensuring parents and pupils are empowered, engaged and truly feel part of the school community.

We have embedded our technology not overlaid it. Our emphases have all been about usage, processes and outcomes, not the technology!

So in this rapidly changing world how can you embed technology successfully?

There are lots of consultants out there providing 'Ten Clever Things to do with an iPad' training but this is merely icing on the cake. A little bit of decoration and short-term engagement with students. These applications also make it hard for teachers, middle and senior leaders and the students themselves to manage learning. What we are seeing is a fragmentation of the use of technology in schools which leads to inconsistency and champion teacher use rather than whole school adoption. These technologies are not inclusive and as we have seen at times, they are making it difficult for staff to show progress within a lesson.

> We need to make sure that every child is empowered and has the capacity to learn to their potential

What we need to focus on is the base of the cake: a good-quality sponge that all teachers and support staff can produce and deliver, that all students can take hold of and add to, ready to decorate. At Shireland we cannot afford to leave things to chance and rely on incidental learning. We need to make sure that every child is empowered and has the capacity to learn to their potential. We have to help support and manage the learning experiences as best as we can. We need to give staff a context for changing learning using these tools not just push them to clever things that will look good but have little lasting effect.

The importance of curriculum design

In the last few years we seem to have forgotten that it is the curriculum design that is the key and not the curriculum prescription. We need to design curriculum programmes for young people that mirror real life, that are based on contexts and competences and not just content. We need to look at the use of time, the difference that technology can make to time and the connectivity of learners and staff.

Technology has been our skeleton, our catalyst and our safety net for many years. The difference that e-learning has made in Shireland has been profound both in terms of improving standards and developing people. Our classroom practices have developed incredibly and the flipped methodology that can be seen to occur so naturally in so many classrooms is causing a fundamental change in the way that our school works and our students learn. Used well technology makes a huge difference – just ask our staff, students and families.

A has been said more than once before, if you get the culture right anything is possible.

Note

1 Evaluation of the ICT Test Bed Project Final Report, DFE June 2007.

6

Exploring System-wide Change: The New York City iZone[1]

David Jackson including a reflection piece on a study tour visit by Jonathan De Suasmarez

Introduction

New York City (NYC) has iconic significance across the world for all sorts of reasons – architecture, business, finance, the arts, fashion . . . and also urban reform. It is no surprise that NYC's educational reform endeavours have particular resonance for schooling systems across urban landscapes internationally. Joel Klein's tenure as Chancellor was characterized by three phases of educational reform. This case study focuses primarily on the third phase – the innovation phase.

To understand this account of the latest phase (the third phase) of NYC's journey since 2010, one has first to appreciate that during the previous decade, from unacceptably poor (and flatlined) levels of achievement, high school drop-out rates, low graduation rates and relatively chaotic system dynamics, New York experienced probably the most rapid and consistent improvement in test scores and graduation rates of any urban jurisdiction in the world. In fact, almost the most remarkable feature of this whole story is that this consistent upward trajectory led not to complacency or quiet satisfaction, but to moral outrage and the desire for a more radical approach.

Convinced by his own life-experience as a poor New Yorker, Joel Klein profoundly believed that education could, and should, do the same for the current generation's poor – those who have consistently been failed by the schooling system. What the data through to 2009 showed was this: if traditional approaches to system-wide school reform in NYC were sustained as successfully for the next decade as for the last, then its schools would still be failing an unacceptably large proportion of its total student body. Worse than that, sub-analysis of data displayed many more alarming features. Although test scores and graduation rates were rising, there was very considerable variation between ethnic and socio-economic groups. More, post-school tracker studies suggested that improved high school graduation rates were being hot-housed by the reforms, and that a disproportionately large number of NYC's College entrants required remediation in College or were among the unacceptably high drop-out rates. It seemed that the success was only partial. Some of it was about schools responding to the reforms by gaming the system.

What was apparent to Joel Klein – passionate, as has been said, about the role of education in transforming lives – and his senior leaders was that a step-change was required; that the traditional model of learning and schooling was inadequate to the challenge of realizing the potential of all New York's youngsters; that school as we know it was not appropriate to the demands or opportunities of the twenty-first century; that while the top-down reform strategies prevalent across the developed world had proved they could drag a chaotic and underachieving system up by its boot-straps, they were failing to harness the energy and creativity of its system actors and were not mobilizing them around the innovation agenda that he now perceived as being critical to system transformation.

Joel Klein's most apparent legacy lies with the stabilization of the NYC system and its progressive improvement during his tenure. His most enduring one may well be the establishment of a system-wide innovation strategy designed to harness the leadership and creativity within the system, to break down the power relations between schools and 'middle tier', to abandon some of the traditional assumptions about schooling and about system relationships and instead to fashion a space in which the most advanced and ambitious sites of practice might innovate on behalf of the wider system.

This is the story of this third phase of NYC's reform – its innovation phase, embodied in the establishment of the New York Innovation Zone. At the outset, let us be clear that this is a story of one of the most ambitious, intentional, strategic, conceptually robust and enlightened system transformation interventions anywhere in the world (outside, perhaps, those prompted by natural disasters such as in New Orleans or Christchurch). It is not only a story of success but also of the complexities and challenges of changing systems.

In its ambition and design and implementation endeavours it has huge amounts of learning to offer urban systems worldwide – the purpose of writing this narrative.

The background story[2]

For most of the second half of the twentieth century, fewer than 50 per cent of NYC public school students graduated in four years, with rates significantly lower for African American and Hispanic students. Corruption and mismanagement were rife and there was no coherent city-wide co-ordination, with responsibility for schools split across 40 district offices.

In November 2001 Michael Bloomberg, the founder and majority owner of the financial news and information services media company Bloomberg, was elected Mayor of NYC and, in 2002, after a protracted campaign by Bloomberg and his predecessor Mayors, the New York State Legislature finally approved mayoral takeover of the NYC public school system. Michael Bloomberg moved quickly to appoint Joel Klein, a lawyer who had been Deputy Counsel to President Clinton and lead prosecutor in the antitrust case against Microsoft, as Chancellor of Education. Together Bloomberg and Klein implemented what turned out to be three phases of reform under the banner of 'Children First'.

The first phase has been characterized as 'depoliticizing and fostering coherence and capacity-building'. It included the restructuring of the NYC public schools in order to stabilize and co-ordinate a disorganized system of schools and involved the consolidation of the 40 city-wide district offices into ten Instructional Divisions. It also included a robust programme of central intervention strategies to address unacceptable levels of teacher, principal and school performance – including school closures, the creation of new schools (both 'charter' and regular schools) and the breaking up of large schools into 'small schools', though generally still within the one building (a programme heavily supported by the Gates Foundation's commitment to the 'small school movement'). More than a quarter of the over 1,500 schools in NYC have opened in the last ten years, although it has to be noted that a far smaller proportion has been closed – one closed large high school yielding many small new schools.

Summarized, the key actions in Phase One were:

- A new management structure: Streamlined bureaucracy, bringing stability and coherence to an unruly system. The ten regions, each headed by a regional superintendent;

- Focus on school leadership: Created the New York Leadership Academy to train and support new and existing principals;

- Enhanced curriculum: Implemented uniform math and English curricula and introduced new curricula in the arts, social studies, and science;

- End of social promotion: Implemented a policy to ensure that promotion is always based on academic preparation and ability;

- Families engaged: Created new parent supports, placing a parent coordinator in every school;

- Schools made safer: Major crimes down more than 13 per cent, other incidents down more than 45 per cent;

- Bureaucracy cut: Between 2002 and 2007 more than $190 million was passported from the bureaucracy to schools and classrooms.

Phase Two of the reform attempted to reduce the level of centralization and operated within three core principles of leadership, empowerment and accountability.

- *The principle of leadership* recognized that the success of empowering schools hinged upon the capacity and capability of school leaders. It built on the introduction of the NYC Leadership Academy (NYCLA) – in particular using radical, intensive new leadership development designs for preparation and placement into some of the most challenging NYC schools, often sourcing its candidates from under-represented groups. A fifth of the NYCLA graduated school leaders have opened new small schools and many more are carrying their learning and experience into leadership across the system – many also sustaining alumni network membership.

- *The principle of empowerment* was founded on the belief that the people closest to the students should be empowered to make school-level educational decisions, such as budget, staffing, curriculum and professional development. The empowerment principle also involved the elimination of an entire layer of district middle-tier management, with the devolution of central functions to quasi-independent learning support organizations and the establishment of networks of schools around these learning support providers. School principals (headteachers) were free to make their own choice of provider and network. An additional $174 million was devolved to schools and classrooms, bringing the total money taken from the bureaucracy and given to schools to more than $350 million.

- *The principle of accountability* recognized that schools and school leaders needed to be held accountable for their performance (against performance review standards) and that the NYC Department of Education (DOE) was reciprocally accountable for providing schools with the tools, resources and capabilities to achieve success. Reciprocal accountability is a key feature of this and the subsequent reform phase.

These elements are represented in Table 6.1.

TABLE 6.1 The principles of accountability/empowerment

Accountability	Empowerment
Holding schools accountable for results: • Progress Reports (Grades A–F); • Learning Environment Surveys; • Quality Reviews; • Rewards and consequences based on results. **Tools for schools:** • ARIS provides student performance data to guide school improvement efforts; • Periodic Assessments help schools identify each student's strengths and weaknesses to target instruction; • Children First Intensive professional development builds school-wide capacity to diagnose student needs and to develop evidence-based individualized instruction, self-evaluation and continuous improvement in student learning; • Leadership development, informed in the components of the reform, builds capacity.	**Decisions made close to students:** • Decisions can be *best for students* when they are happening *close to students* at the school level. **Individualized support options:** • Principals used to get 'support' from regions. Now, they choose what is best for them from more than a dozen DOE and non-profit options; • Networks of schools built around providers create communities of challenge and support. **Schools also have:** • More money and more power over budgets, staffing and programmes, letting schools tailor instruction and programmes to their specific perceived needs; • New funding and more equitable distribution of resources to schools.

Taking stock – dramatic improvement but dissatisfaction

As stated in the introduction, having flatlined for the previous 50 years, between 2002 and 2009 the performance of NYC public schools dramatically improved, with high-school graduation rates (within four years) increasing from around 50 per cent to 68 per cent – one of the most rapid improvements in a schooling system experienced in any urban setting in the world. More students were capable of reading and doing math, and more students were meeting the requirements for high school graduation than ever before. The system was becoming more equitable and professionals more empowered as a result of the two phases of reform.

However, Mayor Bloomberg and Chancellor Klein, and many within the NYC public school system, were not content either with the overall level of attainment or with this rate of increase. Almost a third of high school students were not graduating within four years. And, even though two-thirds were, only 16 per cent had a college ready diploma. For African American and Hispanic students the graduation rate was even lower (around 45%) than for their white and Asian counterparts. And there was huge variation between schools across the city: an issue that the Chancellor highlighted by asking DOE staff whether they would be prepared to have their children randomly assigned to schools.

So, while taking pride in the improvements and past successes, the system's leaders consistently articulated challenge to the present system and re-articulated their aspiration of every student being 'college and career ready'.

They also noticed that while many schools in the city had improved there were some schools that had strikingly better results, often not through strict compliance with central frameworks – not doing what was asked of them or in the ways that were expected of them. Their success appeared to stem from the passions and creativity and commitment of the principals and the teachers – people who seemed to function in some ways as 'creative deviants'. Sandra Stein, then CEO of the New York Leadership Academy, characterized such school leaders as 'renegade principals' who, through the development of practices and methods that often 'broke the rules', were establishing outlier practices.

Against all the odds, these schools were innovating on behalf of their students to significant effect, but they were doing so below the radar and in a way that was publicly invisible and therefore did not yield wider system learning.

In 2009, to nurture, further support and expand such locations of potential innovation, NYC set up its 'Innovation Zone' (mark 1), designed to support a pioneering community of schools in implementing personalized learning environments as a means to accelerate student progress towards college and career readiness. It was, and is, driven by the emphatic belief that both schools and the wider supporting system must change, and that the driver for such change lay in a shift from standardization of learning to more personalized approaches and environments – and that this shift will be enabled by new technologies with the power both to engage and liberate the learner.

This first incarnation established two strands of work. The first strand was focused on innovation around some key 'components' of schooling suggestive of promise – parental involvement, scheduling, student leadership – by inviting (and supporting, incubating and legitimizing) groups of schools to innovate in a loose alliance around these components. The second strand involved innovation around new technological platforms and blended learning approaches.

As the work evolved, and to some extent influenced by insights from other jurisdictions thinking through similar problems via participation in the inter-jurisdictional Global Education Leaders' Program (GELP),[3] they came to two realizations.

The first was that the skills, behaviours and knowledge schools were teaching were too often not those students needed to succeed in the adult world of the twenty-first century (for college and career readiness). The great proportion of their instructional energies was focused on managing groups of students through an industrial-era model of one-size-fits-all courses of study, with standardization as its core tenet: a standard school day, with standard teachers, in standard-size rooms and standard-sized classes – an experience that bears little resemblance to the most positive learning experiences young people (or adults) have outside the classroom, whether through team experiences, artistic creation, entrepreneurship or online networking and journaling.

The second realization was that to effect change across the entire public school system, it would be patently insufficient just to develop a set of exemplary 'components' of innovative practice, or to introduce new blended learning approaches into the conventional school model – or even to identify a number of exemplary schools – without setting this firmly within a diffusion and scaling strategy which held at least the potential to impact on a significant proportion of, and ultimately all, New York schools. This recognition of the need to house its innovation approaches within an ambitious and enlightened strategy for diffusion and scaling has been one of the consistent strengths of NYC's phase 3 work.

Phase three reform

In Spring 2010, recognizing that the 'industrial model' of schooling was exhausted and could not deliver college and career readiness for all students, recognizing the energy, ingenuity and commitment that was present in some schools, and aware that new models of practice were required from which the system could learn, the NYC DOE launched what is quite possibly one of the most ambitious and intentional innovation strategies in education reform (perhaps even public service reform) across the world. The rationale was simple: New York's schooling system perceives a need for its young people to be enabled to achieve higher-order standards that prepare them for post-secondary success by emphasizing higher-order critical thinking, real-world application, and collaboration that will necessitate developing instructional capacity that our schools currently do not have.

The overall aim of the strategy was to transform the learning for the 1 million students in NYC public schools through replacing the 'industrial model', by building schools round the needs, interests and motivations of individual students. Students enter schools as individuals, often now tech-savvy, with a diverse set of needs and capabilities. Therefore, the new logic went, schools needed to reorient themselves to treat students as individual learners, where every child has a unique education plan with his or her own path to personal and academic success. The plan was to make personalization the central approach to educating students – where learning would be about each student mastering skills and capabilities in her own way, at her own pace.

Personalized approaches and mastery-based assessment became new foundation stones. In iZone schools, schooling would no longer be about advancing students through grade levels based on age and time spent in class, but about supporting students in building the skills, knowledge and dispositions they need to be successful:

> We are committed to engage every child in a personalized, rigorous, and engaging learning plan that develops the skills they will need to succeed in the complex real-world situations they will face in college and career. It will motivate them by connecting their learning to real-world contexts and empowering them to define and manage their own academic progress. (http://schools.nyc.gov/community/innovation/izone/default.htm)

At that point, by 2010, the initial version of the innovation zone (iZone) contained the two components described above: iLearn and InnovateNYC.

These two separate but related elements served (and still serve) different functions, then described as:

iLearn – focuses on developing technology enabled and enhanced learning and resources that personalize, extend, and deepen the learning experience of students in participating schools

InnovateNYC – through its schools ecosystem (US DOE grant funded) it identifies and stimulates technology solutions to high-value problems. Working on school component innovations, it evaluates impact on practice and outcomes. It tests and provides feedback on new innovation products. Promising innovations are scaled system-wide.

During the 2010–11 school year this high-level vision for 'personalized mastery learning' was articulated one level further, identifying four pillars or principles:

1 Personalized learning plans and progress;

2 Flexible and real-world learning environments (multiple learning modalities, learning anytime, anywhere, on- and off-line, project-based);

3 Next generation curriculum and assessment;

4 New student and staff roles (advisor, tutor, mentor, designer, facilitator, peer-tutor, etc.).

While retaining the two components of iZone mark 1, the ambition was expanded to include a third component, iZone360, with the following brief:

iZone360 – a community of practice of schools committed to whole school redesign through the integration of components and practices into whole new schooling models of highly successful 21st Century personalized learning – *on behalf of the whole system.*

This is the focus of the final section of this case account.

The three parts of iZone now include more than 250 schools from across the city with over 190,000 students. The iZone serves a higher percentage of students who receive free or reduced price lunch, a higher percentage of students who required special education services, and a higher percentage of English language learners than comparable non-iZone schools. The iZone also is unique to many district initiatives in that schools must opt-in for participation through a rigorous application process.

The programmes piloted in the iZone-empowered teachers, administrators, students and parents with cutting-edge resources and strategies for personalization such as online content, real-time data and a suite of robust educational practices like flexible scheduling and staffing to expand opportunities on how, where and when a student can learn. Some of the tools and strategies piloted included:

- Online and blended learning tools with related training, where real-time data and online content help teachers to differentiate instruction, expand learning time and increase access to courses not offered within a student's home school;

- Mastery-based learning with the support of tools, such as iLearnNYC and Jumprope, and training to change the way students evidence their mastery of content knowledge and skills;

- Adaptive learning software including Time To Know, Pearson SuccessMaker and Compass Learning Odyssey in elementary schools. The software assisted teachers in personalizing learning in English language, arts and math in the third, fourth and fifth grades;

- School of One which uses daily skill assessments to monitor student progress, and algorithm-assisted assignments that adapt a personalized learning plan to best meet students' needs in middle school math. The further innovation is the redesign of the classroom to integrate multiple 'modes' of instruction – live teacher-led lessons, software-based lessons, collaborative activities, virtual tutors, and individual practice – into the same learning space;

- New school schedules, and staff and student roles that are student-centred and designed to facilitate greater personalization;

- Real-world learning, where a significant portion of coursework is completed through internships or other opportunities outside the school building.

Since its launch, the iZone has made significant progress in schools and the broader ecosystem. Key achievements from the iZone incubation period include:

- Identified early indicators of increased student achievement: iZone students demonstrated increases in intrinsic motivation, problem formulation, research, interpretation and communication. These characteristics are linked to college and career readiness and are predictive of eventual increases in traditional student achievement metrics.

- Fostered demand for innovation: The iZone grew from 81 to 250 schools in two years. Schools were chosen through an extensive application process, and each year more schools want to join the iZone than are accepted.

- Deployed new tools to schools: The iZone, working in close partnership with key DOE offices, launched the iLearnNYC platform, an unprecedented, customized learning management system to support online and blended learning. This investment prepared the NYC DOE to quickly and effectively utilize online learning to support students displaced by Hurricane Sandy.

- Made significant progress towards sustainability: The iLearnNYC programme was transitioned from a free resource to a fee-for-service programme, and is on its way to becoming a self-sustaining model. Despite the new cost structure, nearly 200 schools chose to participate in iLearnNYC, up from 140 schools in the prior year.

- Launched Innovate NYC Ecosystem: In January 2013, the iZone launched the Gap App Challenge for middle school math – the first of many challenges in its Ecosystem, a project funded by the US DOE's Investing in Innovation award. The Ecosystem drives smarter investments in education technology on the part of the district, schools, funders and vendors, in order to maximize the potential of the edtech market.

- Successfully advocated for key policy changes: In close collaboration with the Office of Academic Policy, the New York State DOE, and key local partners, iZone has championed policy reforms that facilitate innovation and personalization, including greater flexibility in New York State Textbook Law (NYSTL), funding, the ability to grant credit for learning that happens outside the school building and traditional school day, and the related authorization to determine attendance based on learning anywhere and at any time.

While the NYC DOE has been encouraged by the early success of the iZone, they have learned important lessons that will help to sharpen their focus and refine the execution, particularly as it relates to redesigning existing schools and diffusing promising ideas throughout the system.

iZone 360: Lessons on system transformation[4]

From its outset two things created energy for this bold work. The first was an utterly irrefutable case for change supported by a strong mandate, an impatience for innovation, from the Chancellor. The second was a compelling vision of an alternative pedagogical paradigm and the redesign priciples around which new school models should emerge – well-defined in theory but intentionally open to multiple interpretations in practice. (New York has never set out to create a definitive new model. Pluralism, multiple models, choice possibilities is more the case. The consistency lies in fidelity to the design principles.)

It is said that educational change is technically simple but socially complex. While true, this is also too simple a formulation for the experience of iZone360. The 360 design has proved to be theoretically and technically robust, but the contextual challenges, the embedded social and cultural habits and the dispositional variances – all these have contributed to complexity.

The theory of change was straightforward enough:

- Principals of ambitious and potentially 'renegade' schools willing to engage in radical school redesign within a strong community of practice, working on behalf of the entire system;

- Build the design around a clear diffusion strategy – animate that wider system around the work and connect it such that foundations of a diffusion strategy are present from the outset;

- Create new forums wherein the emergent strategy and implementation challenges can be problem-solved;

- Incubate the schools by utilizing resources flexibly, including service design expertise, multiple professional learning approaches, support from 'model design partners', use of innovation disciplines, provision of innovation coaches and a range of other supports;

- Learn from the work, codifying practices such that they can diffuse and scale across the system.

In addition, the ambition was always to co-design the evolution of this strategy with participant principals, such that the DOE personnel and principals would learn their way forward together – very much in the spirit of a 'systemic action learning strategy'. The significance of this (in theory) is obvious: in the short-term creating radically new school models requires deregulation and safe space – systemically enabling conditions; new policy and practice enablers. Longer-term scaling of these models would involve all system actors learning alongside one another how to adapt expectations, supports and accountabilities to new schooling and learning approaches.

Simple examples of what is implied might be that in new school designs the State's 'seat-time' regulations may become anachronistic; teachers' working conditions might need to change; universal assessment dates (grade-level testing) may become counter-productive; age-cohorting students might be redundant; attendance in learning may be more valuable than attendance in school; the regulation school calendar may be inhibiting. The co-design and shared learning ambitions were designed in part to wrestle with such emergent issues of abandonment – all of which are ones which arose in the early design stages of the work.

This co-design intent and its underpinning trust-based commitment, the community of practice approach, the 'on behalf of the system' moral purpose of the work – and the total belief that professionals have it within their power to be the school and system redesigners, given appropriate license and supports-made 360 an archetypically progressive strategy.

What evolved is both a testament to NYC's ambition and also an illuminating insight into many of the challenges inherent in system transformation endeavours.

A whole school redesign story (2010 to 2012)

The initial strategy for achieving the iZone360 vision (scalable whole-school redesign models) had three key elements: (1) the zone 'mark 2' (iZone360) problem-solving together innovation challenges of designing and implementing new models of schooling within the framework of personalized mastery learning – on behalf of the system;[5] (2) building the capacity of the networks of schools in NYC, established during the empowerment phase of reform, to support the early adoption and adaptation of proven new models; (3) creating the enabling system conditions and dynamics, which would have two dimensions: first the abandonment, redesign and redeployment elements in support of the innovation work; and second new policy, resource and capacity enablers to stimulate and accelerate the diffusion of proven new models to 'early adopter' schools across the New York public school system.

From the outset in year one, for the strategy to be successful it was recognized that:

- At all levels the work as it went forward would need to be co-constructed and problem-solved together;

- The ambition was system change, which meant that all actors, from students and parents through to teachers, leaders and system personnel would need to engage, relate and function differently;

- The DOE, too, would need to learn and adapt in order to co-create the enabling conditions for the iZone's efforts; DOE practices could be part of the solution or a part of the problem for innovative new models;

- Achievement of the ambitions for diffusion and scaling would require a sustained commitment to wider system engagement, mobilization and animation. For the iZone to innovate on behalf of the wider system, the work would need to feel owned by that system.

In its first year iZone360 was a cohort of 26 schools, drawn from five of what were perceived to be the highest capacity networks of schools, each group of schools within a network partnered with an expert external organization. The approach as designed involved the progressive introduction of robust and disciplined methods to design, prototype, evaluate and support the scaling of new school models.

Each of the five networks chosen selected a 'model design partner', an external organization with validated experience of creating a new school design sharing key characteristics with the ambitions of the iZone360 schools in the network. The idea was not for the network to adopt the design partner's model, but to draw from their expertise in creating a distinctive 'next generation' NYC model. Beyond this, 'component partners' were also commissioned to bring expertise in critical elements of the work, which could be anything from technology systems to advisories; simulations to project-based learning; scheduling to community mobilization.

The network was a significant unit in the early strategy and the Network Leader a key role. As well as Network Leaders helping to identify the initial iZone360 schools, each network was to work with the central DOE innovation team to select five 'affiliate schools'. These would partner and help problem-solve the challenges of innovation, and be prime sites for early adoption and adaptation in year two. Not only were Network Leaders to provide direct support and broker connections for and among the iZone360 and affiliate schools – building a network-level 'community of practice' – they would also help develop the processes and mechanisms to promote the adoption and adaptation of proven new models and practices across the network as a whole. To assist the existing network leadership, the DOE secured resources for each participating network also to have an 'Innovation Coach' working across the participating schools.

Another significant element of the early planned strategy was to be the development of conditions, dynamics and relationships to foster innovation and to stimulate and accelerate diffusion. In the early stages of planning, the most mooted vehicle for this was a 'transformational leadership coalition' (bringing together the leaders of iZone360 schools and networks, the central Innovation Team and Innovation Coaches, and positively disposed leaders from across key areas of the DOE). This coalition would anticipate or identify potential barriers to the implementation of personalized mastery learning and problem-solve their removal or mitigation. It would also identify and design potential enablers of innovation, implementation and diffusion.

It was through this iZone360-focused community of practice that it was envisaged the system might cohere around the work and would bring together its learning and knowledge management strategy.

The scope of work of this facilitated coalition was envisaged to include, among other themes, performance management frameworks, accountability and assessment regimes, funding mechanisms and parental, family and community engagement.

Implementation of iZone360 in Year 1

It was always going to be a stretch to get iZone360 up and running to plan for Fall 2011 implementation. Its first year was characterized by some of the 'design in flight' and capacity challenges faced by many significant innovation and system transformation initiatives – identifying and hiring key personnel; securing resource strands in a timely manner; developing effective communication mechanisms; building out the design and implementation model . . . and identifying reasonable indicators or evidence of success.

These are to some extent generic start-up challenges. More significant for this analysis were the achievements in that first full year of implementation (2011–12), and some of the unanticipated or particular fault-lines that might have wider relevance for progressive reformers.

In terms of success, 26 schools were recruited across five NYC networks, as were four supporting Model Design Partners (Kunskapsskolan, New Visions, RISC and Eskolta). Each school identified a core change team, whose members engaged in the design process. This was informed by six workshops (March to June 2011) which culminated in a major 'future state design' sharing workshop attended by the Chancellor. In reality, a proportion of the 26 schools (although far fewer than half) created genuinely radical proposals or had bold aspirations. The Model Design Partners brought new capacity to the work, attending the workshops and supporting the schools between and beyond them. The NYC DOE iTeam matured and gelled quickly and learnt well how to manage the programme and support the work in a manner very different from the traditional DOE-to-school relationship.

Most significantly, 360 generated considerable energy in the system. It broadened and deepened the dialogue about innovation and alternative school designs. There evolved a growing sense of possibility and mission, of peer support, the emergence of an embryonic community of practice and a belief in the legitimacy, feasibility and potential of radically new approaches to schooling. In that first year, about a quarter of the schools were beginning to implement radically different schooling models, but more than half were perhaps doing work of systemic interest.

That having been said, there were also significant fault-lines in the first year's work. Some were challenges of design, others of implementation. Perhaps the most significant, though, for this study were those that may have more generic relevance across systems and cultures.

Design and implementation challenges

The initial commitment to build both the community of practice and the diffusion strategy around NYC's networks ran into unanticipated challenges. The degree of lateral connectivity, collaborative capacity and collegiality vary by network. Therefore the foundations of the diffusion strategy were unreliable, and alternative options needed to be explored to create a more porous boundary between iZone schools and more than 1,300 other schools in the district.

Throughout the first year communication, knowledge management and wider system engagement (students and parents; the wider community of NYC schools) were gradually developed and improved in real time. Everyone was at full stretch getting the show on the road and at times there was insufficient capacity to be devoted to wider engagement activity. This also meant that sometimes schools were being recruited to something about which they had less than a full understanding. More seriously, it also meant that the 'on behalf of' aspirations, a key element in raising demand for diffusion, were compromised. The wider system could not 'own' 360 ambitions if it was not enabled to understand and to participate in some way.

The early demands of implementation were such that it was felt by some that school principals and others had insufficient time capacity to be able to participate.

The Model Design Partners were an important potential capacity, but they began with significant role ambiguity and subsequently adapted to the challenge differentially. (Some were able to abandon their own proprietary 'model' to support schools' ambitions; others found that much more difficult.) iZone360 had some high-potential practices to share, and the most promising have been taken to pilot stages and are on the way to scaling.

For all the challenges, the show was on the road; there was huge learning to be drawn from the experience; the commitment of many of the principals to the systemic ambition of the work was palpable; the case for innovation, for dramatic change in learning and schooling towards a more personalized model, had been well received and internalized. Beyond this, there were early signs that the system was becoming animated around the work.

Wider system challenges

As mentioned earlier, it was clear from the outset that the DOE would need to learn, adapt and become more flexible and enabling of schools' radical intentions for 360 to succeed. It would be either a part of the solution or a part of the problem.

Year one was a steep learning curve! This manifested itself in a number of ways. There was an ongoing effort to ensure the iZone would be owned by the wider DOE. Further, through both the work of 360 and particularly the efforts of the InnovateNYC Ecosystem, many of the DOE's systems (procurement, commissioning, legal, personnel, budget allocation) have needed to flex and adapt to the ambitions of 360 schools and other iZone initiatives. The difficult work of systems-level change can take time, and this at times led to delays from budget approval processes and appointment regulations. Nevertheless, there also have been a number of policy and practice wins, such as allowing students to earn credit for meaningful learning experiences outside the classroom, and the ability for the NYC DOE to use a Challenge model in place of traditional procurement methods.

Along with systemic challenges sustainability was potentially jeopardized by changes in leadership. Within 12 months of the start of the work the Chancellor (Joel Klein, its sponsor and key advocate) left, as did the Deputy Chancellor responsible for iZone.[6] However, turnover is not uncommon in the field, particularly in large urban districts. While the iZone may have lost some traction during leadership transitions, the initiative has a strong team in place and commitment to the work from across the NYC DOE.

Summarizing

It may be helpful here to get a handle on the timeline of events up to and around this time:

- The design and preparation for iZone360 began in earnest in Summer 2010;

- The Chancellor's approval to launch and provide the resource package came in July 2010;

- By March 2011 the programme had been designed, support organizations were being commissioned, some iZone360 appointments made and schools selected;

- The intensive innovation design phase took place between March and July 2011;

- September 2011 saw the implementation launch of cohort one – 26 schools;

- Throughout Year one (2011–12) much site-level work, workshop activity and formative review went on, which led to revisions for Year two;

- February to June 2012 saw a further cycle of school recruitment, contracts with new support organizations and the creation of an innovation and school redesign workshop process – a design partnership between iTeam, Design Partners and Innovation Unit;

- In September 2012 phase two of iZone 360 was launched, making 50 schools committed to collaborative school redesign built around a vision of personalized mastery learning able to meet the needs, strengths and motivations of individual students;

- July 2012 – a new Head of iZone, Andrea Coleman, takes up post (the third in two years) and institutes a radical (and necessary) review of the entire iZone, including 360.

Year 2 iZone 360

At the time of finalizing this case study it is January 2013. The design phase for the second cohort of 25 schools was completed in July and they launched in September 2012. The new schools were selected through an open and robust process (not strongly attached to networks) and there is some confidence that most have the leadership, the internal capacity, the ambition and the will to create innovative new school designs. Many of the participating schools have been enthused by the energy from Year one schools and are already well advanced.

Three more Model Design Partners were recruited (Apple, Big Picture and CSSR) who are contributing capacity and expertise in more informed ways than was possible for the first round. The new schools have some practice models from Year one to build from. iCoaches are in place to act as pollinators and connectors, and they have the collaborative conceptualization of their roles from the first year to strengthen their work.

Additionally, the design component was smarter, tighter and more collaboratively planned and facilitated than in year one. It involved six workshops (most whole day, some half day) as an Innovation Conference – or InnoCon[7] – series moving from Innocon Inspire through Model, Explore, Experiment, Refine & Plan and finally Innocon Share. These events were hosted by notable organizational partners in New York, such as Google, TimeWarner or the NYC Fire Museum, and their expertise was incorporated into the mix as well as that of the Design Partners and Innovation Unit.

Most of the schools had a core innovation team that attended each workshop and an extended group with whom they worked in-between. Model Design Partners were very active participants in Year two: they knew their role; they contributed to design; they were the key supports in the main work (the school redesign and wider stakeholder engagement activity that schools were to undertake between workshops); they were also connectors of people and ideas between schools.

There is also now an iZone Leadership Council intended to facilitate dialogue between principals and the DOE, and there are 'affinity groups', or working groups, drawn from across the cohort of schools to problem-solve the 'wicked problems' of implementation and practice. It is early days and these features will inevitably evolve. It is emergent because that is appropriate for our understandings about the relational dynamics and system kinaesthetic of co-design!

Looking forward, iZone 360 aims to address some the challenges associated with diffusion and scale to maximize its impact across the district.

- The diffusion and scaling strategy will draw on methods such as challenges and accelerators, open to any DOE school, to create more opportunities for 360 schools to diffuse promising practices and spread demand for innovation.

- Wider stakeholder and system engagement within the DOE will also be strengthened by these methods, while the Innovate NYC Ecosystem has made significant inroads into the edtech market and its investors.

- A mutual support relationship between the wider Department and the work of schools in iZone360 is growing sronger.

- New systems to tackle knowledge management and communication challenges are in place, and will be a focus for 2013.

In many ways, as will be obvious, there has been rapid learning in NYC. iZone360 was itself a prototype – a prototype for a different type of system transformation strategy. Like all prototypes, it is entitled to have its failures, as long as it fails fast and is failing forward. This applies to the system's role as designer and custodian of the approach as much as to the work at school level. There are no surprises here. Radical system transformation work is just so hard – challenging, complex, draining, unstable, demanding of courage . . . We know many of the component parts, but those few systems internationally travelling this journey with intent are learning as they go how to fit these moving parts together; how the new system dynamics function; how we can unlearn decades old habitual behaviours; how we unite multiple constituencies around the endeavour. Whoever suggested that it would be easy? It is a work in progress.

What has been presented so far, beyond the narrative sections, is an attempt at a 'balanced scorecard' approach to analysis of the iZone strategy, and 360 in particular. For all its challenges, it offers one of the most promising and optimistic scenarios for urban jurisdictions that we know.

Where might iZone be headed?

This concluding section is both brief and selective. It is included not in the interests of completeness, but in order to bring to the table new thinking around both innovation (used here to describe the creation of new ideas and practices of proven applied value) and the components of system transformation (used to include both the implementation of innovation at scale and the design of the new system dynamics and relationships required for the innovation to flourish and sustain).

With that in mind, although there is no narrative bridge into 2013–14 because that still lies more than six months away (during which time there will be mayoral elections), it might be helpful to conclude by sharing some of the features from initial review work undertaken by iZone's senior leadership between October 2012 and January 2013. All that follows is formative or tentative thinking at the time of writing, but it nonetheless indicates three things:

1 A sustained commitment in NYC to a bold educational innovation strategy as a component in a balanced approach to system transformation;

2 Clarity that NYC does not yet have everything right, combined with a firm determination to learn forward fast;

3   The sense that NYC has every intention of capitalizing on the foundations they have built to achieve just that.

The review process began by creating a set of high-level expectations for new school models – so-called non-negotiables. There were ten of these, but four will indicate the flow of thinking:

- New school models should look radically different from past models;
- The innovation process should give more exposure to the non-education sector;
- The system should design into its role a customized (personalized), demand-led support model;
- Schools should achieve both radically better and different outcomes.

Similarly, among the many 'big questions' the team has set out to answer are the following:

1   How do we strengthen our diffusion strategy? How do we scale to effect systemic change?

2   What does a 'demand-led support model' look like in practice and how do we broker it?

3   How do we maintain the spirit of the iZone as being co-designed?

4   What permissions or deregulation might be necessary for very different models?

5   Where in the world are the potential paradigm-shifting experiences for people to see?

The outcomes of this review are too embryonic to detail here. However, it is fair to say that the work is evolving around three 'levels': innovating with schools, impacting the market (suppliers and supports of schools) and system dynamics for scaling and diffusion.

Within this framework current preoccupations include: developing early or proxy metrics of success, abandoning normative supports for iZone schools – learning how to personalize supports and expectations, maximizing resource deployment to schools and flexibility around resource use, tackling the 'wicked issues' by connecting 'bright spark' innovators, building a system-wide innovation mindset, finding ways to connect across the Department and addressing the scaling challenge in an authentic way.

Final word

This is an attempt at an authentic case study – honest and true to the scale of the ambition and the complexity of realizing it. Working with the New York team has been a privilege. Association with their aspirations for schools and system has been inspiring. Tackling some of the challenges alongside them has been both humbling and exhausting. Engaging with iZone leaders and school leaders on the journey has been the experience of a lifetime.

So this is the last word: NYC's iZone remains one of the most robustly designed, high-potential, strategic, intentional and ambitious system innovation strategies with which we have connected. It almost certainly has implications for public service innovation far more broadly than education. Not only does NYC have an urgent need for the iZone to succeed, but also the rest of the world needs New York to get this as right as is feasible, and to document it for wider learning.

REFLECTION piece by Jonathan DeSausmarez a school leader from England who took part in a study visit in October 2012

New York iZone – where size matters

Jonathan de Sausmarez Executive Principal of Romsey High School shares his experience of visiting two iZone schools during an English School Leaders Study visit October 2012 – one week before Hurricane Sandy.

Our first visit was to a school that was housed in what we quickly found out was an old synagogue converted to an East Brooklyn High School – one of the 'Transfer' schools in the area. The idea was simple: the iZone wants to give all young people a chance to graduate and so this school is open for 16 to 20+ year olds who did not manage to graduate at the high school and can have a second chance. While suitably welcomed by two uniformed officers who sent us through airport-type machines and checked us over very carefully the immediate thought was: *why is it in the United States they want to give young people as many chances as possible to gain academic recognition but in the United Kingdom we are cutting back on coursework assessments and early entry as though somehow this is lowering standards?* In the United Kingdom we have begun the process to make sure that all students up until 18 have a good grounding in English and maths but what of those older people who would like to catch up?

The key features of East Brooklyn High School are:

- 170 students arrive with some credits but not the 44 needed to graduate;
- All courses must have academic aspects and are tailored for students to succeed;
- The curriculum is personalized to help students gain credits, including gardening. Other courses include US history, geometry, living environment, fitness (one assessment includes making a fitness video!);
- Introduction of accelerated catch up – you can take 18 credits in a year instead of the normal 12;
- The Counsellor or form tutor conducts the interview before they arrive, stays with the students and nurtures their progress;
- One student talked about his high school of 4,000 students as 'uncaring' and now 'there is someone looking out for me';
- Every student gets feedback on progress every two weeks. The timetable is divided into six 55-minute lessons;
- Key partnerships with social workers to support wider community issues;
- Formative assessment seen as key; no grades, just conversations with students and constructive feedback.

The seven of us left East Brooklyn with the philosophical commitment to give every young person a chance and also ensure that those students who have difficult teenage years still have a future and can find something that they can feel successful at. In the United Kingdom we appear again to be ridiculing vocational courses and celebrating 'good' schools as those that achieve in the narrowest of curriculums.

Queen's Collegiate High School

The taxi driver's Sat Nav directed us through various neighbourhoods until we reached one of those enormous buildings with flights of stairs which we associate with the best of US schools; it looked and was huge. We duly got out to look for any signs directing us to the high school and we saw nothing. Clearly the iZone had not quite done their work on a corporate approach to signing or in fact in having any signs at all. We looked up at this impressive, large, 1930s buiding to see an enormous sign in concrete, normally associated with a Batman movie, which said 'Jamaica High School'.

The Queen's Collegiate High School, had been created a few years ago when the 2,500-student Jamaica High School had been broken up into four smaller schools, Queen's being just one. This was part of the iZone ethos of creating more personalized schools with a greater focus on teaching and supporting the child. Each of the newly created schools has a speciality for students to choose: 1) Community Leadership; 2) Sciences, 3) Arts and Letters and 4) College Preparation and International affairs (Queen's). This means that young people in the area have a choice of high school suited to their interest while at the same time feel they belong to a smaller unit.

Queens has embraced the iZone ethos of transformational change with a focus on pedagogy; this includes teachers being required to focus their teaching on one particular way of learning. All staff were give a choice of three pedagogical approaches: Project-based learning (guided research, teaching, real-life product), blended learning (mixture of online and in person teaching, student-led) and mastery-based learning (alternative grading practices based on performance). Over three years all teachers should cover each of these so their skill base is increased.

As you walked through the very long and dark corridors you had no sense that transformational change was in evidence. This was a high school that focused on celebrating student achievements; the classrooms were in total contrast to the stark buildings – walls covered with students' work, teaching that is focused on learning with a variety of approaches from students learning with maths software to real independent learning, to teacher-led, whole-class discussions. Students were fully engaged; gone were the long rows of single chairs with flip over desks and we witnessed a plethora of approaches to make learning enjoyable and fun.

The meeting with the Principal quickly highlighted why this high school was so different and reflected the ethos and approach of the iZone. It is well documented that the two things that are required to bring about transformation are quality of teaching and leadership. For the iZone this did not just mean improving teaching but giving more leadership autonomy and it was clear that strong leadership and vision of transformational teaching was central to the success of Queen's. To bring about that transformation the Principal engaged all staff in training with the school closing at one pm on a Wednesday for training, and teachers working in groups every day to plan together.

To enhance the training, Queen's appointed a teacher coach to support the teachers in their transformation and work with them in changing their practice. This level of change meant that you could not simply get rid of the old teachers and have a ready supply of new ones to come into the classrooms. This required existing teachers to buy into the vision and be active participants in change led by the clear vision of the Principal who used her leadership expertise to ensure all teachers were not just embracing change but accountable for the outcomes of their students.

Working in teacher teams means that the best practice is shared and that all staff can take risks and develop their pedagogy. In one particular lesson, it felt like entering the textbook 'Ofsted' lesson, even though Ofsted would never agree to such a thing. We arrived to find the students working on different activities and the teacher immediately gave us one of the most detailed lesson plans we had ever seen. The teacher explained this is what she did for every lesson! The incredulous looks from us clearly baffled the teacher until we realized that her had only one detailed lesson plan per day and teaches four classes that same lesson! She explained that using the model meant that she could refine her plans and adapt and change them throughout the day, very different to UK teachers who have to plan up to five or six lessons a day; and we wonder why some find it difficult to keep up with our expectations.

Not everything was perfect; students in a classroom working on their independent projects found it difficult in a subject like French not to need help. Clearly some areas were more suited to the different styles of learning. The ICT was impressive and similar to that found in the United Kingdom, but like many UK classrooms there is a long way to go to ensure these are used to enhance learning.

Queen's Collegiate High School certainly proved one thing that we can all learn from, namely, that in a school without a playground, but just classrooms on a few corridors, you can bring about transformational educational change through lucid leadership supported by teachers who are able to work together to bring out the very best of practices. At the end of the day the iZone schools will continue to face challenges but in the end it is the young people of Brooklyn who will be the winners.

Notes

1 This case study has been written by David Jackson. It is an adapted and extended version of an earlier piece written in collaboration with David Albury. David Albury is Chair of the Innovation Unit (IU) Board and an international consultant. The IU worked with NYC DOE in the formation and implementation of its innovation and transformation strategy, and most specifically with iZone360.

2 This section draws from NYC's own materials and from Jason Wong et al. 2008.

3 Initially Ontario, Victoria and England; latterly also Finland, South Korea, Chaoyang (Beijing), New Zealand, Brazil, British Columbia, India, Australia at a Commonwealth level, Kentucky and Colorado.

4   Beyond the background and early history section, this case study focuses primarily on iZone360 rather than InnovateNYC and iLearn. Partly this is because IU's work has been primarily with 360. Even more, though, it is because whole school redesign is the ultimate challenge for system transformation.

5   This 'on behalf-ness' – a key feature of the NYC strategy – required the schools to display permeability, connectivity, reciprocity and professional generosity as essential qualities.

6   In December 2010, Joel Klein, prime advocate for and sponsor of the Phase 3 reform innovation emphasis, resigned as Chancellor, and shortly after John White, the Deputy Chancellor who had been the driving force behind the innovation strategy, left to become Superintendent of the Recovery School District in Louisiana.

7   www.izoneshare.org/www/izone/site/Hosting/InTheZone/FebInTheZone.pdf

References and further reading

Wong, J., Sproul, J. and Kosak, S., *Children First in New York: Urban Education Reform in New York City: Challenges, Policies and Implementation* (Harvard: Harvard Graduate School of Education, 2008).

7

Exploring System-wide Change: The Academies of Nashville

Jay Steele, Michelle Wilcox including a reflection piece by Marc Hill

District overview

Metropolitan Nashville Public Schools (MNPS) is a large urban school district with approximately 81,000 students. The majority of students in the system, 74 per cent, qualify for subsidized or free breakfast and lunch. There is no majority ethnicity; the largest population is African American at 46 per cent, and the Hispanic population is the fastest growing. Overall in the district, there are 135 different languages spoken: English, Spanish, Arabic, Kurdish and Somali are the top five. This ethnically diverse and economically disadvantaged population of students presents some unique challenges.

In 2009, an exciting yet terrifying opportunity to lead the transformation of an urban school district's 12 high schools and improve academic achievement of all high school students was accepted. At the time, the MNPS district comprised 24 high schools with nearly 20,000 students, and in position to be taken over by the state. The 12 zoned schools, with more than 16,000 students, were struggling. They were consistently low in performing in reading, language arts, math, and in graduation, with alarming dropout rates. The opportunity was exciting because a small core of high school principals desperately wanted a change; they realized the traditional education and quality of teaching the children received were not increasing academic achievement. The terrifying part of the opportunity was the magnitude of the transformation needed, coupled with the expectation that results would be seen quickly. Self-doubt and concerns about the ability to lead and bring about such an important and large-scale transformation had to be overcome before making a decision to accept the opportunity. The Nashville Area Chamber of Commerce, Alignment Nashville and PENCIL foundations expressed their support and willingness to work hand in hand with the district in the transformational process.

In 26 years in education, never had a business community that was leading and demanding school transformation on such a large scale been encountered. The commitment and dedication of business leaders, foundation leaders and non-profits poised to transform a city's educational system and shape the next generation of citizens was overwhelming and encouraging.

It was evident immediately that there was need for a clear and compelling vision for the impending transformation. The work began in December 2009, with internal and external committee members, in the development of a vision. The agreed upon vision is: 'Metropolitan Nashville Public Schools will provide every student with the knowledge, skills and character necessary for success in college, work and life.' Over an 18-month period, a five-year strategic plan to transform the 12 high schools was crafted by a group of visionary community leaders, with assistance and guidance from leaders working for the Ford Motor Company Fund. Yes, the Ford Motor Company. Why would a car company work with a school district to drive school change? The answer is clear. The Ford Motor Company, through its foundation, determined a serious business commitment to education was needed to provide the impetus for change if failing and struggling school systems were going to improve. Cheryl Carrier, Program Director of 21st Century Education Programs for Ford Motor Company Fund and Community Services, explains.

> Ford's commitment to education goes back to Henry Ford, who was a firm believer in learning-by-doing. Ford Next Generation Learning was developed to help community stakeholders come together to co-create an educational plan that ensure that all students are prepared to be lifelong learners, who are inquisitive and have a thirst for investigation and knowledge. Ford Next Generation Learning is about transformation change in the high school experience. It is about redefining teaching and learning to be more relevant and real-world. It is about fueling students' passion for learning and engaging the entire community in ensuring that every child is prepared for college, career and life. (http://fordpas.org/)

Based on Ford's Next Generation Learning model, the team drafted a strategic five-year plan that addressed three key areas of reform: Redesigning high schools, transforming teaching and learning, and sustaining change through business and civic leadership. The five-year plan became the foundation for all work in MNPS high schools by setting clear priorities for students, teachers, administrators, and community members, centred around student achievement and the district vision. This plan is a living document, revisited and updated quarterly, and continues to guide the transformation.

Redesigning high schools

The traditional design of, and instructional delivery in, many high schools in America continues to be patterned after the compulsory education system established in the mid- to late 1800s. Nashville schools were no exception, and student achievement was low, most noticeably among African American males, who were also being suspended and expelled from school at higher rates than others. Instruction was provided primarily through didactic lecture with students expected to sit in straight rows, and communicate very little. Evidence of learning was primarily through multiple choice and other standard pen and paper tests. There was little focus on formative assessment; instead, teaching to the state tests and keeping just ahead of state takeover seemed to be the goal. The use of rubrics to guide authentic assessment was rarely considered or used.

Nationally, high school teachers have been isolated, concerned about their content and focused only on what takes place within their classrooms. Again, Nashville high school teachers were no different, with the exception of a few schools in which administrators and some teachers had embraced Smaller Learning Communities (SLCs). Although eight schools were part of a federal grant to implement SLCs, they were in varying stages of development, primarily due to a lack of administrative leadership at the district level. As a strategy to improve student achievement in large high schools, SLC grants were awarded by the federal government (US DOE 2012), and MNPS received a grant in 2006. In these schools, there was some evidence of cross-discipline collaboration and teachers working as teams. Otherwise, minimal interaction with colleagues existed outside of faculty meetings or lunch breaks. Students were assigned to counsellors by grade level or by first letter of the student's last name. Assistant principals were assigned to management activities that included textbooks, athletics, facilities or discipline, and often had little influence or direct responsibility in instructional matters. Principals were given very little autonomy to make decisions, or to be innovative and creative. Master schedules were often designed around a teacher's favourite subject or the teacher's desired planning time. The student experience was not the primary consideration in the design and delivery of the curriculum, the design of the mater schedule or the assignment of personnel. Having the qualifications to teach courses in which students were tested for meeting state and national requirements was the deciding factor, not student outcomes.

That model does not support twenty-first-century learners in need of critical thinking, communication, collaboration and creativity skills (Partnership for 21st Century Skills 2011), particularly low-performing urban students who had not been presented with challenging curriculum. Prior to receiving a federal Race to the Top (RTTT) state-wide grant, the content standards were considered to be near the lowest in the United States. New standards had been adopted, but there had been no attempt to transform teaching and learning. Although traditional instruction was the general rule for most students, a few pockets of innovation were sprouting up with visionary principals who were secure enough to make bold changes. However, these leaders were working in isolation, devoid of a clear and compelling district vision. As a collaborative team, with the support of and trust in their new leader, the high school principals agreed there was an exigent need to abandon the traditional school and classroom design, with its patently lacklustre and ineffective instructional methods, if students were to be engaged in their learning at deeper levels to raise academic achievement graduation rates.

Thus, in 2010, the principals rallied around the concept of redesigning all 12-zoned high schools into the SLC model called The Academies of Nashville (AN). This was a decision based on the research by Manpower Demonstration Research Corporation (MDRC), founded in 1974 by The Ford Foundation and several federal agencies. Its implicit purpose was discovering and fostering best instructional practices leading to significant student achievement. SLCs and Career Academies research provide substantive data that validate the benefits to students of this model. The model is driven by the student experience with respect to leadership and facilities use, staffing allocations, resource distribution, master scheduling and, most importantly, quality instruction. Personalized learning is the focus and is expected to drive all decisions made within the school.

The first tasks were to establish a brand, create a brand promise and to design a uniform look and feel for the AN. A branding firm was hired by the Chamber of Commerce to work with leaders to begin this task. As a result of this work, the team designed a brand promise that guides the work in creating the student experience: 'At my academy I choose to learn in an innovative community where I belong, I'm engaged and I am prepared for college, career and the real world.'

After developing the brand promise, the team designed an overall look and feel to logos, a marketing plan to educate various stakeholders and strategic events to inform the community and parents about the transformation called The Academies of Nashville. The team envisioned the ultimate student experience and created the tagline 'My Future. My Way'. The district logo incorporates the AN logo and the tag line. Each school was also provided a logo with school colours and school name, but otherwise the look was the same for branding purposes. From this branding work, the principals worked as a team to create a shared mission and vision to guide all decisions made in each school. This shared vision and mission is at the forefront of all meetings, decisions and discussions:

> Metro Nashville Public High Schools are world class schools that graduate college and career ready students in partnership with the community. MNPS is a district that emerges as a trendsetter in innovative practices where ALL students have the highest level of education and experiences possible. (http://www.mnps.org/)

School curriculum design

The majority of the Nashville's high schools offered the same curricula and programmes in an attempt to be all things to all students. They were aptly called 'comprehensive' high schools. All schools offered culinary and cosmetology, neither of which is considered high skill nor high wage, nor in high demand in the region. Staffing decisions were made based on staffing expertise and traditional offerings. An audit of all offerings in every school was undertaken to determine if programmes offered were aligned with high-skill, high-wage targeted and emerging industries within the city, state and region. This audit relied on the expertise of the business community, not the school personnel. Traditionally, school districts have not aligned programme offerings with workforce data; therefore, this was a paradigm shift for educators. However, the business community welcomed this approach and guided school leaders through the process. Once the audit was completed, it was clear which programmes needed to be abandoned and which schools were lacking in relevant offerings. An important question asked of all administrators was, 'Does the school curriculum create a continuum from 9th grade through college and career with multiple exit points where students can achieve at the highest level?' When answered honestly, using data, it became clear which programmes should be closed, what new programmes were needed and what changes this would mean in personnel. These were difficult and challenging decisions due to the personal investment in existing programmes, and connections to personnel. This approach shifted the staffing and programme offerings from a model based on teacher expertise and tradition to a model based on workforce and postsecondary data with students' futures in mind. New programmes were selected using current and future workforce projections representing the community needs and postsecondary expectations. These new programmes were aligned with postsecondary certificates and degrees creating the continuum for college and career. Business and community partnerships were forged to nurture the new programmes, provide experiences for teachers and rigorous and enriching experiences for students.

An in-depth analysis of district data confirmed a mobility rate as high as 70 per cent in some of the high schools. This meant some students were changing schools seven times during a one-year period and 10 per cent of them were losing one or more credits per year. This negatively impacted the high school graduation rate and the loss of credits often resulted in students dropping out; the graduation rate was 58 per cent in 2006 and has steadily increased. The data made it clear to the leadership the 12 schools had an obligation to students to redesign and unify their master schedules to address the mobility crisis. Prior to this epiphany, schools designed their own master schedules based on principal and teacher preference, resulting in various schedules. The shift in thinking from scheduling based on teacher needs to scheduling based on student needs was a defining moment in the transformation. After much debate and stakeholder input, the principals reached consensus and adopted the A/B block schedule, allowing students to obtain eight credits per year. This schedule requires students to participate in four 90-minute classes per day, alternating daily, similar to a college schedule.

Critical to the new master schedule was to include the creation of appropriate and adequate time for teacher collaboration. Traditionally, teachers planned alone with little collegial and interdisciplinary collaboration. Thus, the master schedule was redesigned to accommodate a 90-minute team planning time every day, allowing for teams of teachers to work together to create meaningful learning experiences for students. Also built into the master schedule was content team planning, allowing for content-specific teachers to collaborate. A team-planning template was developed and teams were required to meet a minimum of once per week to review data and student achievement, plan together and purposefully use the data to drive instruction and interventions, and better meet the needs of students. Available data include attendance, grades, discipline and access to interventions already in place.

Once the unified schedule was determined and programmes were being aligned to community needs and college and career preparation, it was time to redesign the roles and responsibilities of the adults in the building. The schools were divided into multiple teams called academies, similar to the way programmes are configured in a university. A university has several colleges such as the college of engineering, the college of health and the college of business. The academy structure broke down the large high schools into teams, in smaller personalized learning environments where relationships are valued. Each academy was comprised of 150–450 students with a team of teachers, an assigned counsellor and an academy principal. Each academy was designed to function as a school within a school. A freshman academy was created to provide a nurturing home for students as they made the difficult transition from middle to high school. The freshman academy is housed separately in the building, but also has a common team of teachers, a separate counsellor and a freshman academy principal. The upper grades (10–12) are separated into academies aligned with a theme, with a focus on college and career readiness. In addition to the focus on a particular theme, rigour, relevance, relationships and readiness are key to the success of the academy model.

Students select their academy of choice and continue in that academy for three years; they have one opportunity to change at the end of the sophomore year. Teams of teachers representing math, social studies, language arts, science and the thematic pathway are housed together. The academy has a principal and counsellor working with the same group of students for three years. This structure allows teams of teachers to create an environment where students can belong, engage with peers and feel part of a family.

One key position added to the school staff was the academy coach. This position acts as a liaison between the community, the school and the district, aligning all experiences for the students and teachers around the academy themes. Student experiences are woven into the design at all levels beginning with the Freshman Seminar class in the ninth grade. In this class students learn about goal setting, careers, colleges, time management and create a ten-year-plan following each student through high school, college and career. Experiences for upper grades include college visits, internships, career field trips, American College Testing (ACT) prep, academy functions and other activities with business partners designed to prepare students for college and career.

Student experience

Student voice and choice is front and centre in AN. The first student-centred public identity for AN was the creation of the academy ambassadors. A minimum of two students per academy were selected to represent the academy and serve in the ambassador programme. These students were trained in public speaking, presentation skills, marketing skills and how to conduct tours. Ambassadors received an AN blue blazer and were elevated to leadership positions within the school, and quickly became experts in the academy model, their schools and in understanding that their schools, educational experiences and futures were important, not only to them and their parents, but to the community. Today, these students are challenged to develop stories for blogs (http://myacademyblog.com), Facebook and Twitter in order to spread the positive aspects of the student experience. Providing the students a public audience to showcase their talents and skills is a vital marketing tool to use in educating the community. It also provides the students a platform from which to demonstrate mastery, communication skills and gain confidence.

Over the past three years, additional activities have been implemented to showcase students' talents and skills.

Lessons learned

A change in structure doesn't guarantee a change in teaching

Just because there is a change in the structure, there is no guarantee instruction will change.

With the structure institutionalized in each of the 12-zoned high school, it was necessary to focus on the instruction within the structure. One lesson learned: just because there is a change in the structure, there is no guarantee instruction will change. A concerted effort to focus on changing instruction to complement the structure was undertaken. How can we transforming teaching and learning from teacher-centred instruction to student-centred classrooms?

Transforming teaching and learning

Too much emphasis on changing the structure to allow for collaborative teaching, and not enough on actually changing the instruction.

A second lesson learned in this transformation: there was too much emphasis on changing the structure to allow for collaborative teaching, and not enough on actually changing the instruction. Providing the structure to allow collaborative planning and interdisciplinary teaching did not mean teachers knew how to use it, and to plan and deliver instruction in this venue. A clear and intentional approach was required to create professional networks that spurred collaboration and innovation. The key to transforming teaching and learning is to develop instructional leaders.

Instructional leadership

Developing existing and future principals and assistant principals as instructional leaders, rather than the managers.

At the core of transformation was the need to develop existing and future principals and assistant principals as instructional leaders, rather than the managers of facilities, people, discipline, textbooks, buses and lockers. During the first year, the focus was on development of the principals. A new district level Lead Principal was hired to support the vision and help develop principals to meet the new expectations. Two such positions existed to supervise and support the principals in use of data, understanding effective student-centred instruction and interventions and to ensure that district initiatives, including AN and strategies focused on increasing academic achievement. In some cases, it was necessary to make changes in leadership. Several principals were unable or unwilling to move forward with the transformation, and in some cases, student achievement scores dropped to new lows. As changes were made, it became glaringly obvious there were qualified assistant principals who could move into these instructional leadership roles. Their principals had developed them as managers, not instructional leaders, and few of them could articulate how to use data to improve instruction, or how to model instruction for struggling teachers. Their main focus was on discipline. Helping the principals and assistant principals understand that engaging students in the classroom would reduce the need for discipline was a critical next step.

On learning

Tearing down the walls separating education and business, both figuratively and literally became the goal.

The goal was to transform teaching and learning from a traditional didactic delivery method to a model of project-based learning in which students would become deeply engaged in rigorous and relevant learning focused on application and mastery of knowledge and skills necessary to achieve success in college and careers. The schedule and structure were in place for teams of teachers to plan and work together to create the engaging student experiences, enriched through the engagement of the business community in the design and delivery of the instruction. Opening the classroom to the community and the world, through inclusion of a Confucius classroom, use of instructional technology and international businesses, were purposeful actions to create deep, rich, engaging student experiences. Tearing down the walls separating education and business, both figuratively and literally became the goal. Using the vast network of over 200 community and business partners, an experience was developed for teachers to help them understand the connection between their content and what students needed to know in the business world. These teacher externships were conducted during the summer months. The local chamber of commerce convinced key business partners to design a week-long session for teachers to experience the inner workings of a particular business related to their academies. Academy teachers shadowed employees, participated in meetings and learned the industry from bottom to top. After completing the externship, each team of teachers developed projects incorporating the business theme into the curriculum introducing students to more relevant topics. The business partners approved the projects and committed time, personnel and resources to guarantee the project's success. Once the teachers returned to school, the projects were implemented with the partners alongside the teachers.

Now, teacher externships are entrenched in how the teams prepare, and business partners actively design, deliver and enhance the curriculum side by side with the academy teachers. The externship is one of the best professional development experiences for teachers because it brings relevance to the curriculum, provides teachers ways to show applicability to the students' daily lives, engages the students in their learning and fosters trust and collaboration with the community.

Professional development

Focusing on the idea of abandonment as we embraced a new way of teaching and learning.

It was important to focus on the idea of abandonment as we embraced a new way of teaching and learning. Otherwise, many would see it as 'adding more to their plates'. It was important to help teachers and leaders understand this as a different way of teaching, not an additional expectation. To that end, a very strategic approach was taken with professional development.

None of the necessary changes could have taken place without a high quality, extremely well thought out professional development plan. A former academy career and technical educator and district level coordinator was purposefully placed at the helm of curriculum and instruction for high schools. She had earned both her Master of Education and Educational Specialist degrees in curriculum and instruction, and it was evident she was well versed in general education, curriculum and instruction and professional development. She was part of the group that began the academy structure in 2006, and was trusted and respected in the schools and at the district level. It required differentiation in levels of professional development because some schools were more developed in the implementation process than others. Only eight schools had been involved in the original SLC grant and were in various stages of development, and the other four were just beginning.

The plan was created to allow professional development to be embedded in the schools, and a model using instructional coaches was created. Instructional coaches were provided two days of professional development each month to assist them in using research-based instructional strategies to increase student academic achievement as they worked with teachers in the classroom focusing on numeracy and literacy. Consulting teachers, also considered instructional coaches, were used across the content areas in the same way, but with an emphasis on new and/or struggling teachers.

Because high school teachers were being put in teams and expected to plan and deliver integrated and interdisciplinary instruction, it was important to provide professional development in highly effective teaming (HET). The American Alliance for Innovative Schools (AAIS) had been used on a small scale to work with a few schools in prior years, and was selected to provide the HET professional development for all schools. In addition to teaching and working in teams, the schedule had been changed to 90-minute blocks, four periods each day. Teachers also had to learn to 'Teach on the Block', making the best instructional use of a 90-minute period, something many were not used to doing. This required a focus on instructional planning. Standards based interdisciplinary planning was the next step in the professional development plan. Now that teachers were able to function effectively in teams, teach in much longer instructional periods and plan with intention with respect to interdisciplinary units, it became evident that project-based learning was the next step to developing a truly transformational process in which teachers and students could excel. Through the RTTT grant, funds were allotted to initiate this professional development.

> Abandonment of planning alone, teaching by lecture, and assessment solely by test.

Abandonment of planning alone, teaching by lecture and assessment by Scantron tests were necessary if teachers were going to be able to transform the learning experiences for students and increase student achievement. Administrators had to abandon weekly faculty meetings to allow and encourage teams to meet and plan together, and to share information in other, more effective ways. Administrators also had to abandon the focus on discipline and management to be able to focus on being in the classrooms and attending to instructional practices.

Early on, it was evident two groups needed professional development other than the teachers; principals and assistant principals, as well as team leaders, were not all on the same level of understanding of SLCs and there had not been a shift in roles and responsibilities. To provide the professional development needed for these administrators and team leaders, professional learning communities (PLCs) around the academy model and SLCs were established. This was based on the Five Dimensions of PLCs (Hord 2009) which include shared and supportive leadership, shared values and vision, collective learning and application of learning, supportive conditions and shared personal practice. Thus, in teams, schools and in all work with principals and assistant principals, each of these five dimensions exist. The use of PLCs created a level of trust and collaboration that had not existed in past years. Now, although each principal wants the highest academic growth, they also support each other in making sure students in all schools have the opportunity to increase their achievement.

Professional learning communities

Initially, administrators and team leaders participated in PLCs, and in year two, assistant principal meetings became professional development PLCs around Instructional Leadership, Quality Teachers in Every Classroom and Shared Practice. All principal and assistant principal 'meetings' were abandoned and replaced with monthly professional development specific to improving teaching and increasing academic achievement. In addition to HET, Teaching on the Block and Project-Based Learning, professional development was provided for large leadership teams in each school on the Continuous Improvement Model (CIM). This model was used in Texas to turn around low-performing schools and increase achievement gains in schools that had traditionally not been able to meet learning targets (Anderson and Davenport 2002). The focus of the model is on closing the achievement gap and increasing achievement of all students, and requires constant monitoring and adjustment of teaching and learning. Again, this required teachers and administrators to abandon the notion of teaching once and testing for a grade to be able to use formative assessments followed by teaching and re-teaching as needed, and providing enrichment for those who know the content.

This deliberate focus on professional development with teachers, team leaders, academy coaches, instructional coaches, assistant principals and principals made it possible to go to scale with the transformation and use the academy model in all zoned schools. The non-zoned schools, magnets and alternative schools have also embraced continuous improvement, a focus on projects for learning and PLCs, which has in turn increased the collaboration and trust across the high school tier.

A focus on blended learning

Most recently, professional development has become focused on blended learning, in which an online learning management system is used. This allows for students to access class materials, syllabi, messages, learning resources and content 24 hours per day, seven days per week. It also allows students to communicate with one another and their teachers, and to extend their learning to any time, any place and provides them with an environment they will encounter in college. Effective January 2013, all Advanced Placement and International Baccalaureate classes will be taught in a blended environment, and all have completed professional development to make this possible.

Learning environment

As project-based learning grew in the schools, the actual design of the traditional classroom hindered this approach and often stifled the student experience. The classroom configuration and furniture were not designed to support student communication, collaboration or presentation. Therefore, key business partners were selected to help redesign classrooms to support the student experience and mirror the work environment to support collaboration, communication, creativity and critical thinking. The partnerships yielded phenomenal results and one by one, classrooms began to transform into collaborative and flexible learning environments. Science classrooms were redesigned with university and business partners leading the transformation. Local engineers and computer programmers redesigned their respective labs. Traditional furniture orders of small and uncomfortable desks ceased, and orders were replaced with tables and chairs to promote student grouping, student collaboration and student demonstration. This approach flipped the classroom to become student-centred, not teacher-centred. This design is a paradigm shift for many teachers and some teachers find it difficult to give up control of the learning to the students. However, once teachers experienced the power of student-focused learning, returning to the traditional classroom was no longer an option, and the teachers realized the students were the ones doing the work!

Currently, the high schools have begun implementing the blended learning model by extending the learning through online learning platforms spreading student contact to anytime access. Preparing students to learn and succeed in a blended environment is imperative for future success in college and career. Beginning with early adopters, Advanced Placement and International Baccalaureate teachers, a strategic initiative has begun to move students into this learning environment in January 2013. Any teacher who participates in professional development has the opportunity to establish a blended environment, and within five years it is expected that all teachers will be doing so.

Sustaining change through business and civic leadership

The city of Nashville has embraced students through the Chamber of Commerce's work with education, the PENCIL Foundation's efforts with business engagement in education, and Alignment Nashville, an organization that exists solely to support public education. This city supports youth! By providing and fostering deep community involvement, these organizations were the catalyst for the transformation of the MNPS high schools. The old saying, 'It takes a village to raise a child', is evident in Nashville. The Chamber of Commerce perspective is explored by their policy chief Marc Hill in the reflection piece that accompanies this chapter.

Make no mistake, this transformation to the academy model, with a focus on college and career readiness, could not have gone to scale without the strategic and purposeful involvement of the business community.

With over 200 business, community and collegiate partners, students are mentored, provided enrichment and supported to dream, achieve and succeed. However, a transformational movement of this size must have an intentional structure to focus support, and ensure resources are adequate and fairly dispersed, and to develop a system of sustainability.

This structure has brought in the business model of how to operate to the educators, including the use of data, strategic planning, collaboration and teamwork. These leaders are actively involved in the development and implementation of the strategic vision. Partners actively participate and lead strategic planning sessions, goal setting activities and visioning retreats to ensure the school leadership stays focused and action-oriented. Partners are in classrooms every day enhancing and enriching the student experience by providing real-world experiences. Actual student experiences include student-run credit unions, television stations, virtual enterprises, hospital labs, science research projects, biotechnology labs, computer programming classrooms, crime scene and forensic cases, actual student-run courtrooms and many more authentic experiences. This model has fostered mutual trust and respect between students, teachers, partners and business leaders throughout the city. It is truly changing lives every day for every child.

Significant work has been done to change teaching and learning, and students are producing significant projects, increasing their attendance and improving their academic achievement, all the while discipline rates are decreasing.

Accountability is also important to the success of this transformation. Each academy is expected to meet the National Standards of Practice established by the National Career Academy Coalition (NCAC) and become a model academy. To date, seven schools have academies recognized as 'certified' or 'model', and all schools are developing plans for academy evaluation. Additionally, instructional rounds, school and classroom visits, and evaluations occur regularly to ensure everyone is accountable for their roles and responsibilities in each school. Figure 7.1 provides an overview of support for the academies.

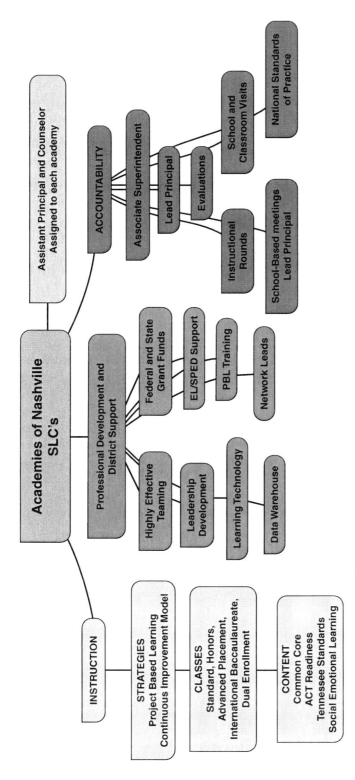

FIGURE 7.1 *Academies of Nashville*

Impact

The transformation has begun to show positive results, not only with respect to academic achievement but also in other significant and tangible ways. Academically, student achievement is increasing, and there are no high schools at risk of state takeover for low student performance. Achievement is up in math as measured by Algebra I, and literacy is flat overall as measured by English II. Writing scores are at their highest point at over 91 per cent proficiency. Figure 7.2 shows the number of students scoring advanced or proficient on state standardized testing over a three year period.

The attendance rate has increased from 94.1 per cent in 2008 to 95.5 per cent in 2012. Discipline incidents, suspensions and expulsions have decreased. The district has measured a 6.8 per cent decrease in the number of students with unexcused absences, a 13.3 per cent decrease in the number of students expelled and remanded to alternative schools and a 2.1 per cent decrease in the number of students receiving out-of-school suspensions.

The graduation rate has increased from 58 per cent in 2004, as shown in Figure 7.3. It should be noted that the graduation rate was changed from a five year calculation to a four year calculation in the middle of the academic year for 2011–12, and the target was achieved.

The dropout rate has been cut in half from 4 per cent to 2 per cent. The transformation is indeed making a significant difference in the success of students.

Nationally, recognition has increased so much that district visits must be scheduled months in advance, and fill as soon as they are announced.

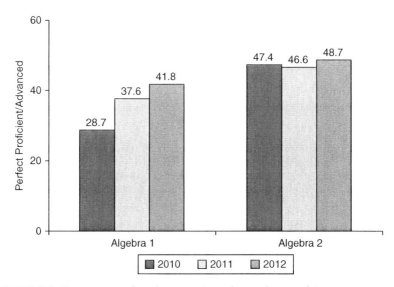

FIGURE 7.2 *Percentages of students scoring advanced or proficient on state standardized testing*

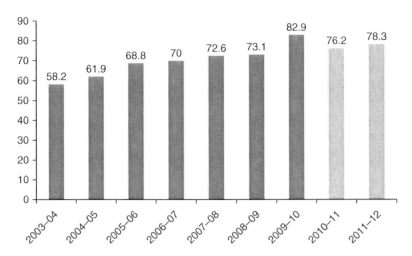

FIGURE 7.3 *Graduation rate*

Districts from as far away as Hawaii have come to examine all components of the transformation, including participation by the Chamber of Commerce, PENCIL, Alignment Nashville, Ford and local business partners. School tours are provided and those who visit are provided access to students, teachers and administrators to discover how they can use this model in their districts. Locally, VIP tours are scheduled and elected officials, school board members and others are invited. Recently, members of private school administration have begun attending, likely due to the declining enrolment of students in their schools as students are returning to the public high schools!

It is evident the transformation is having an impact on teaching and learning. Now, the district must ensure there is an increase in the rate at which academic achievement takes place, and it is going to require a continued focus on a high quality teacher in *every* classroom. The new state evaluation system, a new increase in starting pay for teachers, the strategic system of professional development and focus on accountability support this effort.

REFLECTION piece by Marc Hill of Nashville Chamber of Commerce

The Business perspective – what the Nashville Chamber of Commerce contributed and why they did it.

Educators have come to the realization they cannot be successful on their own.

An important by-product from the era of high-stakes accountability is that educators have come to the realization they cannot be successful on their own. Faced with large numbers of students struggling with the social challenges that can come from living in poverty and the mandate to move all students towards academic proficiency, once-insular public schools have learned to embrace a new kind of assistance from outside. Before the fate of educator's careers became linked to student achievement, community assistance from businesses and parent organizations tended to take the form of a donation. In today's environment, schools need more than just financial resources from the private sector. A community's chamber of commerce or other business organization can play a unique and difference-making role in the success of the education enterprise. Over the past two decades, the chamber in Nashville, Tennessee, has aggressively forged a partnership with its local school system that moves far beyond supplementing public finances and serves as a potential model for true collaboration.

Why should a chamber of commerce make improving elementary and secondary education a top priority?

Increasingly, fewer chambers are wrestling with that question, as the stakes are now fairly self-evident. Traditionally, chambers have housed their K-12 education initiatives within their workforce development strategy. In Nashville, the Chamber produces ten-year workforce projections by job type and industry, with the latest report forecasting a significant shortage in skilled and knowledgeable workers that cannot be solved by in-migration alone. Meeting this challenge will mean producing more post-secondary degrees and certificates, which, in turn, requires a greater proportion of high school graduates to be college-prepared. In certain careers areas, we are experiencing this future shortage today. Nashville is the centre of the country's privately owned health care industry, and there are hundreds of health care information technology jobs today that are unfilled and are being sourced from other places. But beyond the workforce lens, it is clear that families and even businesses consider the quality of public schools in their location decisions. The perception of a school system can brand a community. In Middle Tennessee, the perception of stronger school systems in four of the counties surrounding Nashville helped fuel a 73 per cent increase in population over a ten-year period. As a liability, the consequences of a negative education brand are playing out in large urban centres that are haemorrhaging students and families to charter schools and other communities.

Given the urgency around education improvement, many chambers have, understandably, stepped up their involvement. The Nashville Area Chamber of Commerce plays the part of 'critical friend' to the 81,000-student MNPS. Being a 'friend' manifests itself in numerous ways beyond traditional philanthropy. Because they routinely engage community leadership and typically have staff resources, chambers can often catalyze solutions to unmet needs. The Nashville Chamber helped form a grass-roots coalition called Friend of Metro Schools that lobbies for adequate education funding at the local and state level. Supporting a mayor who has prioritized education spending, the end result has been a school system budget that has not only weathered a national recession, but enjoyed annual budget increases in four of the last five years. The Chamber also led the creation of a public campaign and Website called www.onenashville.org that encourages citizens to volunteer, donate or advocate on behalf of public schools, resulting in a 30 per cent increase of those activities. And in 2002, the chamber sparked the formation of a new non-profit, Alignment Nashville, to coordinate and focus the efforts of the city's many non-profits and community organizations – initially to better support the strategic direction of the school system, but soon branching out to other areas such as children's health and out-of-school youth.

Being a critical friend

The 'critical' part of the chamber's relationship with MNPS is just as important, and it is a role that few other organizations are equipped to play. In 1993, the Nashville Chamber began holding the school system accountable for results by producing its own annual report of the district's progress. At a time when Tennessee and other states were just beginning to compile student data that was accessible to the general public, a committee of 13 Chamber volunteers, supported by staff, offered a concise, readable, 14-page accounting of MNPS's performance. Recognition of successful district programmes and a coherent plan for improvement were balanced by admonishment for an 'unacceptably high drop-out rate' and a scarcity of instructional materials. Twenty years later the Chamber's annual report card is now a 64-page effort that includes results from an opinion poll that tracks public perception of the school system over time. Each release continues to highlight commendations and shortcomings, along with five recommendations for improvement that are tracked for implementation. A myriad of charts containing student academic and demographic information has made the report a go-to resource for non-profit grant writers in the city. The committee of 25 volunteers now begins work each August, culminating in a presentation to the school board, director of schools and mayor in December.

Both aspects of the critical friend role are evident in the Chamber's support for MNPS's high school reform effort, the AN. First initiated to turn around the district's 12 zoned high schools in 2006 and phased in over several years, Nashville's high school academies are schools within a school, tied to a career or thematic focus. 16,000 students and 1,000 teachers organized into 43 academies across the 12 high schools – necessitated a thoughtful and robustly supported structure for hundreds of business-school partnerships.

If the partnerships are focused and impactful, businesses should eventually see the return on their investment.

Although the chamber recruits academy partners from its membership by referring them to the PENCIL Foundation, the chamber is directly responsible for two additional tiers of business engagement, which provide system-wide strategic support. Five industry-based partnership councils, consisting of business volunteers, postsecondary officials and educators from the academies are convened by the chamber on a quarterly basis. As an example, the Hospitality & Tourism partnership council consists of representatives from the city's lodging, entertainment and dining industry, as well as educators from the five schools that have a hospitality and tourism-related academy. The partnership council discusses industry trends, workplace skills and academy offerings. In addition to providing advice, the partnership councils serve as a resource to academies by recruiting new partners and marshalling volunteers for a career exploration fair or academy showcase. But the partnership councils are also part of a system of accountability designed to ensure that progress is made towards the goal of every high school graduate being prepared for postsecondary education and an eventual career. The chamber works with MNPS and PENCIL Foundation staff to produce a dashboard of indicators that is reviewed at every meeting. The dashboard updates student attendance, annual performance on the ACT college entrance exam and academy partnership activity. Knowing that a dozen or so stakeholders from outside the district are looking at your activities and performance on a regular basis elevates the importance of maintaining these partnerships. And, if the partnerships are focused and impactful, businesses should eventually see the return on their investment.

CEO champions

The third tier of business engagement tied to the AN is a Chief Executive Officer (CEO)-level group modelled after a similar entity in Philadelphia. In Nashville, the CEO Champions is a chamber committee co-chaired by the mayor and a prominent business leader, with MNPS's director of schools serving as one of 22 members. Just as the partnership councils each have a dashboard of their related academies; the CEO Champions have a dashboard of district-wide information spanning all 43 academies. As their name implies, the members of the committee participate in press conferences, serve as spokespeople in the community and author opinion pieces in the daily newspaper. Important as their cheerleading role is, the purpose of the group is also to protect and sustain successful education reform. The CEO Champions are in a position to evaluate the school system's commitment to their own strategy by looking for that support in the district's operating budget. Even greater than the threat of under resourcing reform, is surviving changes in school district or city leadership. New leaders are tempted to scrap existing strategies and start anew, and the education reform landscape is littered with the carcasses of silver-bullet solutions and cure-all programmes. By design, the CEO Champions are a group with sufficient gravitas to focus the attention of any new leader on the results to date and the merits of continuing a successful reform, irrespective of who might get credit for its initiation or success.

While the Nashville Chamber's extensive partnership with the school system is specific to local context and history, there are at least four broad lessons that educators and businesses can adapt to fit their own community's circumstances.

Four broad lessons for others

Everybody needs a 'critical friend'

Having spent most of my career, since the mid-1990s, working on improving public education from within government and now in the private sector, I am convinced that bureaucracies, which large school systems are, will not and cannot change without constant outside pressure. In America, much of that pressure comes from the formal systems of accountability put in place in the 50 states as the result of the 2001 'No Child Left Behind' federal legislation. But positive pressure for continuous improvement must also come from a local community. Unfortunately, these local sources of positive pressure rarely materialize on their own. Parents who are disappointed in their school's performance usually vote with their feet by moving to another school zone or enrolling their child in private school, and the ones who cannot leave tend to lack organization and clout. In addition, most community organizations lack the capacity or stature to be an effective critic of the schools, or, being critical is contrary to carrying out their mission to provide unqualified support for the school district.

Local chambers can play the critical friend role to their school district if they are willing to take it on. Successful chambers are connected to significant resources in a community, whether it is community leadership, philanthropic resources or access to news media. And while there are inevitably community members who question the motives behind every chamber activity, our polling in Nashville indicates that the average citizen is four times more likely to have a positive impression of the Chamber's activity, as compared to a negative perception. Being well-regarded does not mean that a critical friend relationship is easy. In the case of the education report card, it requires talking candidly in public about successes, but also about the deficiencies of the school district. It also means accepting a certain amount of permanent tension in the partnership. The upside for the school district is that when their critic offers a commendation or defends the school system, it does so with tremendous credibility. On the positive side for the chamber, there is a balance to the relationship with the district that comes from the knowledge that either partner has the ability to walk away and be missed by the other, which other community organizations may find difficult to replicate.

An anecdote from the early stages of the AN high school reform illustrates how the Nashville Chamber has played this role. While the academies were expanded in 2007 to include all 12 zoned high schools, a year of interim district leadership in 2008 led to uneven implementation as the reform was being phased in. School principals who had bought into the academy concept from the very beginning forged ahead; school leaders who resisted the change were allowed to do nothing. Presented only a month into the new superintendent's tenure, the 2008 report card called the school district out, stating 'this high school redesign effort needs renewed commitment and clear leadership from the school board and director of schools, and a committed administrative team at every participating school, if it is to deliver on its promise to our students and the Nashville community.'

Business-education partnerships must be adequately resourced

Volunteers are absolutely vital to a chamber's effectiveness in the community. In fact, while I believe that the staff's professional experience and expertise at the Nashville Chamber ensures a baseline of success, it is the personal involvement of business leaders that gives the organization the highest level of credibility. Organizations that recruit volunteers to deliver programmes directly in schools, such as student mentoring, rely even more on donated time. However, any significant business-school partnership that runs solely on the backs of volunteers is bound to falter. The reason is obvious: business volunteers have their full-time job to attend to. The job of a chamber, or other community organization managing volunteers, is to make it easy for volunteers to be involved. This means that we have the engagement opportunity identified and vetted beforehand, we understand clearly how the school system plans to interact with the partner, and we provide the right level of support throughout the partnership – such as collecting data to show whether the activity is making an impact – so that it can be sustained.

A coordinating organization managing partners at a significant scale can also offer volunteers an additional support: peer networking. In the AN example, the five industry-based partnership councils convened by the chamber consist mostly of companies that are also academy partners through the PENCIL Foundation. At their meetings, these volunteers share best practices and lessons learned across the many academy partnerships in the district, mutually reinforcing the importance of continued involvement and, often, spurring a healthy competition for the most exemplary partnership.

Just as importantly, chambers and other intermediaries offer businesses a degree of separation from the messiest parts of the policy process. Reforming education is not only difficult, it is often controversial. Changing the way teachers are evaluated and compensated, opening up public education to new delivery models and calling out low performance all involve taking on entrenched bureaucracies or organized interest groups. And while many business leaders want and, indeed, expect these battles to be waged, they are understandably less interested in having their company's brand associated with the public rhetoric. One such controversy raging in several states is the creation of school voucher programmes, which are taxpayer-funded tuition payments for students to attend private school. What we know from two years of polling this issue in our community is that the public is evenly divided on school vouchers. And, remarkably for an education reform issue, a majority of respondents have strong feelings on either side, with only 4 per cent not knowing enough to register an opinion. In 2011, the Nashville Chamber opposed school voucher legislation in the Tennessee state legislature because the amount of the voucher was too low to offer real choice to most of the city's private schools and the programme did not mirror the state's accountability system for students attending public schools. Our position was fully supported by our volunteer leadership and board, but the Chamber paid a price for its visible opposition. After the bill died in committee, we were lambasted by not only the bill's supporters but also by a lead editorial in the *Wall Street Journal*, which accused the opposing chambers of restricting 'freedom and opportunity' by supposedly conspiring with the teachers union to kill the legislation. Not only was the Nashville chamber strong enough to absorb this hit and stand by its policy position, there is every likelihood that a Tennessee voucher programme, if it is enacted, will bear features that address many of our business community's concerns.

Chambers rely on the annual support of their members to be an effective driver for education improvement. The vast majority of these investors, which also include foundations, understand the critical role that chambers can and do play in reforming systems, even though much of the activity may not take the form of student programmes.

Think beyond the cheque

Too often, educators think of partnerships with the business community in terms of receiving a financial or material donation. There is nothing inherently wrong with a purely transactional relationship, and for some businesses, this may be the preferred way, or even the only way, they can contribute. But schools and school systems that do not also consider asking their local business community for expertise and advocacy are leaving valuable resources on the table. Outside specialized career and technical programmes, secondary schools in particular have struggled to provide meaningful roles for business partners. That has changed in Nashville with the advent of the academies approach, in which all students participate in an academy programme with a career or thematic focus. Prior to the academies, a business volunteer wanting to work directly with students was channelled to the elementary grades as a reader or a math tutor. Rewarding and helpful to be sure, but the same role could be provided by a parent volunteer or a student peer. With academies, business persons are able to share their industry knowledge and expertise, their career and college path and the passion they have for their work with high school students who are beginning to think seriously about their own life choices.

At a system level, educators would do well to enlist their local chamber's power and influence to help shape the regulatory environment. Many chambers have a government affairs function at the local, state and sometimes national level. In 2008, the Nashville chamber helped MNPS remove a legal barrier to reorganizing its high schools. A key element of the academy model is to create teams of teachers that have common planning time in order to develop real-world connections across the curriculum and plan student interventions. The problem was that Tennessee state law had varying class size requirements for different types of teachers, making it nearly impossible for a principal to create a master class schedule that accomplished the necessary teaming. Once Nashville chamber staff became aware of the issue, we initiated meetings with state officials, drafted legislation that provided MNPS with class size flexibility within the academies, lined up bill sponsors and successfully lobbied for its passage.

Each business community should also push its thinking beyond the traditional ways it supports education improvement. Business people understand that effective leadership at every level, particularly at the top, is critical to the success of any large enterprise. A high-functioning school board that understands its governance role provides strategic direction for the district and accountability for the system's performance in all areas. A dysfunctional board focuses on endless, inconsequential issues and the political aspirations of its members, sending a message to every educator in the system that other issues take priority over student achievement. With most school districts in the United States led by an elected board of education, the business community can often play a difference-making role in what tend to be off-year, low turnout elections. In the late 1990s the Nashville Chamber set up a political action committee (PAC) focused solely on school board elections. SuccessPAC is a separate legal entity from the chamber that interviews all candidates for Nashville's school board, makes endorsement decisions that are then communicated to Nashville's business community and the news media and contributes funds to political campaigns. Prior to SuccessPAC's formation the only organized resources available to school board candidates came from labour unions. The PAC has had a clear track record of success, having endorsed seven of the nine current school board members.

Getting involved in school board elections is important, but the best way to elect an effective school board is to begin by recruiting good candidates. Given the trials of modern-day electoral politics, it takes extraordinary commitment and toughness to offer oneself up for public service. A retired CEO or a current executive with experience managing a large organization would add tremendous value to a school board that oversees an annual budget in hundreds of millions of dollars. Chambers know how to find these talented individuals, but historically it has been a difficult sell to convince them to run. That now seems to be turning, thanks to the dramatic changes wrought by the education reform movement. In the August 2012 Nashville school board election, the field of candidates included a former gubernatorial staffer, a national Teach for America executive and a senior executive at one of the city's largest companies. At the individual school level, Chambers can also play a role in recruiting volunteers to serve on the non-profit boards that oversee charter schools.

Create genuine shared ownership

The AN are getting attention from educators across the country because they are beginning to show real results. The graduate rate has steadily risen because students are more engaged in their learning, and the percentage of students deemed 'college ready' on a national test (the ACT) has ticked up each of the last three years. But the defining feature of Nashville's academies has been the widespread participation of the business community at multiple levels, and that participation continues to broaden and deepen. How did the business community become so invested in the reform? In simple terms, the school district was willing to share ownership. Appropriately, it was MNPS that chose the academy model and provided the vision for what high school education needed to become. Those decisions are the district's responsibility. But, wisely, from the very beginning the school system reached out to the chamber and other key community organizations and asked for their help in creating a plan of action. It was this collaborative planning that resulted in the three-tier structure of business engagement. Sharing ownership meant it was okay for the CEO Champions to be a Chamber committee rather than a school system-led group, and that the industry-based partnership councils would advocate more effectively if they were chaired by business leaders rather than district staff.

MNPS experienced the power of this shared ownership approach during the only significant controversy surrounding the implementation of the academy model. In early 2011, the district announced that the long-time International Baccalaureate (IB) coordinator at one of the high schools was being transferred, involuntarily, to another role at a different school. There was soon a vocal and organized protest from some students, parents, alumni and a couple of elected officials. News media reports hinted that the teacher's unwillingness to support the school's move towards academies was the reason behind the transfer, resulting in some of the teacher's defenders attacking the academy concept and mischaracterizing the reform as 'vocational education'. As the school district stood its ground on the transfer throughout the summer, the chamber, PENCIL Foundation and Alignment Nashville publicly countered the misinformation being spread about the academy approach. Business volunteers serving on the partnership councils took it upon themselves to correct the elected officials who were weighing in on the controversy but seemed to have little first-hand knowledge of the academies. Eventually, the teacher decided to accept the transfer, most of the protesters came to realize that MNPS was still committed to the success of the IB programme, and teachers and students at the school brought the focus back to teaching and learning in the academy model.

The episode highlighted the value of having articulate and influential partners who are not afraid to take a public stand. For the partners, the experience revealed a need to organize a comprehensive, multi-year communications and outreach campaign to make sure the public understood the academy approach. The chamber funded the services of a professional firm to help the district create the plan, and then companies involved in the academies pitched in to privately fund the first-year outreach activities. In addition, during the following school year, the chamber organized a series of academy VIP tours in six of the high schools targeted towards community leaders and opinion makers. Over 40 state and local elected officials attended the tours, as well as leaders of faith congregations, neighbourhood associations and parent groups.

Reflections on three wider questions

Accountability

There is no doubt that the formal systems of accountability put in place over the past decade have forced much-needed change in education, but it is important to acknowledge their limits. Test results and state administrators certainly influence behaviour and decisions at the local level, but that pressure tends to be isolated into a few key moments during the year, such as immediately before student testing takes place or immediately after the release of the results. A chamber of commerce playing the critical friend role, on the other hand, is also the neighbour, the shopkeeper, the quotable source in the daily newspaper explaining what academic results actually mean to a local community. Formal accountability systems provide crucial information to stakeholders about performance, but are less helpful in gauging whether schools are making the necessary adjustments, whether they have a coherent plan for improvement, and whether the right leadership is in place. A locally-based critical friend is in a much better position to make those more subjective assessments, and apply pressure for change if they are found wanting.

> Accountability systems are good at punishing, but less effective at rewarding and motivating performance.

Another such limitation is that accountability systems are good at punishing, but less effective at rewarding and motivating performance. In fact, one of the ironies of the accountability system under the federal No Child Left Behind law was that failing schools received substantial additional resources, but once a school started improving, the resources were yanked away. Four years into our high school reform effort, the Nashville Chamber started an annual awards programme modelled after the Academy Awards in Hollywood, complete with a red carpet reception, cocktail reception, dinner and trophies recognizing outstanding educators, administrators and academy partnerships. Atypical of most recognition events in education, educators not only appreciated the special attention, many of them were vowing to win an award the following year, precisely the kind of response we were hoping for.

Perhaps most frustratingly to non-educators, formal accountability systems tend to change every few years, making long-term comparisons impossible, or, accountability systems simply do not include measurements that are meaningful to the world outside education.

Perhaps most frustratingly to non-educators, formal accountability systems tend to change every few years, making long-term comparisons impossible, or, accountability systems simply do not include measurements that are meaningful to the world outside education. Of course there are perfectly good reasons for re-norming a test or adopting a completely different test to measure new academic standards. But the end result tends to be that the slate is wiped clean for low performing schools and it is left up to the local critical friend to keep everyone honest about the pace of progress. It is often said that business is the ultimate 'consumer' of the K-12 education system, as high school graduates move on, hopefully, to a postsecondary credential and into the workforce, but Tennessee's high stakes accountability measures for high schools tells a business very little about the quality of the 'product'. High schools are judged by on-time graduation rates and two courses completed fairly early in a student's high school career: Algebra I and English II. Proficiency levels on these tests might be useful feedback for the math and English departments, but what 80 per cent proficiency in ninth grade algebra is supposed to tell an employer, a college or parent is much less clear. Oddly, improvement on the ACT college entrance exam is absent from the state accountability system, despite the fact that nearly every Tennessee high school student takes it, it determines eligibility for the state scholarship programme and it is a reliable predictor of postsecondary success. That is why the Nashville Chamber digs into the district's ACT report each year to compute the percentage of students attaining a 21 or higher on the test. An accountability environment that includes a local critical friend increases the likelihood that important measures receive the proper attention.

On continuity and change – community stakeholders can also promotes policy continuity by helping a school system focus on succession at every level

Continuity from top leadership is important, but community stakeholders can also promote policy continuity by helping a school system focus on succession at every level across the district. Business in particular is focused on ensuring continuity from succession planning, while such a practice is almost antithetical to government agencies that change course with every election. In the early years of the AN high school reform, principal vacancies were filled by recruiting experienced leaders from other schools or districts who may not have been experienced in the academy model. More recently, executive principal vacancies have been filled by assistant principals groomed in the district's high school academies. The Chamber has also worked with the district to push understanding and awareness of the academy model to the elementary and middle school tiers, with the target audience of its second round of Academy VIP Tours being the principals of feeder schools and optional programmes.

Getting buy-in

We know from our annual public opinion polling that more than 80 per cent of Nashvillians feel improving K-12 education is 'personally important' to them, so convincing companies that they should be involved has not been an issue. But even so, businesses do not have the time or patience to figure it out on their own. In most cases, a business wants to be told exactly what the school wants them to do, oftentimes with some sort of metrics that will quantify the impact of their involvement. If they cannot provide a requested service to the school, they will say so, but schools are sometimes reluctant to make the ask. That is why intermediaries that specialize in school-business partnerships can play a valuable role in bridging the culture gap between the two sectors. A Chamber or non-profit can coach school staff on how to make a focused partnership pitch, while also protecting a prospective business partner from wasting time with a school partner who is not yet ready.

Looking to the future

While the substantial momentum around the AN high school reform is encouraging and the Nashville Chamber intends to continue its substantial support, we are also seeing opportunity for engagement on both ends of the high school years. For a successful business, it is imperative to begin with the end in mind and align an entire system to produce the best possible product. Yet, I have watched Nashville's public school system develop an elementary school strategy, a middle school strategy and a high school strategy completely independent of each other, despite the district having established measurable goals for each high school graduate. There is a clear need to connect the high school strategy to the earlier grades so that students are adequately prepared for secondary education, and the chamber can potentially play a supporting role. In addition, there is also an opportunity to create a more seamless connection between high school and postsecondary education. One way to do this is to expand student opportunities to earn postsecondary credit while still in high school. Students who take dual enrolment, which in Tennessee means a class in which a student earns both high school and transcriptable college credit for the same course, are more likely to attend and complete postsecondary education. While the State of Tennessee provides assistance for some dual enrolment, the programme does not cover the full tuition amount or the cost of textbooks, creating a potential barrier for students living in poverty. The Nashville Chamber is among a group of state and national partners commissioning an independent study of Tennessee's dual enrolment programme in comparison to peer states, with a report issuing recommendations for improving participation in the programme to be released in 2013.

> A deep partnership between schools and business can be a powerful force for education improvement.

The Nashville example shows that a partnership between schools and business can be a powerful force for education improvement. Both parties need to be willing to think and act a bit differently in order to realize all the advantages that such a relationship can offer. With each passing year this is becoming the rule, rather than the exception. Best practices on how to engage in education are springing up from local chambers across the United States, and the national organizations that support these local chambers are visibly more engaged in supporting this work at the community level. Initially compelled to collaborate with business and community organizations to meet the challenges of a high-stakes accountability environment, school districts see even greater value in these partnerships as they compete for students in what is fast-becoming an open market for education.

References and further reading

Anderson, G. and Davenport, P., *Closing the Achievement Gap: No Excuses* (Houston, TX: American Productivity and Quality Center, 2002).

Blackboard, Inc., *Thought Leadership: Edu-views, Blended Learning* (2012). Retrieved 1 November 2012 from www.blackboard.com/Markets/K-12/Thought-Leadership/eduviews.aspx

Gangopadhyay, P., *Innovation Resources for Teaching and Learning at The Henry Ford* (2010). Retrieved 4 October 2012, from www.thehenryford.org/education/pdf/article_innovationResourcesTeaching.pdf

Hord, S. M., *Professional Learning Communities: Communities of Continuous Inquiry and Improvement.* (Austin, TX: Southwest Educational Development Laboratory, 1997).

Hord, S. and Somers W., *Leading Professional Learning Communities: Voices from Research and Practice* (Thousand Oaks, CA: Corwin Press, 2008).

MDRC, *Career Academies: Long-term Impacts on Work, Education, and Transitions to Adulthood* (2008). Retrieved 5 November 2012, from www.mdrc.org/career-academies-5

National Career Academy Coalition, *National Standards of Practice* (2012). Retrieved 15 October 2012 from www.ncacinc.com/index.php?option=com_content&view=article&id=15&Itemid=10

Partnership for 21st Century Skills,. *Framework for 21st Century Learning* (Washington, DC: P21, 2011).

United States Department of Education, *Smaller Learning Communities Program* (2012). Retrieved 27 October 2012, from www2.ed.gov/programs/slcp/index.html

PART THREE

Creating an Empowered System

8

Autonomy and Professional Courage: Rational, Emotional and Political Aspects of Change

Pat Collarbone and Simon Edkins

Around the world schools are facing structural and financial changes on a scale unprecedented in the past 60 years. All of us who work in and around the sector are acutely aware of this. While for some it is threatening, many of us feel excited and energized by this opportunity and challenge. What we are most passionate about – and what we have spent the past ten years exploring, refining and delivering – is the facilitation of cultural change at both a local and system level. Change that impacts on how people work and behave, that delivers efficient and effective services as well as improving the life chances of young people.

Everywhere the watchword is autonomy. At its simplest this is about self-government, whether you are talking about a whole system or a single individual. In this chapter we will argue that the challenges faced by the education sector as it becomes more 'autonomous' are similar at a system, school and individual level. Our hypothesis is that transformation is only ever sustainable if the rational, emotional and political aspects of change are all fully addressed. This type of cultural change takes courage and perseverance.

Current structural and financial changes mean that schools need to do things differently. We may or may not welcome it, but we have a once-in-a-generation opportunity to really change the way the education sector is led, works and thinks about itself and its role in society. For many years a culture of command and control accompanied by excessive bureaucracy cascaded down through the system so that we are now in a position where many people do not know what it means to take up their own authority, to take a risk in the service of educating their students. This has in some cases led to inefficiency, poor staff morale and a dependency culture. The challenge we all face is to change this culture and release the potential that is undoubtedly already within our schools.

It is Principals (in the United Kingdom known as Headteachers) and their senior leadership teams who set strategy and direction, and changes in schools are down to their willingness to adapt. It is often very hard and painful for them to discard ways of working they have developed over many years and that have served them well in the past. They not only have to recognize and make personal changes but, in order for their organizations to thrive, they have to find ways of encouraging teacher's passion, initiative and creativity. This calls for professional as well as personal courage.

Michael Barber[1] goes so far as to say that teachers 'will find it difficult to change or even see why they should'.

Without a coherent and structured approach to change though we are concerned we will miss this opportunity and end up with less, rather than *more for less*. Our schools need to address the way they are doing things in a way that delivers more for less, ensures the greater involvement of all staff in the running of their schools, promotes collaboration with other schools and organizations and ensures a better education for all students.

We all know from personal experience that the way leaders lead or resist change, and how they engage with their staff, sets the climate of an organization that either promotes trust and innovation or reinforces rigidity and resistance to change. This sounds like common sense (well it is common sense), but is often deeply counter-cultural in the public sector.

The nub of the matter, *how* to bring about sustainable change, is rarely mentioned other than in vague terms. We believe that in every organization there already exists the potential to address this through improved leadership and engaging more employees in tackling key challenges.

Any intelligent fool can make things bigger and more complex . . . It takes a touch of genius – and a lot of courage to move in the opposite direction. Albert Einstein

Professional courage and accountability

The development of a culture of autonomy involves embedding a system of distributed leadership that empowers the whole workforce (including leaders), where all staff are encouraged to contribute fully, to use their initiative and take responsibility. A culture where feedback is honest, welcome and constructive and where meaningful aims and outcomes are defined across organizations and measurable at both a system and organization level. Enhancing leadership in schools is at the heart of this. Changing the way leaders lead facilitates the development of organizations that allows them to thrive in a climate of autonomy, with a culture of trust, interdependency and mutual respect.

Principals and senior leaders have a pivotal role in this new way of working. They continue to set the direction of their organizations, ensure that the right people are in the right jobs, explicitly define managerial authority and accountability and clearly articulate measurable outcomes and reward effort appropriately. They still lead but, crucially, the *way* they lead changes.

By engaging staff in critical decisions and the implementation of change, leaders build authority within individuals and increase leadership capacity and capability at all levels. This frees everyone to work at their full potential, including leaders themselves, creating increased efficiency, effectiveness and motivation.

The alternative (which really is no alternative at all) is retaining a dependency model, where a lack of discretionary effort and an unwillingness to take risks mean that at best organizations maintain the status quo, at worst their standards fall and students suffer. This erosion of individual responsibility and trust also has a significant negative financial implication.

It is important to understand that a culture of autonomy is not about leaders giving their power away; rather it is about them getting the balance right between control and freedom as Figure 8.1 shows and, ultimately, becoming far more effective leaders. The challenge is that when under pressure people usually revert to a command and control leadership style. What then is needed is a robust way of leading change that contains the anxiety of leaders and others engaged in change, so that real work and innovation can take place and ideas are allowed to flourish. A certain level of failure and a great deal of trust is the price that has to be paid for innovation.

Creating Tomorrow Ltd 2011.

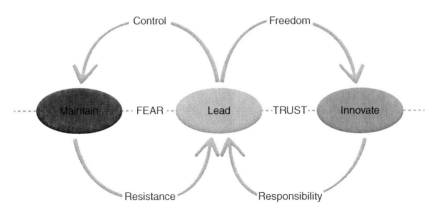

FIGURE 8.1 *Maintain/lead/innovate*

Inevitably when cuts are deep there is uncertainty and fear, and this is often a time when leaders retreat to their offices rather than leading from the front. So having a process that promotes transparency and honesty is essential. With a robust change process in place leaders are able to support their staff to develop a shared view of the future, encourage the analysis and benchmarking of performance and give them the opportunity to introduce new ways of working.

Distributed leadership and the need to promote and develop authority and accountability at all levels is a hot topic. Certainly leading and being involved in change can provide a unique opportunity for personal, professional and organizational development.

An effective change process must incorporate professional and organizational development. It is characterized by a focus on learning by doing, learning from each other, with each other and for each other. This ensures staff involvement and support and leads to sustainable change. We call this model Distributed Leadership Development, as shown in Figure 8.2.

Everyone involved in change, wherever they are in an organization's hierarchy, will have people above them who will delegate authority to them and people below who will sanction their position. They will all also face the challenge of taking up their own authority.

Getting this right means the motivation for change and the skills to bring it about are distributed throughout the organization and the whole system. This facilitates a change in culture through the *process* of change itself, and embeds effective distributed leadership into an organization in a natural and experiential way.

Model adapted from Obholzer, A.[2]

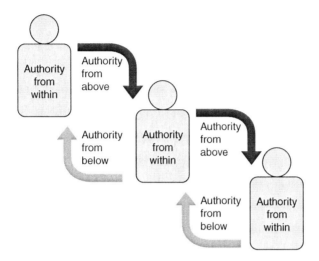

FIGURE 8.2 *Authority from within*

The rational description of authority is that leaders have certain rights over their subordinates, including giving orders, rewards and discipline – authority from above. At the same time they are accountable for both their own actions and those of their subordinates. For their part subordinates are obliged to do as they are asked, thus from the rational point of view authority and accountability are not attached to individuals but invested in roles. Leaders therefore need to develop the skills associated with sponsorship, delegation, challenge and support.

Followership, authority from below, although always important, has become even more crucial with the advent of the information age and dramatic social changes in the workplace. The political and emotional aspects of change play an important role. Individuals are more inclined to follow leaders who inspire self-confidence and encourage people to take up their own authority than to submit arbitrary rules and regulations. Leaders need to practice developing trust, collaborating, creating and developing teams.

Crucially individuals may be appointed to positions of authority, sanctioned from below, yet still be unable to exercise authority. They can be undermined by their own self-doubt or have an inflated ego resulting in authoritarian attitudes and behaviour. They lack authority from within. Leaders need to reflect on their practice, encourage honest feedback and develop their resilience.

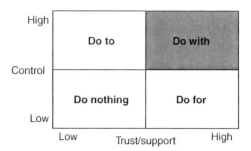

FIGURE 8.3 *Control-trust/support*

As Figure 8.3 illustrates 'Human beings are happier, more cooperative and productive, and more likely to make positive changes in their behavior when those in positions of authority do things with them, rather than to them or for them.'[3]

Working with others requires the giving and receiving of constructive feedback. Without it, and the development of a culture where it is welcome, it is impossible to create a truly effective system of distributed leadership.

Giving and receiving feedback is not a simple transaction, it implies judgement and this has profound implications for our self-esteem. It takes trust and courage. If we get it right it can be incredibly constructive and empowering. If we get it wrong it can destroy confidence and encourage dysfunction and stasis in an organization.

We all know experientially, though, that many people find feedback confronting and threatening, especially when it is between peers rather than between a manager and a subordinate. There have been many attempts to overcome this based either on anonymity, for example, 'multirate' 360 degree feedback, or 'scientific testing' such as scaled competencies.

However both approaches treat the symptom and not the cause. They avoid the fundamental developmental issue of interacting as an adult with another adult. The challenge we face is to place healthy human relations at the centre of the debate and encourage a culture of open and constructive feedback, facilitating a real and sustainable change from dependency to autonomy within organizations.

This movement from a dependency culture of command and control, to an organization-wide culture of trust, of distributed leadership and open feedback, is fundamental to successful and sustainable change. The personal and organizational freedom it encourages helps release creativity and ensures staff feel they are working on something fundamentally worthwhile and are being treated as adults.

Collective courage and maturity

In addition to leading in their own schools Principals are, in greater numbers, taking up a role in improving the system as a whole. There is significant growth in schools working together and with other agencies. Although this is nothing new it is happening to a much greater extent today than ever before. In the United Kingdom, for example, the Department for Education is clear there are significant educational benefits to be gained from promoting and supporting collaboration. It has funded initiatives such as London Challenge, National Leaders of Education, Federations, Teaching Schools and the National Schools Linking Programme.

Similar initiatives are to be found in the United States and in many other countries around the world. They all aim to improve the educational experience of students and reverse some of the worst tendencies of the past. There are many other benefits too, such as professional development for staff, knowledge transfer, raising standards and helping schools that are in difficulty.

Up until the late 1970s most public service institutions were dominated by a dependency culture, in which an individual's relationship to the state and their employer was similar to that of an infant to its mother. When times became tough individuals and organizations would revert to co-dependent behaviour rebelling against their enforced dependence rather like badly behaved teenagers.

Our maturity model shown in Figure 8.4 describes the characteristics of the co-dependent and dependent individual or team, but applies equally to organizations and even whole sectors. The last 30 years has seen institutions coming to terms with this failed dependency culture by becoming more independent and most recently interdependent.

	Co-dependence	Dependence	Independence	Interdependence
System focus	Confused	Centralized	Localized	Personalized
Leadership based upon	Fear	Control	Responsibility	Trust
Accountability	Remedial action	Inspection	Self-evaluation	Peer view
Ways of working	Conflict	Negotiation	Consultation	Partnership
Approach to change	Status quo	Reactive	Proactive	Creative
Workforce response	Denial	Compliance	Development	Professionalism

Maturity of the individual, team, organization and sector

FIGURE 8.4 *Co-dependence-dependence-independence-interdependence*

Initially, in the private sector, this meant many organizations simply going out of business. There was a surge in outsourcing, off shoring and self-employment. In the public sector the pace of change has been slower but no less radical. Wherever we go in the world we see similar challenges, the need to do more for less, to use new technology creatively and for individuals to take up their own authority and go the extra mile.

Hargreaves and Fink[4] argue that strong networked learning communities that have a compelling sense of purpose and work within clear parameters of collective, multiple and light touch forms of accountability, are one of the many strategies for restoring the rich diversity that years of standardization have depleted or destroyed.

A school working with other schools is just one type of collaboration. Another is schools collaborating with other agencies.

The Every Child Matters agenda in the United Kingdom, for example, had a focus on schools working closely with other agencies. Other examples include vertical integration, where a headteacher has responsibility from nursery right through to 19, and schools work more closely with their local communities and parents.

All of this has profound implications for leadership. The transition from being the leader of a school to leading a complex interaction of relationships is very challenging.

Any movement towards collaborative and integrated working involves not only rational issues such as structure and funding, but political issues of status and power and emotional issues of loss and ego. But the benefits are so compelling that new ways of developing leaders with the skills to work in this way have become critical.

Fullan[5] (2004) puts it like this:

A new kind of leadership is necessary for breaking through the status quo. Systemic forces, sometimes called inertia, have the upper hand in preventing system shifts. Therefore it will take powerful, proactive forces to change the existing system. . . . To change organisations and systems will require leaders to get experience in linking to other parts of the system. These leaders in turn must develop other leaders with similar characteristics.

Interdependence is less about command and control and more about working within complex and diverse systems. The reductionist view of leadership, which simply looks at competencies and individual traits, and ignores systemic thinking and relationships, results in structures where individuals play their part without taking responsibility for the whole.

Peter Senge[6] says that the leadership of the future 'will not be provided simply by individuals but by groups, institutions, communities and networks'.

Interdependence also involves rethinking what success means. It is not simply being interested in the outcomes for your own organization but for the wider system as a whole. It is recognizing, for example, in England, that a school cannot be held solely accountable for safeguarding of children.

Schools are, of course, in part accountable, but to hold them solely responsible and therefore accountable for this would of course be counterproductive. A broad number of partners and stakeholders need to become involved for achieving such ends. The responsibility of the school is therefore to work with a team of partners to create a strategy that makes all children as safe as possible.

However, in our experience, professional learning communities and networks when examined closely sometimes reveal ineffectual leadership hiding behind the rhetoric of collegiality and equality, unwilling to face up to the emotional and political realities of working together. Effective partnerships demand high levels of trust and mutual understanding; conditions that take much investment to create and very little time at all to destroy.

The HayGroup[7] worry that there is too much 'false rhetoric around partnership' that devalues the concept and can lead to wasted time and resources simply getting to know each other rather than working together productively.

It has long been recognized that people are more likely to be trustworthy if they are trusted. The same is true in partnerships. This does not imply blind faith, but partners need to build into the design the space for each party to make their own choices about how they deliver.

For alliances to work there needs to be agreement between schools on what they wish to achieve for a particular group and how they will know that they have delivered it. They need to focus on aligning vision, values and outcomes with data-driven strategies and community engagement.

Change on this scale cannot be left to chance. The question is how do you bring about system-wide change, school by school, so that the results are context-specific and designed locally? We believe the answer lies not in providing solutions but in building sustainable capacity, capability and leadership at a local level.

Leading change, changing leadership – A school led theory of action

We do not believe you can learn about leading change from a book; you have to actually do it. However, it is commonly acknowledged that over 70 per cent of change initiatives fail and the reasons for this have been well documented.

Such a high failure rate means that existing ways of managing change do not address these reasons.

The approach we have found to work, which we have refined with others over the past decade, facilitates a change in the way leaders lead and, as a consequence, changes ways of working across organizations. This six step change process – Change[2] – uses tools and techniques that, rather than being prescriptive, allow organizations to tackle their challenges in the way most appropriate for them.

Central to this approach to change is the concept of learning by doing. When leaders and staff work together on real problems, in new ways, the culture of their organization will change.

To be effective, any change process must include appropriate governance and social partnership, robust quality control, independent monitoring and evaluation of progress, unambiguous measures of performance and efficient online systems of data capture, analysis and reporting. This ensures that all changes are based on evidence, that they have a measurable impact and that they are sustainable.

A robust change process clearly defines roles, contains anxiety and allows learning to take place. The Change[2] model illustrated in figure 8.5 below is built to address the rational, emotional and political aspects of change. It recognizes that there will be times when the going gets tough but by following the steps a team will come out of the dip with creative solutions and plans for the future.

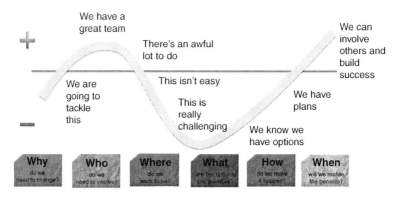

FIGURE 8.5 *The Change[2] journey – Creating Tomorrow LTD 2011*

Change[2] is as Hargreaves and Shirley[8] describe, 'a democratic and professional path to improvement that builds from the bottom, steers from the top, and provides support from the sides'.

In a short space of time a well-structured change process can not only deliver strategic and operational objectives but also bring about cultural and behavioural change at all levels in an organization.

Here we describe two examples of the use of Change[2]. In the first case a network of cross phase schools worked together to improve writing for every student. The second example is where our change process is being cascaded through a whole system in advance of a major IT implementation.

Case study – The North Bunbury Network of public schools, Western Australia

A restructuring of The Department of Education, Western Australia, in 2010 resulted in 21 State Education Districts being reduced to eight very large and diverse regions. Regional Directors in consultation with school Principals, established school networks with the intention of creating structures to support school development appropriate for each of their unique contexts. These networks were given more autonomy and operational flexibility. Professional support and teacher development opportunities previously provided from the Department of Education had now to be sourced from within school networks.

One of these, The North Bunbury Network of Public Schools, is a large education precinct located on the South-West coast covering approximately 1,200 square kilometres comprising two senior high schools, one community college, one agricultural college and ten primary schools. This network was yet to develop a clear direction for their school support programmes so there was a unique opportunity to build sustainable change using Change[2]. Nigel Wakefield, Deputy Principal, Australind Senior High School facilitated an initial workshop to establish the focus for the programme and it was agreed that quality teaching would be the vehicle to improve Writing performance across the Network.

A Change Team was selected by a Steering Group of Principals, with a diverse range of talented classroom practitioners and school leaders chosen from each of the Network schools. Seed funding of $50,000 was granted to the project.

Over a period of six months the Change Team met and worked through the Change[2] process. The result was a comprehensive plan to improve writing across the Network guided by the vision to 'support every teacher in every classroom to inspire excellence'. The plan included a focus on four main drivers for change:

1 Seamless transition in writing from kindergarten to year 12;
2 Scope and sequence curriculum documents aligned to National Standards;
3 Common assessment tasks organized by year level;
4 Transitions through key phases of educational development.

The presentation of the final plan to the Steering Group was very well received and the plans and actions exceeded expectations. The shared vision about how to improve writing performance includes sharing data, teacher expertise and common resources. Interschool moderation has been organized for May 2013 where 300 teachers across the 14 schools will meet at one campus to examine and discuss writing performance and improvement strategies across the Network.

'The Change[2] Team has established a strong interdependent bond driven by a common purpose to inspire excellence in teaching practice. The Network Principals have developed great trust in their Change Team and are actively supporting the Change[2] initiative within their schools'. Nigel Wakefield, Change[2] Master Facilitator

The Steering Group have held preliminary discussions to use the Change[2] process to improve Numeracy across the Network.

Case study – The Catholic Education Commission Victoria, Australia

Fullan[9] argues that technology can transform performance but only if it is integrated with deep understanding of what makes good teaching and knowledge of how to reform education systems.

The Catholic Education Commission Victoria (CECV) is introducing a new computer system ICON into all of their schools. It is a very ambitious project that will deliver radical new ways of both managing schools and using the latest technology for teaching and learning linking 13 000 teachers, 190 000 students and their parents in over 470 schools.

This will be a transformational change for the sector and as such will evoke emotional and political responses as well as the purely rational. Change[2] is designed to assist schools prepare for such change.

A pilot was held between November 2011 and March 2012. Thirty-two facilitators were given three and half day's intensive training in the delivery of Change[2]. Immediately following the training, Principals from 14 schools were briefed about the pilot and the process. The Principal is the sponsor and chair of the Steering Committee, but does not take an active part in the Change Team.

A number of Principals felt uncomfortable at not being in direct control of or being a member of the Change Team. However, when talking about the impact of the change journey on them personally, most acknowledged that it provided a profound learning experience and agreed that the structure – not being in the Change Team – was absolutely the right thing to do.

> . . . this is what I saw as we went through the process and it made me realise, as a leader, that I didn't need to be on that team. Because if I was on it then perhaps my voice and my perceptions do flavour, do colour what other people do and say, so for me that was a real learning. And I was excited because I think that it made me really look at myself as a leader and think well what is my leadership style and what does our school truly need in this time? How do we build capacity of our staff? Deb Egan, Principal St Luke's Blackburn South

The facilitators, working in pairs in schools took a Change Team through seven two- to three-hour workshops. They were asked to choose one of two themes directly related to preparing for ICON, to explore this during the pilot and develop a plan for introducing a significant change. The themes were: collaborative learning for students and teachers, designing student learning.

The process proved to be sufficiently flexible to allow schools to tackle issues, of importance to them, within their own unique context.

ICON was unavailable during the pilot but this did not detract from the fact that schools found the process powerful in bringing about cultural change and developing sound business cases and plans.

Since April 2012 70 facilitators have been trained and 40 schools and the central office have been through the process. It is planned that another 90 schools will take part next year and over 60 more facilitators will be trained. Facilitators are drawn from the central office and regional offices as well as schools. ICON will be rolled out over the next three years and each school will use Change² to prepare themselves.

This is life altering stuff for an organisation, that's what I'm seeing, this really making a difference and you don't always get the benefit of seeing the outcomes of your labour yet we are seeing it here. It is a very significant piece of work for Catholic education in Victoria. (Debra Punton, Assistant Director, School Services CECV)

A courageous future

We are all united in our aim to develop a culture appropriate for twenty-first-century education for all our children. This is a culture that is student-focused, flexible and self-regulating and one that delivers high-quality teaching and learning, with value for money.

Achieving this is dependent upon continuous improvement from each member of staff, whatever their role, taking full responsibility for what they do and being committed to the values of their organization.

This does not mean that education needs to become 'more like a business'. As Jim Collins (2005)[10] notes, this is not the answer, and we agree. He points out that many accepted business practices correlate with mediocrity rather than 'greatness' and that the real distinction is not between 'business and social' organizations but between 'good and great' ones.

Our aim must be to create great schools – schools that deliver superior performance and make a distinctive impact over a long period of time, schools that are led and managed well, that are rewarding places to work and to learn and that provide the best possible education for our children.

Notes

1 Barber et al. 2012, 58.

2 Obholzer and Roberts 1994, 39–41.

3 International Institute for Restorative Practices.

4 Hargreaves and Fink 2006.

5 Fullan 2004.

6 Senge et al. 2004, 185.

7 Haygroup 2008, 4.

8 Hargreaves and Shirley 2009, 107.

9 Fullan 2012.

10 Collins 2005.

References and further reading

Barber, M., et al., *Oceans of Innovation: The Atlantic, the Pacific, Global Leadership and the Future of Education* (London: Institute of Public Policy Research, 2012), 58.

Collins. J., *Good to Great and the Social Sectors, Why Business Thinking Is not the Answer* (USA and England: Harper Collins, 2005, 2006).

Fullan, M., *System Thinkers in Action, Moving Beyond the Standards Plateau* (London/ Nottingham: DfES Innovation Unit/National College for School Leadership, 2004) , 7.

— *Stratosphere. Integrating Technology, Pedagogy, and Change Knowledge* (Canada: Pearson, 2012).

Hargreaves, A. and Fink, D., *Journal of Educational Change: Sustainable Leadership* (San Francisco, CA: Jossey-Bass, 2006).

Hargreaves, A. and Shirley, D., *The Fourth Way. The Inspiring Future of Educational Change* (Thousand Oaks, CA: Corwin, 2009), 107.

Haygroup, *The Art of Alliance: Creating Partnerships that Work* (London: The Hay Group, 2008), 4.

— *Building the New Leader. Leadership Challenges of the Future Revealed* (London: The Hay Group 2012),5.

Obholzer, A. and Roberts, V. Z., *The Unconscious at Work* (London: Routledge, 1994), 39–41.

Senge, P., Scharmer, C. O., Jaworski, J. and Flowers, E. S., *Presence Exploring Profound Change in People, Organisations and Society* (London: Nicholas Brealey, 2004), 185.

9

Approaches to Accountability

Jeff Hale with James Park

Introduction

Before the 1988 Education Act Her Majesties Inspectors (HMI) inspected a sample of schools in-depth or on particular themes and produced reports to guide the system. Individual inspections were not available to the public though they were provided for the schools that were inspected. From 1988 every school was to be inspected every four years and the reports were put in the public domain. The original post-1988 model was comprehensive: data was less significant, an inspection team would usually contain a subject specialist in each area and every teacher would be observed at least once. There is no doubt that this was a 'Rolls Royce' model. Further it recognized while a number of elements of school improvement are generic and about leadership, a key element relates to pedagogy and the specifics of the delivery of teaching and learning that are subject-specific. Inspection professionalized judgements about teaching quality and led to widespread teacher observation by school leaders and peers using the Office for Standards in Education, Children's Services and Skills (Ofsted) criteria. In the main teachers and schools have valued the contribution of inspection too as the National Foundation for Educational Research (NFER) report in 2008[1] involving 18 school visits and a wider sample of 126 schools illustrated. What they valued most is significant:

- **84 per cent** classroom observation important – particularly dialogue with inspectors and paired lesson observation between schools and inspectors;

- **99 per cent** views of pupils important;
- **58 per cent** improved own teaching;
- **85 per cent** improved teaching in the school.

The new streamlined and lower-cost inspections still cover every school but are data focused and arguably have the answers before they arrive. The team no longer contains a specialist in every discipline and may not even contain a specialist in all the core areas. This raises the question of whether Ofsted now is able to do as good a job as it used to, and whether the data tells the system all it really needs to know in terms of accountability? It surely would be unusual for an inspector to say a school was better than its data and saying it was worse would probably give grounds for appeal. The current Ofsted model is a good fit for a top-down system, with pre-defined curriculum standards. It is an effective way of ensuring compliance with government policy too but is this sort of approach still fit for purpose and the best way to create a world-class system?

Public accountability is clearly important but is this essentially old fashioned quality control model the best way and the best value for money?

Public accountability is clearly important but is this essentially old fashioned quality control model the best way and the best value for money? As we move away from pre-defined curriculum and pedagogy, and if we accept the best way for a system to move from good to great is greater informed professionalism, there may be a better and different role for HMI in helping the profession to be better informed. As described in an earlier chapter, Finland, one of the world's most successful systems, does not even have a word for accountability and its focus is on 'professional responsibility'[2] and forms of what they call 'smart accountability'. Genuine self-assessment benchmarked by good data which Ofsted began to embrace is a powerful tool but it is an uneasy bedfellow of traditional public accountability and can lead to some unintended consequences. There is also a widely shared view that Ofsted does not make enough of its knowledge base although reductions in the scale of its inspections have of course reduced this knowledge. Yet research-informed practice development needs to be a key focus area if pedagogy is to improve. Samples may in fact yield more. The English schools' inspection system is certainly one of the most comprehensive in the world, but is it really designed to service a Second or at best a Third Way? It may help raise the floor but can it help raise the ceiling and foster creativity and innovation? The question remains as to the best combination of levers to enable England to move from a good towards a world-class system – the answers may well lie in those systems that already are world class. This chapter consists of two opinion pieces. The first is by Jeff Hale, a former teacher and school adviser who now regularly inspects schools and reflects on what he views as the limitations of the current system and on how we can build a new approach. The second from James Park argues the current system is 'toxic' and that the time is right to consider an even more radical way.

Too much accountability not enough trust – building a new approach

JEFF HALE

School improvement in England has lost its way. While it is undoubtedly right that schools managing large budgets should be held to account for their impact and effectiveness, the degree of accountability heads are now subjected to is counterproductive. Taken together, the raft of national strategies, 'no-notice' and one-to-three year variable Ofsted inspections, HMI curriculum monitoring visits, floor and other statutory targets, national tests, endless small-group comparative progress measures, 'critical friend' governors, local authority, academy improvement officers, parental choice, performance tables, attendance officers, safeguarding officers, auditors, health and safety officers and the interests of national media campaigns, particularly in relation to allegations that examination standards have been watered down, have combined to place many headteachers needlessly on the back foot. Schools have become national scapegoats for all society's ills, not least those riots.

> Fault is more readily identified than need; challenge offered more instinctively than support.

Fault, consequently, is more readily identified than need; challenge from all sides, both to the institution and to the individual pupil, is offered more instinctively than support. The right of schools to define the purposes of education for themselves and to take ownership of that vision is discouraged. There is room for but one goal: the centrally directed one of raising standards. This is not a recipe for genuine growth. Schools cannot and do not expect carte blanche but this degree of unremitting oversight risks inhibiting ambition to an unwarranted and unhelpful degree.

We cannot go on like this. There is an urgent need for a framework based on very different assumptions amounting to a wholly new 'paradigm' of school improvement if the profession is to make the improvements beyond 'satisfactory' than are now insisted on.

No single all-encompassing model of school practice should be promoted centrally. Instead, schools should be encouraged to develop beyond the baseline of a simple pursuit of equality of opportunity and entitlement and develop the ability to innovate and experiment. Though still operating within with a clear framework of accountability that is appropriately (but not excessively) rigorous, schools of known quality will consistently have the vision and leadership capacity to define their priorities and practices for themselves. A far better approach would be to avoid offering additional or more stringent sets of mandatory techniques to 'drill down' even further into school quality but instead to endorse the importance of encouraging schools and teachers *who have proved their worth* to develop the flexibility to be more selective in their use of recommended techniques and to favour those that play to their strengths. This acknowledges that schools operate in markedly different contexts and face very different challenges. 'One size' operating from Dover to Durham will not do for all. Provided a secure baseline is in place, for example, reasonable standards, strong subject knowledge, purposeful marking and planning, good behaviour management and consistently high expectations, there is more room for individuality in teaching and provision than is currently acknowledged in much outsider-driven school improvement and by many inspectors. Teaching has to be more personalized if it is to be compelling.

Altering the focus of inspection and quality assurance

Standards matter, of course they do, and all heads accept this. This is a battle that has long since been won. However, defining school effectiveness *exclusively* in terms of teaching's impact on achievement is to ignore all the highly significant forces that research has long shown inevitably affect the performance of any one individual in the classroom. We cannot ignore class, culture, values, home background, language use, social deprivation, frequency and type of reading matter, peer pressure and the effectiveness of previous teachers any longer. We know that these things can all make a huge difference. For all that schools must do all they can to overcome these constraints and 'fight the good fight', we cannot assume they will always or all equally succeed. What, then, is the point of performance management and inspection systems that concentrate so narrowly on just one pupil/student outcome? We need something better, more wide-ranging, more inspiring.

Five key messages

1   Learning, specifically pupils' attitudes to learning, motivation and engagement, is as much a priority as achievement and should be seen as an equally key measure of teaching's effectiveness and impact. It is learning that offers the most striking and secure evidence of any one teacher's quality and should replace achievement as the focus of all short-term individual lesson observations.

2   Judgements of progress should be more explicitly related to the knowledge and skills evident in pupils' work in books and in class, not just to data based on untested and hypothetical models of so-say 'age-related' or termly expectations. It is whether pupils and students ultimately reach the right standards that matters in the long run not how much movement they make at any one moment. No model of expected progress should be promoted unless it is backed by clear research evidence that this is how children actually learn.

3   No one model of good teaching should be imposed on a school from outside. Provided a baseline of competence is in place, teaching should be assessed exclusively on whether it works, not whether any particular checklist of supposedly required features has been followed. 'Momentum' and 'purpose' are more helpful terms than 'pace'. Extensive, passionately conveyed subject knowledge is better than simply setting targets and challenges. The impact of teaching on achievement should be determined over time. The key unit is not the lesson but the series of lessons over a week, fortnight or month.

4   Performance data is valuable but its role in inspection, particularly pre-inspection, needs to be significantly curtailed. Inspection needs to be neutral and seen to be neutral. All schools should be inspected on the same schedule to prevent the possibility of bias and, unless there are compelling and urgent grounds to move quickly, inspection should always start with an 'assumption of innocence'.

5   The tightly drawn procedures used to ensure ineffective schools are brought to the point where they are satisfactory are unlikely to be able to help them become good. For schools to go on to flourish they need the freedom to determine their priorities and practices for themselves to a significant degree. Good schools should be encouraged to be innovative as well as ambitious. Outstanding schools are a rarity and often short-lived but at their peak they change all the rules, and their wider influence on our understanding of what education can provide at its best is marked.

The centrality of learning

Four key concepts dominate the educational landscape: *achievement*, *attainment*, *progress* and *learning*. Interestingly a fifth – *intelligence*, probably the most significant elephant that is not in the room – barely gets a mention. However, our main concern in this section will be with the centrality of learning because it is learning, and specifically pupils' attitudes to learning, rather than progress or standards, that is most directly under the teacher's control. It is the hub around which everything else revolves. It is the tangible buzz you feel when you are in a class or school that is working well. You can see it in the faces of staff and students and at its best it can make your hair stand on end. Learning is why we come into the job and why we are all still there at the end. It is this that is our heartbeat, not standards. If we are to be successful in our strategic aim of significantly raising achievement, getting pupils' attitudes to learning right does not just matter, *it matters most*.

> Our present strategy of endlessly raising standards for its own sake is flawed.

Our present strategy of endlessly raising standards for its own sake is flawed. Too easily we have accepted a relative definition of standards that merely relates one school's results to another, whether or not they are deemed 'similar'. Good schools, we are told, are 'above average', poor schools below. In so doing we ignore the fundamental question of whether the average itself is high or good enough, or so low as to be a concern – we fail to find the absolute measure of standards that is so essential in deciding whether pupils are performing as we need them to. What is needed is an answer to a single core question: are *knowledge and skills levels good enough in themselves*, irrespective of where they sit regarding averages?

Losing sleep worrying about the achievement of the most able, narrowly defined as the acquisition of the highest grades, is futile if we promptly disparage their validity in an annual act of educational masochism when the results are published. The purpose of statutory targets is to ensure that nationally we do not have a problem and that our education system is generally fit for purpose; floor targets (ideally individualized) should be used to reduce any unacceptable levels of variation between schools. High grades are nice for students but evidence that the more able are being properly challenged is as likely to be found in the numbers gaining their qualifications not only in, for example, physics, mathematics and mandarin but also obtaining grade 8 in a musical instrument; or in sixth formers producing the school play and playing with the local youth orchestra. The existence of a flourishing public speaking and debating society and chess or astronomy clubs are not bad pointers either. Primary schools can just as easily list the experiences and activities that define their most able pupils, too. Gaining additional points/scores just for the sake of it or to enhance the school's profile is meaningless. We have to stop worrying about why everyone is not above expectations. 'Expectations' means exactly what it says. If you get precisely the Christmas present you asked for, it is not good tactics to keep on whining!

We should therefore focus instead much more strongly on the presence or absence of key qualities such as determination, perseverance, intellectual curiosity, thoughtfulness, attentiveness, reflection, an eagerness to 'get it right and see it through', listening to and respect for others, a willingness to look to the long-term and the capacity to work independently. Developing these qualities in young learners is the key task of teaching; it is the most successful strategy for raising achievement and restoring the professionalism and morale of schools. Much more than has been acknowledged, they form the cornerstone around which school success can be built. Where schools have established a profound and consistently promoted culture of endeavour, standards will be in good hands.

> The primary purpose of all education is to so inspire the young that they want to continue to learn.

The primary purpose of all education is not to seek endlessly to raise standards for their own sake but to so inspire the young that they want to continue to learn long after they have left us and develop the maturity of outlook and steadfastness of purpose to do so. Successful education is something children should remember, look back on with fondness, carry forward for themselves and above all, *value*. It means providing the young not only with the skills and knowledge to succeed but also the values whereby they can recognize the importance of the journey that they have made and have yet to make. Education goes hand-in-hand with the development of humility. We teach children the immenseness of what they do not yet know and, in doing this, we help them become properly reflective and to appreciate the nature of their own and others' achievements. Education is the antithesis of arrogance, of too easily acquired certainty, of the mind that is closed and 'knows all it needs to know'. Education acknowledges the primacy of detail, depth, complexity, endeavour, perseverance and *uncertainty*. That is why we should take such pleasure in being proved wrong by the success of ex-pupils who have surpassed our expectations of them. They have gone beyond us and our view of them, and the better teacher instinctively recognizes that this is good. They continued to learn!

The notion of learning underlying so much of our current methodology assumes that (1) children learn through a pre-determinable escalator or hierarchy of steps, that (2) their progress up this minutely sub-divided slope can be reliably assessed by inspectors and others on the basis of fleeting observations and evidence and that (3) their motivation to learn can be stimulated through a series of academic and abstract targets related to the curriculum thus defined. All three assumptions are highly contentious. We *know* children learn in different ways and patterns and in frequently random spurts. Yet we have persisted in pursuing the one-track 'escalator model' despite the pretty static national picture of English and mathematics results for the primary phase for much of the past decade. So, if the methodology does not work, why – other than for ideological reasons – does it continue to hold such sway? We need a different understanding of what it is to help children learn.

By asking whether pupils have made enough learning, Ofsted confuses learning and knowledge. Learning is not a 'quantum' but a process, and is frequently mysterious. If we are honest we will recognize that we seldom really know why our teaching suddenly, often inexplicably, pays off. we are not always able to fathom or bottle what happens on those occasions when light dawns. Whenever it worked, however, this was probably because the teachers had so caught their students' interest and imagination that they began to ask questions for themselves; read for themselves; explored and tried out ideas for themselves; thought for themselves and debated among themselves. They also stuck at it when the going got tough, asked for help without embarrassment and looked to make corrections. In other words, they saw education as their responsibility and for their benefit and enjoyment, not something that belonged to others, something that others 'delivered'. In the process, they came to realize there are no easy answers – you have to work at it. The quality of pupils' own contribution is crucial. *What they do* matters more than is acknowledged in the current debates about teaching quality and school leadership. We have lost sight of the fact that children have to *deserve* success. Learning takes time and personal effort! It is inseparable from motivation, which requires pupil engagement on the one hand and independence of thought and study on the other. Past a certain point, as we have learnt to our cost, you cannot 'drive up' standards by force of will alone. But done sensitively, you can entice them!

> The greatest single mistake Ofsted inspectors and others still make, is to assume that the key unit of currency is the individual lesson. It is not.

The greatest single mistake Ofsted inspectors and others still make, is to assume that the key unit of currency is the individual lesson. It is not. What schools should evaluate is not the individual lesson but the *series of lessons* across a week, fortnight and possibly month. Ofsted's own position, made more difficult than it needs to be by the much reduced time allocated to an inspection of even the largest secondary schools, is compromised by the fact that it has to come to its judgements in a mere two days. But headteachers are in a far more favourable position, being in school all the time, and need not therefore seek to 'ape' their self-appointed betters so slavishly. They should look instead to identify the impact of a teacher *over time*, not in an arbitrarily chosen 30–60 minutes. They need to assess whether teaching ensures pupils develop the right kinds of *lasting* attitudes and whether they can combine and apply their skills subsequently on demand in unseen contexts, not merely within the span of a single lesson. 'Teaching for learning' is a more helpful concept than 'assessment for learning', and the new approach will involve a better balance than is often seen between learning by listening and learning by doing.

Judging teaching should not just involve looking at the data alone or a single lesson in isolation. We are on safer ground if we have direct evidence that it has tangibly succeeded or failed over time. If we conclude something is wrong this should be because there is clear evidence in pupils' books or responses in class that teaching has been dull or poorly prepared or that the teacher is incapable of controlling behaviour, or that pupils' work is allowed to be slapdash, needlessly error-strewn or too-frequently unfinished. The data can raise interesting questions in advance, to be sure, but only a properly constituted, and that means sufficiently well-informed, review of pupils' work over time can answer them. Any judgement of teaching quality ought to be cumulative and broad-based. 'Does it work?' is the question we should pursue, not 'Does the school use all of the currently in vogue tracking and target-setting techniques?'

The qualities that go to make up good teaching are perfectly straightforward. Teaching is, after all, a relatively simple affair and we must avoid making it overcomplicated – as those who insist on aims, objectives, stepping stones, assessment outcomes, challenging questions, pace, differentiation, use of ICT, marking guidance and success criteria and continuous adaptations of the planned activity *in every lesson* have tried to do. The use of targets for example is optional and frequently over-rated. They suit some pupils but generally these are older, more able and already committed. The less able are usually just as perplexed after getting them as they were before. If I am a teenager struggling to understand calculus, being set a target in it is unlikely to help. I need to be *shown* how to improve not simply *challenged* to do so.

At its best, teaching is a flexible not a mechanistic thing.

Good teaching does not involve a driven experience for pupils. At its best, teaching is a flexible not a mechanistic thing. Teaching for learning means that, at regular intervals, the teacher has to shut up and let the children get on with it, and work at or just practise tasks that genuinely extend or support them. The key is to get them to do more than briefly *encounter* specific concepts or skills before rushing on to the next set but to let these sink in so that students can *apply and combine them unaided and recall them at a later date.* And that requires practice and reinforcement. Consolidation should not be seen as a waste of time, something done once at speed proves little – it is what lasts that matters. We are very good at providing pupils with opportunities to acquire key building bricks; we are much less prepared to give them the time they need to build the wall. The test, however, quite rightly, emphasizes the latter. You do not pass your driving test by producing assessment certificates that show you drove up a hill and reversed round a corner during separate lessons some weeks previously but because you can and do draw your skills together at once, on demand, in unforeseen circumstances on a given day. School teaching is no different.

Teaching for learning does not preclude teaching from the front, or the current vogue for questioning at pace, when appropriate, but it does require a *range* of approaches and a proper balance between teaching methodology and independent working. That balance is frequently missing from our current nostrums of how-it-should-be-done. The (semi) official and consequently much overused standard package delivered 'from the front' places a huge premium of motivation and understanding. Much of this teaching goes well over the heads of the very pupils who need to improve. Hence the hiatus in the national rise in primary school standards. We are teaching (and preaching) very successfully to the converted but, as for the others.. . . well, just look at the lines of sight of less able.

Particularly in Key Stage 1 and the early part of Key Stage 2, *we do far too much learning by listening!* Pupils need to *see* how something is put together, not merely hear it, and they need to be able to refer to it later. All pupils, but particularly the less able, need permanent models of what it looks like when it is right that they can go back to, particularly in mathematics or when writing at length. If too often it is the teacher who is the most active participant in the lesson, the balance is likely to be wrong. The excessive and wholly misplaced emphasis on what goes on in a single lesson is also the cause of the confusion over satisfactory teaching. If too much teaching is below par, it is *unsatisfactory*, pure and simple but this is quite different to the case of a single lesson being judged satisfactory. A teacher who is excellent may nonetheless teach a number of (perfectly) satisfactory lessons. There is no contradiction here. Some topics – the apostrophe or algebra, for example – cannot necessarily be made exciting just because children would like them to be. Pupils just have to learn them, and learn also that nothing, least of all mastery and skill, is gained without effort – in this case, *by them*. The pay-off (deferred gratification) will come later. It is hugely important that a proportion of lessons are 'measured', since time has to be allowed for consolidation and the correction of errors, and for pupils to combine and apply their skills to new material and read and write extensively, and this is impossible if every lesson must break new ground. How else can we find time for genuine assessment? When otherwise will students find the time to become reflective?

Because inspection has too easily confused satisfactory with dull or ill-prepared teaching, schools now assume that each individual lesson has to be much the same, contain all the politically approved bells and whistles and, at least in an inspection week, be conducted at breakneck pace with the teacher talking too much at the front and pupils gabbling unreflectively from the rear. 'Pace' has replaced 'purpose' and uniformity become the norm with too little evidence of substantial or lasting learning being made by the majority.

What we actually need is not 'pace' for its own sake but a sustained *sense of momentum and purpose* in our classrooms, and this will unlock our understanding of learning. Our enemy is not lack of pace but pupil 'drift', which is something quite different. This can certainly be the result of poor organization by the teacher or the failure to look to interest or excite, and if so this is something that needs to be challenged. But it can equally be the result of a failure to engage by the pupils themselves and though this still represents a proper challenge for the school to try to confront, it does not imply that we should automatically rush to judgement about teaching quality. For a variety of reasons outside the teacher's control, some youngsters are just plain difficult! We need schools to do all they can to respond to these challenges and this means being well-organized and purposeful in all that they do. But, once this is in place, we should not then define school effectiveness entirely by their success or failure, however key this regard. A well-organized good try is as much as any school can guarantee. Whether it pays off is quite another matter. Pupils have to earn their success the hard way. There are no guarantees!

A note about capacity

In recent years, inspection has frequently confused overall effectiveness with capacity, to the disadvantage of the school and the fairness of the report. Undoubtedly, the benefits of successful leadership must in time show up in a school's overall standards but there is a clear difference between this and saying that, until this happens, it necessarily lacks evidence of the capacity to improve.

Overall effectiveness is a *backwards* looking judgement; it takes stock of what has been happening and draws it all together into a formal statement at a given time about how things have been up to this point. This is a hugely significant and valid judgement and inspection quite rightly concentrates upon it. Schools have to account for their record. However, 'capacity' reflects a *forward* looking judgement and primarily concerns provision. It takes stock of what is happening *now* and projects forward into a likely outcome, assuming this is sustained. Overall effectiveness is asking 'Has it worked up to now?' Capacity is asking 'Is it likely to in the future?' The evidence to be accrued to answer the second question will be different to that used to answer the first.

Inspectors have generally resisted this approach because they wish to avoid what they see as evidence-free or highly speculative judgements. Typically, the scenario they have in mind occurs where the head has been in post a mere five or six weeks and the school has not yet had time to write a new chapter. Fair enough. However, the overemphasis on past effectiveness, defined in terms of results, that typically forms a key element in this kind of model means that the 'capacity' judgement frequently fails to do justice to a school where there is substantial evidence that a more established head has sharply improved other features of school life, such as teaching quality, behaviour, governance and middle management. If successes here are too easily ignored until the next set of results comes in, that is wrong.

Three steps to outstanding: Equality and entitlement; innovation and ambition; self-sustaining excellence

Satisfactory' should not be used as a pejorative term nor be deemed as requiring improvement.

Satisfactory schools are *good enough*; this is what the Latin terms 'satis' and 'facio' *mean*. 'Satisfactory' should not be used as a pejorative term and it has nothing in common with 'mediocre'. Good schools and teachers are better than satisfactory and all should aim to achieve this higher status and be rewarded when they do but satisfactory schools do their job. The efforts of satisfactory schools are properly organized and purposeful and ensure that, whether or not they are always successful, they give it their best shot' at all times. Satisfactory schools guarantee pupils their entitlement: an equal opportunity to succeed. Whether they take it, of course, is up to them, but the offer is undeniably there.

Although there are never any guarantees of success, in satisfactory schools we are looking at a well-organized good try. More may be desirable certainly and it deserves to be rewarded if it is achieved, but this is *good enough*.

Good schools: Innovation and ambition

'Good' schools do more than this of course. Good schools tend to have high standards (defined as above target *not* as above average) but this is clearly easier for schools with advantaged catchments to achieve so it is not the overriding hallmark of their quality. What sets good schools apart from the rest is their *ambition*, their capacity for *innovation* and the *marked progress* made by their pupils. Inevitably, these three qualities are interlinked.

Schools with economically or linguistically deprived catchments can still be deemed 'good'. They have gone beyond merely offering the required opportunity to achieve and have ensured it is taken up with some alacrity. All credit to them. Our praise should be unstinting.

Outstanding schools: Self-sustaining excellence

There is no simple template to define outstanding, no blueprint for excellence. Excellence is multifaceted, generally a rarity and, when encountered, astonishes us. It may flourish unexpectedly and sometimes dies young. It invariably involves a coming together of all the strengths exhibited by good schools into a sudden qualitative leap forward that ensures the school, for a brief period, is truly remarkable. Undoubtedly, extraordinary vision and leadership are at the centre of an outstanding school as are the commitment, intelligence and organization of staff. Pupils are likely to be above average in ability and keen and eager to use it. Results will be high. But good schools have these qualities too and not all show the same remarkable ability to dominate the educational landscape and capture what education can offer at its peak. Outstanding schools become beacons and redraw the educational possibilities for others. They set up new courses, make new links, devise new training programmes. They are the birthplace of new ideas, developing countless staff who leave to take the message elsewhere. They use their resources to maximize connections with employers and higher and vocational education providers and work exhaustively with needy families. They fill the vacuums left by gaps in public policy. They leave a lasting mark on the experiences of those pupils and staff fortunate to attend them at the peak of their flowering, and the education they provide is a memorable one not just for the children and young people attending them but for the whole community they serve. But the intensity of what they do is often not sustainable and in time staff turnover and sheer exhaustion take their toll and they slip back to 'good'.

Good schools and satisfactory schools are both effective and fit for purpose. Further the majority students will do just as well at a satisfactory school as they will do at a good one. Perhaps a better, more simple and more just distinction is effective and less-effective schools. The American definition of making Adequate Yearly Progress (AYP), while not inspiring, does simply say they are doing the job they are required to.

Ineffective schools

There is, of course, another side: educational failure. School improvement was not invented on a whim. That it has become too diffuse, too urgent, should not deflect us from recognizing its former and continuing necessity. Ineffective schools undoubtedly exist and need purposeful action. Children must receive their entitlement. Ineffective schools are characterized by leadership that has run out of ideas and lost its way and is consequently failing to generate consistency and commitment, let alone dynamism, creativity or enthusiasm from its teaching staff. There is too much unresolved weak teaching. Policies are not in place, or are implemented inconsistently if they are or have lapsed. Pupils' behaviour is not well managed. Results are consistently below floor targets. The poor progress of key individuals and groups is not identified, let alone resolved. Parents lack confidence in the school and communication with them is weak.

Not all 'below target' schools are necessarily failing – where there is a capacity to improve, the school should be given time to respond, but schools have to accept that they are there to pursue and secure decent outcomes, and if they cannot, ultimately some other leadership team, some other pattern of organization and funding will have to be tried instead. Driving instructors are meant to get you through. The aim of the game is to ensure you meet the required standard before you are allowed on the road. It is the same for schools.

Detoxifying the accountability system

JAMES PARK

The accountability system we have now is toxic because it compels school leaders and young people to focus on improving a set of inter-related metrics that provide proxy indicators of whether a school is a great place in which to learn, and whether students are developing as individuals capable of making the richest possible contribution to a sustainable economy and a vibrant society. The new approach to accountability we need would allow schools to focus directly on being great places to learn, and students to focus on becoming great learners.

> Schools are complex organizational systems, and the development of individual learners is a subtle and sophisticated process.

The current system is attractive to policymakers and other stakeholders because the delivery of judgements on schools and individuals is made easy through its deployment of comparable criteria, whether these are the numbers of students achieving particular grades in particular qualifications, or the ratings formulated by inspectors as a result of their visits. But schools are complex organizational systems, and the development of individual learners is a subtle and sophisticated process. It has become increasingly clear that forcing them to organize themselves around simplistic criteria, for the convenience of the accountability system, is constricting to both.

> We need a system that monitors the performance of schools against a clear definition of education's purpose, rather than system that directs the energy of leaders, teachers and students towards achieving things that are easy to measure.

Andy Hargreaves and Dennis Shirley say in *The Fourth Way*[3] that we need accountability to be 'the conscience or superego of the system that checks it', rather than 'the ego or id that drives it'. This argues the need for a system that monitors the performance of schools against a clear definition of education's purpose, rather than a system that directs the energy of leaders, teachers and students towards achieving things that are easy to measure.

The argument presented below states that a healthy approach to accountability can only derive from empowering young people, from a young age, to generate idiosyncratic strategies for their lives through the conversations they have with parents and teachers, and from whole school communities coming together to find where the opportunities for improvement lie. This is because parents, teachers, other staff and students will always know more about what is happening than any external agency.

Toxic beliefs

There are two powerful beliefs that need to be challenged in order to displace the current system:

1   The first of these is that it makes sense, in a complex world where there is a need to maximize the development of diverse skills and varied forms of creativity, to measure the achievement of schools by their capacity to get all students up to a particular level in a particular set of 'core' subjects, measured by a particular set of qualifications (or their 'equivalences'), at a particular stage in their development.

2   The second is that the strengths and weaknesses of schools are most effectively brought to light by commissioning teams of 'experts' to write up reports on what they have learned as a result of their having spent a few days reviewing data, talking with school leaders, dropping in on lessons and following a few vulnerable people around to gain some insight into their experience.

Passion and aptitude

The UK government recently introduced a phonics test for children aged five to six in their first full year of schooling, on the basis that this would identify schools which were not providing children with sufficient additional support. This was in defiance of clear evidence that *some* children learn to read only when they are aged seven or eight, without any apparent detriment to their intellectual development (Albert Einstein being the most commonly used example), and through no lack of attention to their learning by parents or teachers. It is just a consequence of their brains developing differently to others of their peers.

Measuring the performance of schools by their capacity to get students up to average expected levels of performance in English and Maths at Key Stage 2 and 4 suffers from the same problem as the phonics test. The imperative to maximize the numbers reaching particular levels leads to considerable energy being expended on getting *some* students to perform in areas which currently do not provoke their interest or match their aptitude. There is obviously an opportunity lost to do *other* things. It does not follow from the vital importance of reading, writing and arithmetic to life and work in the modern world that it is an indicator of the system's effectiveness to have all students achieving the same levels at the same time. Some may take more time; others may benefit from taking a route that involves the development of other skills. We usually accept that, when young children show early brilliance on the piano or violin, it is good to let them focus intensely on their instrument to the exclusion of other things. This is not because we do not think they need other skills, it is just that we assume from the way they are developing their self-confidence and capacity to learn they will easily acquire those skills when they are ready. Imagine, then, how different would be the design of our accountability system if schools were charged with finding for *every* student a specialism that they were passionate about, and could become brilliant at through hours of dedicated practice.

What most commentators tell us about the future world of work is that interpersonal competence will be as 'basic' as reading and writing, that successful employees will be those who can build flexible packages of skills around areas of intense specialism and their ability to keep on learning in collaboration with others and that the big prizes will go to mavericks with high levels of creativity and resourcefulness. Somehow, we need to develop an accountability system that finds out how well schools are preparing young people to thrive in such a world. Take away the assumption that a school's effectiveness should be measured by its ability to get students through a particular set of tests at a particular time. Ask instead how well students are being prepared for the future by looking at their success in enabling young people to put together portfolios of qualifications and achievements that display sets of skills that they have worked out will be relevant to them.

Operating in such a different system, schools would start to see their role as being about helping young people develop strategies for their lives that turned their enthusiasms and aptitudes into pathways towards fulfilling learning and employment. They would need to engage their students in deep conversations about who they are and what they want to become, about what skills they need to develop, what qualifications they need to acquire and how best they might go about doing so. Business organizations regularly produce reports lamenting that schools and colleges are not producing young people with the range of skills and qualities they need, and universities less frequently say something similar. One way to address this would be to set up an agency gathering and communicating the latest data on the skills being looked for in particular types of work or higher education, and the qualifications that were taken to demonstrate those skills. Good systems for sorting, channelling and bundling this information could be deployed by young people and their mentors to chart each individual's course through school, college and on in to the world of work.

The data resource would act as a form of exchange, matching sets of qualifications to particular pathways in an organic, ever-evolving way. Around such an exchange, there would develop an ongoing debate about what the purposes of education should be, and how these could be most effectively delivered. And parents, as well as policymakers, would be able continuously to review how well individual schools were doing at equipping their students to seize the opportunities available. Having a system to track the progress of each student cohort through the first ten or so years of their careers (which would presumably be quite easy to do through the National Insurance system) would give policymakers and stakeholders much deeper insight into the effectiveness of the education system as a whole than the current narrowly focused approach.

Another way . . .

If a healthy accountability system is one which recognizes that young people, given the right mentoring support, can work out the most effective way to realize their potential, without needing to operate within the parameters laid down by an education minister, so too are school communities better placed to determine where their possibilities for improvement lie than are a group of inspectors who have just come back from a brief visit. The current system is built around the belief that external inspectors are required to judge whether a school is 'good', 'outstanding' or 'in need of special measures'. This is because they can look objectively upon faults or virtues, and compare each school with others they have visited. But if you were to collect together, and sort through, all the knowledge about a school that is held by its parents, students and staff, you would get a picture of where it is strong and where it is less strong that was considerably richer than anything an external inspector could gather. This could be achieved through an online platform that provided all members of the school community with a regular opportunity to describe their experience in complete confidence (with everybody understanding that that this was a genuine opportunity for participation, and it was in their interest to take part). This would comprise a research-validated survey that probed areas of leadership, culture and learning very similar to those currently explored by Ofsted inspectors, together with opportunities for people to write freely about their experiences and how they informed the ratings they had given.

This data could then be used to inform a whole school discussion based on a report that brought together all the quantitative and qualitative information that had been gathered – the positive messages as well as the tough ones that might make some people uncomfortable. What dimensions are rated strong? What dimensions are rated less strong? How does our school compare against other schools in the same category? How do our results this year compare to last year? Who do different year groups or staff groups compare with each other? What are people saying about their experience that explains the numbers? As staff, students and parents explored the questions thrown up by this report, developed explanations for the top-level findings and moved towards what they could do that would make the school an even better place in which to teach, work and learn, they could consult with other schools to find out how well they perform on particular criteria, what solutions they have found to particular issues. Again, a central data resource could help to match up schools to organizations that might help them better understand the issues they face or find answers to the questions they are asking.

> The analysis and the solutions would be generated from within the school, rather than imposed on the school.

What sharply differentiates this process from the current model is that the analysis and the solutions would be generated from *within* the school, rather than imposed *on* the school. A series of structured conversations would draw the community together around a shared picture of what was happening that they wanted to change, and creative thinking about what would make the school even better. Enabling everyone to contribute to the emerging improvement plan would ensure there was real buy-in for whatever strategy emerged. This is a long way from what happens now, especially when a school is judged to be failing its students – rightly or wrongly (the claim that every report is 100% fair defies credulity).

A number of elements in the process would ensure that the self-generated reports were honest, open and fair. They would have to explain quantitative data (which does not mean explaining it away) and be validated by all staff, students and parents. If any felt their views sidelined by the process that was followed, they would be free to explain them online in a qualifying note to the report. A remodelled inspection agency could read the reports, ask questions about the argument being put forward, and supply resource to build the school's capacity to bring about the improvement it was seeking. It is not, after all, as if the current system guarantees full honesty, with its incentive for schools to present the best possible face to the inspectors so as to secure the kitemark represented by a 'good' or 'outstanding' Ofsted judgement, or to avoid being plunged into organizational upheaval by a less positive rating.

Such a model of accountability would provide staff, students and parents with the opportunity to practise a much more active model of engagement in school life than is currently allowed for: dinner ladies and teaching assistants conversing with teachers about how children should be spoken to; parents providing input from their professional experience to questions of pedagogy and management; children having the opportunities to develop a sense of personal agency through participating in discussions about the management of the playground or the organization of learning that are seen to make a real difference. By mandating the whole school community to gather around and sort out a creative way of moving forward, it would locate the responsibility for making each school the best it could possibly be in a place where an effective strategy is most likely to be found. And the reports emerging from each school would provide parents, policymakers and other stakeholders with a much richer account of each school's strengths and weaknesses than the formulaic statements which currently emerge from Ofsted.

Conclusions

Overall we need an accountability system which at the very least is without preconceptions and one that has a greater presumption of innocence; an approach that recognizes the fact that most schools are also effective even though they may still need help. We must replace the notion of fault with that of need. It is reasonable to advise how schools might become stronger and how struggling or less-able youngsters might be helped to improve even further but the current culture of unremitting fault, criticism and blame has to end. There is too much suspicion in the system, indeed, too much smugness. That is wrong.

Further there is a case for a whole new approach, incorporating something like the principles outlined above. Schools must also be given the time to make the difference that is being sought and it is absurd to suppose that lasting improvement can be gained within the single 12-month period assumed by the usual frameworks governing 'category' schools. It is unlikely that the current inspectorate, locked as it is into instinctive, data-driven negativity, is capable of developing the change in outlook that will be needed. An effective accountability system that is designed to enable a system move from good to great is needed to help our schools regain their sense of confidence and self-worth and to re-awaken the store of creativity and energy that once so typified at least the better half of our profession.

Notes

1 NFER 2009.
2 Sahlsberg.
3 Hargreaves and Shirley 2009.

References and further reading

Hargreaves, A. and Shirley, D., *The Fourth Way* (Thousand Oaks, CA: Corwin, 2009).
NFER, *Evaluation of the Effect of Section 5 Inspections – Strand 3* (England, NFER: 2009).
Park J., 'Detoxifying School Accountability', London: Demos, 2013.
Sahlsberg, P., *Finnish Lessons* (New York and London: Teachers College Press, 2011).

10

Being Data Informed Rather than Data Driven

David Crossley including a case study by James Park

Few could deny the importance of data in the information age. In education, data can enable teachers to know every student and know their potential. It can and does inform our decisions. Personal experiences have informed my own thinking about the value and use of performance data. My first personal engagement with both was during my first headship when two academics visited my school and asked if we knew why students did better there than similar students in similar schools – we did not. They knew it was happening because they had studied Intelligence Quotient (IQ) data over 25 years, but they did not know why either. They carried out research in the school which led to my early engagement with the concept of value added. Its benefits came four years later when I experienced my first full Office for Standards in Education, (Ofsted) school inspection. A formidable lead inspector remarked that the school appeared to have one of the largest differences between boy and girl attainment and they were going to make it a focus of the inspection. I could say I already knew that the boys had an average IQ of 89 compared to the girl average of 101, and we had been both studying and working on strategies to improve boys' attainment for four years. At the end of the inspection they said they could observe no difference between boys' and girls' performance. This was the beginning of my confirmed belief in the importance of use of data and research.

At its best, good use of data enables us to:

- know every student and their potential;
- project future performance based on past experience;
- compare like with like;
- benchmark the progress of similar students in similar schools and learn what works for them;
- validate and learn from successes in different contexts with a school, between schools, between systems both nationally and, increasingly, internationally too.

Learn more, improve more, judge less

Performance data is increasingly a key element in most accountability systems but the danger is we can become dominated by what are not necessarily the best or most appropriate measures. To me the key lesson could be *learn more, improve more, judge less.* Hargreaves and Shirley[1] cite three concerns as a result of the extravagant promises that have been made about what the data can do and how *an over-reliance on data distorts the system* and leads it to ignore and marginalize the importance of moral judgement and self-reflection.

1 Misleading data: In schools and school systems the data used mostly comes down to standardized test scores in literacy, mathematics and sometimes science. Technocrats value what they measure instead of measuring what they value.

2 They narrow the curriculum, prioritize the tested basics and turn a blind eye to teaching to the test. Because tests vary between districts, states and nations, schools can frustratingly find themselves performing well on one set and catastrophically on another.

3 There are also inconsistencies and contradictions over time. Like the 638 failing secondary schools that formed England's National Challenge. Many of them had scored well under one year's floor target only to be deemed as failing the following year when the government moved the goalposts and raised the floor. This is not to say that raising the bar is a bad thing but to harshly name and shame the schools who fall below is.

In their view 'the data should *contribute* rather than *dictate* what needs to be done'. So they argue for using data intelligently, invitationally and inclusively. Of course teacher judgement alone is not enough and data brings many benefits; as most things it is best used in conjunction with other factors. In addition we need to ensure that we do not only value what we measure. I have also been reflecting on Brian Caldwell's comment, 'henceforth the unit of organization should be the student not the school not the system',[2] what that might mean and how this could change our use of data. The dangers of just focusing on specific failing schools were brought home to me working in a previous role when I was responsible for work on system-wide data. The statistical truism that there are more students failing in the generality of schools than in failing schools became clear. It is interesting to reflect on how approaches to school improvement and enabling every child to achieve would be designed if data was used and calculated at the student level across an area or even system rather than the school level.

What matters is to better know and understand the things that make more difference. Teachers instinctively know what is working in their classroom but knowing why and how to make it better can take it to scale, both strengthens and validates it and offers the opportunity for wider impact. It also motivates us, professionalizes what we do and helps us improve. This is what being world-class involves and the power to make a real difference is in our own hands; it is what teachers in the very best systems are doing already.

> Good use of data helps students, teachers, schools and systems to understand where they are and what they need to do next.

Good use of data helps students, teachers, schools and systems to understand where they are and what they need to do next. It also plays a valuable role in accountability. Governments have a clear right to say what they expect from a system and good use of data enables an open and objective form of accountability. The key word here is 'good'. Effective use of value-added data to both analyse and project future performance became a key strategy in the Raising Achievement Transforming Learning programme (RATL) that I led in England between 2004 and 2008.[3] It was also used as the initial objective criteria to choose the schools that mentored and supported schools on the programme. The schools on the programme had lower than average raw results at age 15 and were in the bottom 20 per cent of value-added scores so we selected schools in the top 25 per cent to begin the selection process of those who provided support. Interestingly, many of the group of 70 mentor schools that supported the programme including those who had previously made significant improvements against the odds said that good data use was the main thing that had enabled them to improve and sustain improvement. True, you can argue that of all data but in the words of Jim Collins, 'What matters is not finding the perfect indicator, but settling upon a consistent and intelligent way of assessing your output results, and then tracking your trajectory with rigour.'[4]

In the United States Hargreaves and Shirley argue that 'despite its urgent insistence on improvement and equity, NCLB (No Child Left Behind) legislation alongside endless and also contradictory systems of state-wide and district testing, has narrowed and dumbed-down the curriculum.'[5] Fear of failure on data measures that track narrowing achievement gaps between subgroups of students can lead to intended and unintended consequences of schools either targeting students close to gap boundaries or worse still holding back some students so the gap appears to have narrowed. The funding that has been offered to states and then districts and schools through initiatives like Race to the Top (RTT)[6] has come with the attached strings of near-impossible improvement deadlines that produce panic-driven measures of short-term change. My experience in Nashville allowed me to experience first-hand the pressures this brings but also the value of a more in-tune federal and state approach in which they allowed a waiver on the rigidity of the federal assessment requirement too. In England the understandable desire to keep raising the bar led to 600 high schools that had been deemed as failing to meet the then floor target in 2000, reducing in number to 40 by 2005 just to be told the bar had been raised and now they were all named and shamed as being below the new floor target. This is hardly a way to motivate those leading our more challenging schools. In addition the undue focus on floor targets at 11 and 16 has led to far less emphasis on other, wider performance indicators. The whole system now focuses at getting a student a grade C at 16 as it is the key accountability measure. Worse still it distorts teaching, learning and system energy from the achievement of the most able and least able at the same age. More seriously it allows the system to neglect focusing on what students go on to do. Further, a focus on the school as a whole and schools that fail to meet floor targets ends up ignoring a statistical truism that more students are failing in the generality of schools than in failing schools; not all students succeed in outstanding schools either. This takes the focus away from collaborative and collective solutions to improve outcomes in a community, town, district or city.

Value-added assessments are a more just measure than simple raw scores but if misused even these can lead to misjudgements rather than informed judgements. Some also argue that value-added data can lead to under-expectations of students from disadvantaged backgrounds but this blurs the appropriate use of value-added data to judge schools more fairly with the inappropriate use which can lead to lower expectations of certain groups of students.

Consider these two hypothetical analogies.

Comparing two teachers responses to the same data

- Teacher 1 to student – The data shows only 20 per cent of students like you get a Grade A – 75 per cent of students like you based on your prior attainment get a C – so your target is a C. I will also set you work and give you a text book that focuses on C grade work.
- Teacher 2 to student – 1 in 5 students like you get an A – do you think you could, do you want to be one of them – I think we should target an A and if you want to I will set and help you with the work that will help you get an A.

One limits potential and one is empowering and energizing.

The Holy-grail of performance-related pay . . .

Teachers also become uneasy when faced by some politicians' or administrators' holy grail of performance-related pay. The trouble is data is at its least reliable when the sample is small and a class of students is a small sample. Further, it is not just the teachers in the year the test takes place that make the only or arguably the most contribution to a student's success. The larger the sample the more reliable the predications and hence judgements are. In fact at a system level most students do as we expect in most schools so why do we worry at all! What is needed is a realistic and sensible evaluation which takes into account a range of factors at a teacher, school and system level. This involves give and take, sensitivity and a genuine understanding and honesty by both system leaders and educators. It requires an end to an excuse culture on the part of educators, a genuine desire and aspiration to be best in class and a culture of continuous improvement. At a system level it requires greater trust and a combination of both challenge and support in equal proportions. As I have remarked in a previous chapter no one comes in to teaching to help students do worse at school. It happens though it should not; but what is the best way of avoiding it? Good use of data can lead to informed discussion; informed planning; deepening and developing learning opportunities for students; clearer understanding of what works and what is making the most difference; creating professional learning communities; linking student outcomes and the wholly laudable academic and practitioner research. In Hargreaves and Shirley's words, 'the danger of data driven decision making ends up driving teachers to distraction . . . turning a much needed precision and focus into an obsession'.[7]

We must begin to value and use a wider range of data. Here the key words are value and use. In the case study in the next section of this chapter James Park reflects on other data that we might value.

School leaders have become skilled in recent decades at collecting and analysing data about the achievement levels of individual students and groups of students. Data that compares the performance of individual students with that of others in their cohort can help schools provide every child and young person with the best possible opportunity to learn and to grow.

Data that allows comparisons between the performance of a school's students and similar groups in other schools, or in other countries, provides leaders with opportunities to see where they might usefully up their game, and also where sources of fresh thinking might be found. One of the problems resulting from the way we currently use data is that too much time can be spent compiling information of minimal value: a lot of teachers feel that the hours they currently allocate to spreadsheets and reports would be more productively spent interacting with students or designing exciting lessons. Another problem is that data is often used to inform simplistic judgements by people outside the school, and to justify the setting of unrealistic and damaging targets that provoke excessively high levels of anxiety in those expected to implement them.

Case study – Human Scale Education's PROGRESS enquiry tool

JAMES PARK

The problem of 'attribution error'
A key problem is of data being used to reach incorrect conclusions about cause and remedy, as a result of what social psychologists call 'attribution error'. This arises because someone inside or outside a school simply assumes they know what a particular data finding means, and what will ameliorate the issue they think it identifies. An individual teacher might be criticized for poor performance that could be better explained by a series of unfortunate management decisions, or a new school leadership team might gain the credit for the accumulated effort over many years of parents, teachers and non-teaching staff. The consequences – whether it is a teacher demoralized or a leadership team buoyed up by unjustified self-confidence – are clearly unhelpful for schools seeking to steadily improve. School leaders seeking to avoid 'attribution error' will start by recognizing that data is useful because it provides good *questions*. Good answers can only be found by

drawing out, through enquiry, the tacit knowledge possessed by staff and students as a result of their daily experience of being in the school.

A rich picture of what is happening is more likely to emerge if this enquiry is informed by data about things other than achievement levels, which can open up thinking about the question 'why'. The right sort of data can help people get under the surface of overt behaviours and simplistic explanations of those behaviours, leading to an analysis that goes sufficiently deep to point towards effective ways of moving forward. The work of developing Human Scale Education's PROGRESS enquiry tool was inspired by a case of attribution error at a school in the London Borough of Newham. A group of consultants were asked to sort out a group of year 9 students who were regarded as a 'nightmare class'. Their apparent lack of interest in learning was draining energy and optimism away from their teachers. It was assumed that these students did not know how to listen and learn: the consultants were asked to take them away and teach them how to do so.

A survey issued by the consultants quickly established that these students were individually skilled at listening and learning. Their difficulty arose only from the experience of being together on a daily basis. As students and consultants explored why this was, it transpired that, in their first weeks at the school, the class's tutor had gone off long-term sick. For months, this class had been 'looked after' by a succession of supply teachers. What they collectively concluded from this experience was that the school did not care about them. For eight consecutive terms, they had dealt with the difficult feelings this provoked in them by shouting at each other, and their teachers, pretty much all the time. But what monitoring system could the school put in place that would ensure no group of students were ever again left to waste two years' of education as a result of an unhappy group experience? How could they provide students with an outlet through which to describe the feelings they were having? And how could this information be shaped into a form that would enable people to think deeply about it, so that they could discover the source of the problem and the solutions to it?

Thinking about this question led to the development of a 'school climate survey' that asks students to rate their relationships with each other, and with adults. It also asks whether they experience the school as Responsive (capable of sorting out the things that might get in the way of their learning), and Confidence-building (setting clear expectations and providing the resources that enable them to deliver on those expectations). Professor Robin Banerjee at the University of Sussex has subsequently established through an analysis of data from approximately 90 schools (involving nearly 30,000 pupils), that these perceptions of school climate significantly predict variations in headline Key Stage 2 and Key Stage 4 attainment results. Subsequently, a range of other dimensions have been built into PROGRESS to throw light on *why* these perceptions of climate predict achievement.

Generally, where students perceive the school's systems and structures to be responsive, they are more likely to report being resilient and creative in their learning. How far they perceive the school to be confidence-building will affect how well they rate themselves on working in teams, planning their work and taking on challenge. A number of other dimensions are explored through the tool, from controlling anger to being honest and acting with integrity. A school in South London decided to administer PROGRESS to all its students in year 7. When their eight tutors were gathered to hear the report, the first question they asked was: 'Why do students have a voice in this process, when we do not?' The staff version of PROGRESS that we developed asks questions like: Do teachers receive feedback that enables them to do the best job they can? Are things organized in a way that enables them to get things done without becoming over-stressed? How does their experience affect the interactions they have with students around learning or behaviour? And how far do non-teaching staff feel that their views are taken into account when decisions are made, or that they are given the level of responsibility they need to carry out the tasks that are allocated to them?

Subsequent experience has confirmed the value of looking across the experience of staff and students, charting the experience of how different groups interact, often in an escalating way. At another South London secondary school, the headteacher encouraged teachers to work together in groups on ways of making lessons engaging and exciting. The school timetable started late on two days of the week so that teachers could meet to share experiences and develop ideas. What nobody recognized was how the confusion that resulted from the varying daily timetable contributed to young people concluding that teachers were more interested in their projects than their students. Some were already expressing their irritation by misbehaving in lessons, provoking frustration in teachers who felt that they were being blocked from trying out their more interactive ideas.

The benefits of using a wider range of data

What makes this sort of deep data useful? – the light it casts upon the deeper feelings that shape behaviour – may also make it difficult to handle. It may generate accounts of what is happening that differ significantly from what people want to believe. It may cause people to feel that their own efforts are being judged and have been found wanting. Additionally, some leaders resist the process of involving staff and students in thinking what the data means, and what can be done to address it, for fear that it will undermine their authority. But none of these issues diminish the value of developing an account of what is *really going on* in the school, and using this to shape a strategy that addresses real issues rather than imagined ones; or the value of involving the whole school community in thinking together. The issues are best dealt with by encouraging an attitude of shared responsibility built around the perspective that we *all* have to deal with the stresses created by external realities and our own histories; and that we are more likely to create an organization that works for everybody if we can pool what we know and the solutions we can create.

The use of a wide range of deep data, alongside topline information on grades and levels, enables the school to become reflective rather than reactive.

One argument for mining this sort of data and exploring it in this way is that schools can thereby model the sort of robust learning skills that will serve young people best as they move into adult life – grappling with complexity rather than making do with simplified accounts of things; being tough-minded in resisting easy explanations or quick-fix solutions; drawing on all the resources available in finding solutions to sticky real-life problems; working collaboratively together to achieve shared goals. Another argument is that it integrates the processes of research into the daily life of teachers and other staff. Styles of teaching and learning can be fine-tuned around an exploration of the learning profiles of particular classes. Teachers and lunchtime staff can have an interesting conversation about how the interpersonal dynamics of the playground are then played out in the classroom. Teachers and students can think creatively about how these dynamics can be used to stimulate an even richer experience of learning. Leadership teams can reflect how their own dynamics are reverberating through the school's organizational processes in ways that would not otherwise become apparent. Ultimately, the use of a wide range of deep data, alongside topline information on grades and levels, enables the school to become reflective rather than reactive. This supports the development of intelligent forms of accountability (see Chapter 9) while enabling schools to become steadily better at addressing the learning needs of all their students.

International lessons

Given the increasing focus on the Programme for International Student Assessment (PISA) and the extent to which it is informing education policy and strategy this section provides some background to the tests, a brief commentary on the outcomes and considers its implications for school improvement.

PISA is a worldwide study and comparison of attainment organized by the Organisation for Economic Co-operation and Development (OECD) of 15-year-old school pupils' performance in mathematics, science, and reading in member and non-member nations. Developed from 1997, the first PISA assessment was carried out in 2000 and then repeated every three years. The results of each period of assessment take about an year and a half to be analysed. The Trends in International Mathematics and Science Study (TIMSS)[8] and the Progress in International Reading Literacy Study (PIRLS) by the International Association for the Evaluation of Educational Achievement are similar studies. The tables of the 2006 and 2009 PISA assessment of 15-year-olds show the most successful countries. The United Kingdom performs around the average in reading and mathematics and above the average in science among the 34 OECD countries as the table below shows. There was little if any change in these outcomes from 2006. Similarly the United States performs around the average too.

It is also interesting to consider other facets of the report. This reveals that relatively few OECD countries spend more per student than the United Kingdom and United States. The data links to the McKinsey conclusions that both the United Kingdom and United States are 'good' systems in terms of their classification. This raises the question for politicians and educationalists of what the systems that are outperforming them are doing, and is what they are doing replicable? It also provides a useful benchmark against which to judge progress. The results also provoked controversy and debate as for the United Kingdom there was a significant decline in their ranking when compared with the 2000 table when the United Kingdom was in the top ten. This inevitably raised the question of whether there had been a decline in outcomes over that period and as to whether there had been a dramatic decline in outcomes in the United Kingdom and United States between 2000 and 2009? This is clearly unlikely to be the case and closer evaluation suggests that while both systems are still improving they are not improving at as fast a rate as the best-performing systems. A research paper[9] by John Jerrin of the Institute of Education in London (IOE) sought to compare PISA and TIMSS and focus on England's outcomes. Results suggest that England's drop in the PISA international ranking is not replicated in TIMSS, and he views that this contrast may well be due to data limitations in both surveys. Consequently, he argues that the current coalition government should not base educational policies on the assumption that the performance of England's secondary school pupils has declined (relative to that of its international competitors) over the past decade. He shows how different surveys can produce markedly different results.

Differences between PISA and TIMSS

Whereas TIMSS focuses on children's ability to meet an internationally agreed curriculum, PISA examines functional ability – how well young people can use the skills in 'real-life' situations.

The major issue is that the total number of countries in PISA has, however, risen from 43 in 2000 to 65 in 2009 (a large number of non-OECD members have been added). The implication of this is that one of the reasons England has 'plummeted' down the international rankings is because more countries are now included. In Jerrin's view it is easier to come tenth in a league of 43 than it is in a league of 65. The TIMSS eigth-grade study has been conducted four times (1995, 1999, 2003 and 2007) with mathematics and science but not reading skills examined, using approximately the same number of questions. However, in contrast with PISA, not all of the OECD countries take part.

Inevitably what are intended as politically neutral evaluations can become highly political and as ever with use of data the devil can lie in the detail, as does the most useful information. The current coalition government in England opened the 2010 Schools White Paper by stating that:

> The truth is, at the moment we are standing still while others race past. In the most recent OECD PISA survey in 2006 we fell from 4th in the world in the 2000 survey to 14th in science, 7th to 17th in literacy, and 8th to 24th in mathematics.

Jerrin argues that PISA and TIMSS (where England has not seen such a decline in outcomes) are problematic for studying change in average test performance in England over time and sweeping statements are in his view based upon flawed interpretations of the underlying data. He argues that England's movement in the international achievement league tables neither supports nor refutes policymakers' calls for change. He also illustrates in Figure 10.1 the unusual lack of correlation between the PISA and TIMMS scores compared with other countries which, at the very least, suggest the need for caution.

This need for caution was also expressed by Andrew Dilnott, Chair of The UK Statistics Authority, who commented 'those commenting on data in this area should take particular care to avoid making comparisons which could be interpreted as statistically problematic'.[10] He argues that conclusions should not be based on PISA alone, and that other evidence (including TIMMS) contradicts the findings of the PISA study and therefore it may be difficult to treat an apparent decline in secondary school pupils' performance as 'a statistically robust result'.[11]

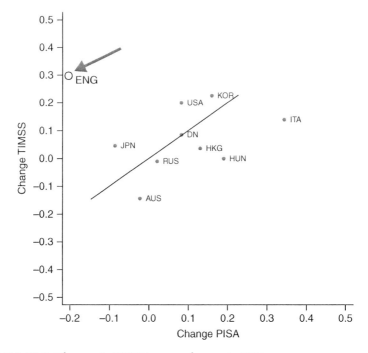

FIGURE 10.1 *Changes in TIMSS versus changes in PISA*

This likely inaccuracy of overly-critical judgements on the performance of the English system was further compounded in a recent study published by Pearson[12] where the rankings and weightings prepared by the Economist Intelligence Unit created a composite of all the recent international tests which went further to state England was sixth after Finland, South Korea, Hong Kong, Japan and Singapore. England was top of the above average group including New Zealand, Canada and Ireland and ahead of the average group including the United States, Germany and France. Sir Michael Barber, Pearson's chief education adviser commented that this was 'the start of something significant – providing a practical resource for policy makers wanting to learn from other countries'.

What does this all mean for those involved in school improvement?

So what does this all mean for those involved in school improvement? It certainly does not suggest we should ignore the data whether it is from schools, systems or international studies, rather we should make good and informed use of it, to test hypotheses, to challenge where we are relative to others, reflect on and where appropriate learn from and apply what others are doing. There is a broad consensus about the best and how quickly they are moving forward. So, most of all the best use of the data is to help schools and systems improve by learning from each other. Above all it is important to avoiding simplistic judgements or using limited data sets to justify actions which could of course make things worse rather than better. To me the overall conclusion is: use data for what it is good at, recognize its limitations and do not use it in isolation. Jim Collins captured this well in his comment

> All indicators are flawed, whether qualitative or quantitative. Test scores are flawed, mammograms are flawed, crime data are flawed, customer service data are flawed, patient outcome data are flawed. What matters is not finding the perfect indicators, but settling on a consistent and intelligent method of assessing your output results and then tracking your trajectory with rigour.[13]

At a system level governments quite rightly identify what they want from the school system and data on these outcomes is probably the most effective way to judge success. It is a cost-effective way of dealing with the requirements of governments for accountability. It is for the government to decide and gain a consensus on what it seeks to judge its schools by. However, in my view it is both useful and important to separate its accountability 'post mortem' role from school improvement which is about supporting improvement and tracking progress. Clearly global measures will increasingly grow in importance. However, far more work needs to be done on how far what is currently taught and when it is taught is aligned with these international assessments. No one would practice for an important football game by playing a different sport or the same game on a different set of rules. It is also unfair to both students and teachers if they are to be judged by these measures but are not trained to understand what they are and what they are testing.

At a school and system level there is room for a more honest analysis of what is and is not possible. There is a tendency to set unrealistic goals based on the performance of a small number of outliers that are probably impossible to achieve. All this leads to is disappointment. While it is an important goal for society that every child achieves, every child is not the same, nor do they have the same skills, interests and aptitudes. Further, while as societies we see Contextual Value Added measures as a much fairer way of judging progress, they are complex and they risk under-expectation of underperforming groups. That is why I personally have long preferred more simple progress–based, value-added measures that have the same expectations of those with similar prior attainment. Contextual information is best used to track performance of specific groups, look where they are being more or less successful rather than to target outcomes.

At a school and classroom level good data really does allow a teacher to know every student and their potential and to benchmark against similar students within the school and wider system. Good use of data can play a role in predicting future performance too.

At a system level the old saying 'societies measure what they value and value what they measure' does raise the concern that we measure and value too limited a range of indicators at present. For example, in England a measure at age 16, which records average performance at what is no longer the school-leaving age has undue importance, whereas measures for the subsequent years including destinations information is tracked with far less vigour and consequently has far less focus and impact.

The need to integrate performance data with research

However while performance data gives us the equivalent of a post-mortem as well as hypotheses to test, data derived from research allows us to learn from and apply improvement strategies that are known to have impact. Earlier in my career I had the privilege of developing and leading a major government-funded raising achievement programme that involved 700 secondary schools, as described in Chapter 2. From the beginning we were informed by research involved leading academics including Professor David Hargreaves whose thinking, writing[14] and practical involvement informed our approach to network development and Professor David Jesson[15] who developed what is perhaps the most simple to understand and effective value-added analysis. We also commissioned Professors Andrew Hargreaves and Dennis Shirley and a team from Boston College to evaluate the first two years of the programme and to inform its future development.[16] Much of the strength and depth of that work and its ongoing significance was informed by their research.

> Fostering and embedding better use of data and research at a leadership and classroom level is the key lever to help both an individual school and our system become truly world-class.

In my view fostering and embedding better use of data and research at a leadership and classroom level is the key lever to help both an individual school and our system become truly world-class. It is a 'both and' not an 'either or'. Performance data offers a post-mortem and if used well enables us to project forward. Academic research and analysis of what works in practice enables us to really understand and reflect on what will help us to improve. As we move and take to scale what I call 'school-led system leadership' through the Teaching Schools initiative and the delivery of all the National College's programmes this becomes all the more important. I was delighted recently when visiting one school on another matter to see both an engagement with the impact on student outcomes and a commitment to use of research truly embedded in the end-of-course celebration of the school cluster-led Middle Leadership Development Programme. It bodes well for the future. There is one final example I will use to argue the case for better use of research and data, John Hattie's impressive work *Visible Learning*.[17] He has analysed and reflected on some 800 meta-analyses relating to achievement. He concluded that virtually all initiatives make a difference but many make little more difference than would be made anyway if nothing had changed. What matters is to better know and understand the things that make more difference. As previously remarked, teachers instinctively know what is working in their classroom but knowing why and how to make it better and/or take it to scale strengthens it, validates it and offers the opportunity for wider impact. It also motivates us, professionalizes what we do and helps us improve. This is what being world-class involves; the power to make a real difference is in our own hands and it is what teachers in the very best systems are doing already.

Notes

1 Hargreaves and Shirley 2009.

2 Caldwell 15.

3 RATL – the government funded programme that supported 700 schools between 2004 and 2008.

4 Collins 2005, 8.

5 Hargreaves and Shirley 2009, 31.

6 RTT Race to the Top the US Federal Funding programme.

7 Hargreaves and Shirley 2009, 41.

8 TIMMS – http://nces.ed.gov/timss/ – TIMMS data has been collected in 1995, 1999, 2003, and 2007 and involved 60 countries in the latest analysis in 2011.

9 John Jerrim, 'England's plummeting PISA test scores between 2000 and 2009: Is the performance of our secondary school pupils really in relative decline?' Dept of Quantitative Social Science DoQSS Working Paper No. 11–09 London: IOE, December 2011.

10 Dilnott 2012.

11 Dilnott 2012.

12 http://thelearningcurve.pearson.com

13 Collins 2005.

14　Hargreaves.

15　Jesson.

16　The Long and the Short of School Improvement quoted in *The Fourth Way* Hargreaves and Shirley 2009.

17　Hattie.

References and further reading

Caldwell, B., *Re-Imagining Educational Leadership*, (London: Sage, 2006) 15.

Collins, J., *Good to Great in the Social Sectors* (UK: Random House, 2006), 8.

Dilnott, A., 'Chair Of the UK Statistics Authority', November 2012, London.

Hargreaves, A. and Shirley, D., *The Fourth Way* (USA: Corwin, 2009).

Hattie, J., *Visible Learning for Teachers* (London and New York: Routledge, Taylor and Francis group, 2009).

11

Exploring and Defining the Evolving Roles of the Middle Tier in a School Led System

Jonathan Crossley-Holland with a case study by David Carter

Introduction

The 2010 McKinsey report[1] stressed *the critical role that the mediating layer* plays between school delivery and the centre. They identified four types of mediating layers among their 20 improving systems: a geographic mediating layer, school clusters, subject-based mediating layers and level-based mediating layers.[2] This becomes an interesting area in an autonomous system like that in England. This chapter, through a study of five locality areas explores examples of evolving and emerging mediating tiers and the ever more significant role of schools in providing support for other schools.

One thing is clear: this demonstrates a very different way from the conventional local government, state, district or jurisdiction-led systems that represent the most common way of managing individual state schools internationally. One other way and form of mediating tier in England are the Academy chains of schools similar to US charter groups. These are hard federations with formal governance and control mechanisms. It is interesting that a number of these are led by successful headteachers one of whom, David Carter, the leader of the Cabot Learning Federation (CLF), a chain of ten of schools in the South west of England, provides a case study in this chapter. The major work on analysing these chains by Robert Hill[3] cites two key characteristics of chains as having:

- clear vision and values which capture and describe the central driving educational ethos of the chain; describing how it sees the mission going beyond the boundaries of an individual institution

- a distinct teaching and learning model: which he sees as the crucial defining feature that makes a school chain a chain, and distinguishes it from other groups of schools that are working together in addition to shared governance.

They often exhibit many of the characteristics of the successful networks including a way of doing things. He views the harder, more formalized nature of chains are at present the most effective form of networks. To date the most successful chains tend to be relatively small and geographically focused. They also provide many of the services that would have traditionally been provided by local authorities for their schools. The years ahead will see significant growth in some chains and it will be interesting to track their effectiveness as they go to scale, especially as they will be operating in what is an increasingly demanding accountability environment. Of great interest too is how well those schools in chains that have improved will sustain their improvement and whether the same models that have enabled them to show initial gains will still apply as they seek to move all the formerly failing schools in their chain from good to great.

There is another way – a study of the response of five local authorities areas in England

Of course not all schools will become part of academy chains and this chapter focuses on how some innovative Local Authorities (LAs) working in partnership with schools in their locality are responding to this school-led agenda. Further, it will explore the lessons that are emerging about how they need to be led and managed. These lessons have wider national and international relevance. The networks that are emerging in these contexts are often more lateral and sometimes less formal. They are of two broad kinds; *base or core* networks which are the focus for day-to-day school-to-school support, and *strategic networks* which provide equally crucial wider linkages and support. Typically, schools see the need for both kinds and are often members of three or four networks. Some of them take on aspects of the role of a traditional 'Middle or Mediating Tier' – interpreting and delivering government initiatives and ensuring they are integrated in local or national arrangements for the benefit of schools – although their focus is supporting bottom-up initiatives and making links across schools, rather than looking up. They are much more than simple mechanisms for enabling central directives to be disseminated. This chapter draws on recent action research undertaken with National Foundation for Educational Research (NFER)[4] in five English LAs-*Hertfordshire*, *Wigan*, *Southend*, *Brighton and Hove* and *York*. They were chosen because they are advanced in their thinking about how to support inter-school partnerships and, even in these difficult times, they had the ambition to reflect on their practice with others and push forward.

The key message of this chapter is that there is excellent practice to be learnt from, especially from the growing expertise in school-to-school support underpinned by school and stakeholder networks. Further, that this can be much more cost effective than traditional school improvement but requires LAs in England, districts or jurisdictions and other system shapers to be prepared to lead in a different way and adopt radically different models. More than ever, long-term success will require this emerging system to look beyond the requirements of a top-down standards compliance agenda. Finally, there is a need for a particular style of effective leadership at all levels and emerging lessons to understand, explore and apply if the enthusiasm for the potential shown in the initial success of school-to-school support can be embedded and sustained.

Working in 'messy' or diverse systems

The system in England is indeed a very 'messy' or diverse one at the moment and many schools interviewed in the five case study areas were exercised as to where school improvement support was going to come from in the future. Those who like simple comprehensive one-size-fits-all models will not feel comfortable in this sort of system. While there are clear and obvious disadvantages there are significant advantages too. The positive side of the 'messy' picture, which was very apparent in the areas researched, was that LAs are adapting to their new roles and are seeking to develop a school-enabled system which is inclusive of all schools. There was evidence that Teaching School Alliances (TSAs) are beginning to find their feet and many entrepreneurial headteachers are revelling in the opportunities that are being provided. This system, 'messy' or otherwise, needs to help schools and networks achieve high standards. One of the key questions for the school and stakeholder networks is what is meant by that. As already explored in an earlier chapter, one of the encouraging things about the current situation is that there is a broad consensus on the *kind of learning children need* to thrive in the twenty-first century, about the *kind of teaching* that will create that learning and very importantly the *kind of conditions* that will enable such teaching to flourish. A key task for leaders is, therefore, to provide the incentives for collaboration, for robust peer to peer support and to embed systems that are necessary so it becomes 'the way we do things around here'.

> The core principles that draw on and build professional capital in schools are the same as those that cultivate and circulate professional capital throughout the system.

Andy Hargreaves and Michael Fullan make the very important point that 'the core principles that draw on and build professional capital in schools are the same as those that cultivate and circulate professional capital throughout the system'.[5] As one primary Head from Southend put it, very succinctly, when his colleagues were searching for reasons why one network was struggling with achieving effective challenge between schools: 'If there is insufficient challenge *within* their schools how do we expect it to happen with other schools?'[6] The interconnectedness of the management of change in the member schools and the network as a whole is sometimes overlooked. Therefore strategies for strengthening school-to-school support need to focus just as much on building capacity *within* individual schools as on what they do together.

In the five case study areas the system leaders and schools were reflecting on their need to develop their vision and strategy. Networks, strategic and core, have not yet, generally, adopted long-term whole systems approaches. LAs that might have been expected to be able to stand back, have become so focused on what the Head of Southend School for Boys called their 'Accident and Emergency Functions', that they have reinforced their focus on short-term strategies to get schools out of trouble and are only now beginning to raise their heads. This limited focus is reflected in the vision and strategies for the Strategic Networks, whether promoted by LAs or by schools. There may have been a loss of confidence that they, with their Heads, can agree on a more comprehensive vision and strategy for teaching and learning. This is a challenge facing school and stakeholder networks in other areas too. In fact these five case study areas are doing more than most to seek to engage with the whole learning agenda with all schools and with a long-term vision and strategy for improving teaching and learning which is comprehensive and leads to sustainable change. Sir Michael Barber's challenge[7] is that you need to and can do both!

Common features of emerging locality networks

Fluidity

The five case study areas have demonstrated that the situation is very fluid. Many of the inter-school networks looked at have only existed in their current form for less than two years. TSAs are a good example: the first ones were set up in July 2011. The networks set up for one purpose can rapidly take on another role as a result of growing confidence and the needs of the system. A number of the Brighton and Hove networks, for example, started life supporting the after-school clubs as part of the extended school programme. In the last 18 months they have taken on teaching and learning functions for their own group of schools and are now looking at offering services for the LA to commission for intervention and to other networks. Wigan's eight consortia, organized to tackle schools causing concern, are now looking at the good to outstanding agenda.

Multiple membership

It is also very clear that leading schools belong to three or four networks, for example, a network-focused on a shared-learning agenda, sometimes across the area, a locally based one, often cross-phase with the family of schools, membership of a local or national strategic partnership network.

Not really a middle tier

The term 'Middle Tier' for these networks is a misnomer, with the implication that the main task of the structures growing up to enable school-to-school support is to look upwards to central government. There are such functions, including helping interpret Department For Education (DFE) policy and seeking to make government initiatives coherent at the local level. They are better seen as structures that are responding to bottom-up initiatives and the need to link across schools. The description *School and Stakeholder Networks* seems more useful.

Types of networks

Core or base networks are the centre of most of the day-to-day school improvement. Three types of these have been identified in the research areas: School Federations or clusters, LA-led networks and TSAs. There were also what can be described as overarching *Strategic Networks* which provide a collective vision and strategy, ensure cohesive provision, the link to the place, can pick up on cross area issues, can engage in brokerage and links with agencies. Critically, they are often seen or have been designed to have a degree of impartiality and, therefore, better able to challenge, although this does not always happen. There are two types of these among our case studies: Strategic Learning Partnerships like York and Brighton and Hove and School-led Partnerships like the Southend Educational Trust and the planned Hertfordshire Learning Trust. Outside our case study areas some local and national academy chains often combine both functions too. The importance of strategic partnerships is seriously undervalued.

What differentiates the networks is their specific purpose and the nature of their governance arrangements. The focus of what follows is on four distinct types of local network: LA-led school-to-school Support Networks, TSAs, School Clusters and Overarching Strategic Partnerships.

LA-led networks

Their purpose is to enable the LA to meet its statutory duties for schools causing concern. In the case study areas these were relatively small numbers, less than 10 per cent of the schools. All the LAs collected data which enabled them to categorize schools. The LAs, increasingly, were commissioning schools to support intervention, using Executive Heads, hard federations and encouraging local Academies or inviting national academy chains to sponsor failing schools. Hertfordshire estimated that 75 per cent of the services to fulfil their statutory role for secondary schools causing concern is commissioned from other schools. The scope of this is becoming increasingly ambitious and innovative, it goes further than tackling schools with old style negative judgements but would embrace schools falling into the new category of 'Requires Improvement'. It was mutually agreed, for example, by the LA and all six Stevenage secondary schools that there was a lack of capacity within the town to drive improvement. The solution was to audit the schools' needs and then match them with secondary schools from other parts of the county that could meet those needs. They included one of the county's six Teaching Schools. The supporting schools are brought together by the LA to learn from each other and identify common themes. One of the things that is striking is the way supporting schools are learning the skills of working in a way that their support is accepted and not seen as something to be resisted. In Hertfordshire they underline how important it is to have a sufficient number of outstanding schools for school-to-school support to work. It is very important that there is as much a focus on increasing the number of outstanding schools, in developing a self-enabling system, to provide what David Hargreaves would call the 'Social Capital' and Andy Hargreaves and Michael Fullan 'The Professional Capital' to support change. The top is as important as the bottom!

The most radical example of developing the capacity of schools to better meet the LA's statutory duties is demonstrated by Wigan LA. It is also a good example of a strategic network co-owned by the LA and Schools. They have in effect adopted a zero-based approach by abandoning their existing provision of support advisers provided by the centre and redeploying resources to school-led clusters. The initiative is in its early days – two years old, but the enthusiasm of the schools – especially the primaries – combined with the improved results are very impressive. A 7 per cent improvement across all levels this year – no secondary school below the new 40 per cent floor targets and only one school in an Office for Standards in Education, Children's Services and Skills (Ofsted) category and on the way to coming out.

Wigan – A radical or 'zero-based' approach

You do have to be confident enough to let go; if you don't, you get found out very quickly as your actions reveal your real intention – you have be confident to do it but be clear about the terms you are letting go – not 1000 flowers bloom or wilt – this is a formal relationship.[8]

With a population of about 300,000 across an area of 77 square miles, Wigan is the largest urban district in Greater Manchester in the northwest of England. The borough is based around the two main towns of Wigan and Leigh, and several smaller towns and villages.

Brief description of approach to school improvement

School-to-school support is the model adopted by Wigan to meet both the statutory LA functions and to enable a self-sustaining school system. A very small, highly valued LA core team of one and a half people (the Head of Service has other responsibilities beyond school improvement) work through eight consortia – five primary and three secondary (note that the phases are treated separately) – who are responsible for the performance of their schools, including delivering interventions. They are held accountable through an Improvement Board, convened by the LA. It is also the body that agrees the school categorization. The focus of the LA team is on monitoring school performance largely based on data: the production of annual school performance profiles based on methods agreed with schools and discussed with them. On this basis schools are categorized to identify low-performing/ underperforming schools which support a school-to-school approach driven through primary and secondary consortia. They also co-ordinate communication across the eight consortia, contract with consortia and provide additional funding to undertake interventions for schools jointly identified as in need and, as a fallback, to provide challenge where a consortium feels unable to do so effectively and can procure someone from an approved list or involve the LA as a last resort. In addition they quality assure the consortia services system, help to broker Academy sponsors/Primary Federations and maintain a directory of good practice.

> The commitment to partnership working is driving the role of the LA which changed the services it still provided to support the model put in place too.

It was not just that the LA has distributed leadership to the clusters; the clusters distribute leadership within themselves too. As one remarked, 'You also don't have to do it all yourself it is about looking for talent both within and across consortia creating almost a shared directory consisting of support from successful schools but also schools that were supported and are now strong and can offer support too.' The primary cluster leads convey a real sense of responsibility not just for their own school but the cluster as a whole. This was observed at a recent meeting in London when the call from Ofsted came – a head rushed back to Wigan, not for her school but for one of her cluster schools! In addition flexibility and evolving systems and processes seem to have generated a model of continuous improvement. The philosophy and approach of one remaining key member of the LA team has played a critical role in the success of the model. She sees the LA's role as providing leadership and redesign of services to provide the infrastructure which enables this radical model to operate. When asked if it would be easier for her if she had more central staff she says no as she focused her time and depends on the school's leaders more. In her words,

> the commitment to partnership working is driving the role of the LA which changed the services it still provided to support the model put in

place too. For example data services investment increased and governor services increased as did intervention monitoring. So a key process was the development of a fit for purpose infrastructure to support partnerships to deliver.[9]

Our independent review of Wigan (2012)[10] conducted with NFER as part of the five areas we studied concluded that the key facets which contributed to the success were:

- Long-term good relationship between the LA and its schools which helped overcome any initial resistance and the subtle underlying question in the words of the DCS, 'Does Wigan want to continue to take responsibility for its own destiny or leave it to chance?'

- Leadership, leadership style, and distribution of leadership and genuine transfer of power, resources and responsibility;

- A clear vision and focus on one specific function rather than all possible functions on the notion you can do anything but never everything;

- Pragmatism rather than idealism – illustrated by initial separation of primary and secondary schools into separate clusters;

- The creation and nature of clusters including the way the cluster leads were chosen based on National Leaders of Education (NLE) type incontestable criteria, creating a cluster lead team through the school improvement boards, transfer of funding, payment of leads and the freedom for the clusters to invest in and undertake wider work with all schools in their clusters;

- A degree of flexibility and adaptability in response to perceived needs – for example, clusters can commission other clusters and go outside Wigan too;

- The size of the LA and profile with relatively few failing schools;

- Clarity over respective roles and responsibilities;

- An inclusive approach in two distinct ways: first, the aim of the clusters to involve and embrace all schools in their cluster and secondly, the LA aim embracing Academies and other emerging structures;

- Philosophy, approach, culture and relationships.

Finally the fact this is an improving system model not just targeted at under-performance but enabling good schools to become outstanding too.

Teaching School Alliances

These are seen as key system leaders along with the nationally designated NLEs, Local leaders of Education (LLEs) and now Subject Leaders of Education (SLEs). Heads of Teaching Schools have to be NLEs. All the case study areas have at least one. Brighton and Hove, Wigan and Southend have one, York two and Hertfordshire four, with two more on the way. They have been given six key roles: Initial Teacher Training (ITT); Supporting School Direct (other schools training teachers); support for succession planning and leadership development; Continuing Professional Development (CPD); Research and Development and school-to-school support (this can include support for intervention in or out of the LA area).They are encouraged to form a TSA with a cluster of local schools which are expected to show improvements from the base line. The initiative is in its very early days – the first 100 were only established in July 2011. A further 120 were added in March 2012 and the aim is to have 500, each with an alliance of up to 40 schools. In the case study areas they varied between 18 and 30. In the light of evidence about the best size for strong school improvement partnerships, which points to about 12 schools being the optimum size, the ambition of 40 may look unrealistic. The Teaching School is intended to work across a wider area for its other functions, for example, ITT. The CPD offer was seen as important. In Brighton and Hove it was seen as an opportunity to meet the need for curriculum leads in core subjects previously available through National Strategy funding. The relationship with the Alliance schools at this stage seemed to be one of providing services in response to need identified by the Teaching School, the LA or by the school in need. This is some way from the kind of deep school improvement partnerships, with embedded evaluation and challenge, outlined by David Hargreaves.[11] What was very noticeable was how all the Teaching Schools encountered spoke of the importance of the partnerships with their LAs; that is, the need for a supporting strategic network at this stage. All the case study areas had worked hard to incorporate the Teaching Schools. At this stage Teaching Schools particularly looked to LAs in these areas:

- To help identify schools' needs;
- To help commission services;
- To underpin sustainability;
- To broker in other services if the Teaching School offer is too limited.

In one LA the TSA's borrowed protocols for school engagement developed for work with Academies as models to use.

What was also apparent was that at this stage of the roll out of the National Teaching Schools' local concerns, such as the evenness of distribution, were not much considered. What was also very evident was the energy and enthusiasm they have released for school-to-school support. They have been given a huge range of tasks, with very little core funding. It is hard to see how they will be able to deliver on all of them without significant additional funding and a better distribution. It may make sense, as one Head suggested, for them to specialize where there are a number of Teaching Schools.

Cluster or consortia networks

These are groupings of schools; they can be cross-phase and include special schools or single phase. Their purpose usually starts with a focus on the challenges of moving teaching and learning from satisfactory to outstanding. In the five case study areas their focus included: exploring the use of single gender maths groups; succession planning; continuity of pedagogy in years 6–7; improving literacy and numeracy; developing information technology (IT) teaching to meet the new requirements. They are not bound by formal governance arrangements. They may be serving the same local area or have come together from a wider area, attracted by a common learning agenda. They typically comprise 5–12 schools. They are the most common form of school-to-school support in terms of the numbers of schools involved. There are many examples of weak and flabby partnerships. Many of the heads interviewed identified as their biggest concern the problem of heads acting as barriers and not wanting their school to engage with others. They are, potentially, able to challenge the idea that school-to-school support only works when it is strongly directed from outside and provided some of the best examples of joint practice development in our research. The indication from the evidence is that they need the right kind of strategic networks, providing the right framework which they have helped to develop, to enable them to do so. It needs to comprise:

- A short and long-term strategy;
- How the school-to-school network can be developed to maturity;
- Quality assurance of inputs and outputs and training.

What was striking in three of the five case study areas that had school-led clusters was that there was far less attention to the 'inputs' than the outcome, even where there was significant funding from the LA or the School-led partnerships; for example, there was not a clear indisputable criteria for appointing cluster leaders, funding to give them time to lead, or process for holding them and the cluster to account. The same tended to apply for the process of choosing teaching support.

Strategic partnerships

These have invariably been set up by LAs in a response to increased school autonomy and the challenge of coordinating the 'messy' world of school improvement. Wigan (see case study on Page 219) and the cities of York and Brighton and Hove have such a partnership and there are many variations of them up and down the country. They are not usually a legal entity. They bring together the key stakeholders in education: Higher Education (HE), Further Education (FE), Voluntary Sector, not just schools, but with schools as represented by Heads and Governors having the majority representation. Their purpose is:

- To provide a collective education vision and strategy for teaching and learning and an accountability framework;

- To provide a forum which embodies the sense of place and provides the opportunity for issues of concern to the whole area to be aired, involving stakeholders and agencies and resources mobilized to tackle them;

- To prevent the schools sector fragmenting and ensure there is effective brokerage and co-ordination of the school improvement system. This can give them a role in advising on potential providers for new schools and plans for managing schools' places and on meeting the needs of vulnerable pupils. Academies and Free Schools are treated as equal partners;

- To demonstrate the LA's acceptance of its changed role from being in charge to supporting;

- To take on limited executive functions of commissioning school interventions and resource allocation.

Education leaders at a national level seriously underplay the importance of this local loyalty as a force for good.

There is no doubt from the five case study areas that many schools are attracted to strategic partnerships where relationships between schools and the LA, or School-led Network, are sound, because it gives them a connection to the wider community to which they and their children belong. This was very apparent both in relatively small, compact urban areas like Wigan, York, Southend and Brighton and Hove, but also in Hertfordshire which is in many ways a very disparate county of small urban areas. There, the competence of the county and the strength of relationships is very evident, not least in the sign up to the new Hertfordshire Learning Trust which will be taking over from September 2013. This is a radical response to the new world. A company, 80 per cent owned by schools and 20 per cent by the LA, will take over all the school improvement tasks, including the LA statutory duties. It will have a turnover of about £15m because of the very healthy position of the LA's Traded Services for Schools. This loyalty to a place, beyond the immediate community the school serves, is a very important dimension of system leaders' sense of moral purpose, as everyone knows who has asked for help in working with another school, especially when there are few resources. Education leaders at a national level seriously underplay the importance of this local loyalty as a force for good and they fail to recognize the LA's role, crucial as it still is and likely to be for a long time, not least for harnessing local commitment to school improvement. The big challenge for Learning Partnerships is that school improvement has become – except for schools causing concern – a bottom-up, dynamic, school-driven process. Schools Networks will be fluid and constantly shifting their focus and will have most of the resources themselves. This means that Learning Partnerships, if they are to remain relevant to schools, will have to be explicit about the value they add. It is very clear from the five case study areas that schools will also expect a vision for the area, will want to ensure there is effective challenge for coasting schools, good commissioning and brokerage of support and that there is a channel to support from outside the area.

York – A strategic partnership serving 68 schools

The York urban area had a population of 137,505. There are 65 LA schools with over 23,000 pupils in the City of York Council area.

Brief description of approach to school improvement

York's Leadership recognized the national direction of travel and wanted to avoid a more autonomous system becoming a more fragmented system. They were also concerned about the potential of progress made in improvement being undermined. However it was stressed that it was not about protecting the status quo but was about responding to the question of whether they were making best use of capacity available in the education community and on where resources were and whether they were best used. Underpinning all this was a strong sense of place and a shared vision. York, following a thorough consultation with schools, set up York Education Partnership (YEP) to provide a collective vision for education in the authority and to respond to the desire among schools for a sector-led approach to running a self-sustaining system. Here the LA adopted quite a different leadership role, distributing leadership through creating an organization that was a guardian of a wider vision and mission for York and its young people. It is in the early days but it is generating a lot of enthusiasm. Schools are in the majority. There is an independent chair, David Cameron, a highly respected former Director of Education from Scotland selected by the schools. FE and HE institutions are also represented. The LA are present but do not have a vote and see themselves as 'the servant' of the YEP. It strengthens coherence and reduces bureaucracy by subsuming the Schools Forum, the 14–19 Partnership and the Admissions Forum. The YEP oversees school-based education policy and commissions all school improvement. It is a whole system approach for all schools including Academies. In the words of the former Director of Adults, Children and Education Peter Dwyer, 'The YEP has opened a genuine agenda between schools around the harder issues'.[12] This raises the question of the potential and value of a separate body that sits alongside the LA. York describes itself as a proactive LA, for example, in their response to Teaching Schools they thought about it as a system with an inclusive approach – every head is involved in the EBOR TA Alliance, which is bigger than the two teaching schools. Key to delivery is the 'Hub' made up of highly regarded LA staff which is responsible for monitoring, school performance, the impact of interventions in school (including Academies where Department for Education agree), providing support for maintained schools below floor targets and those at-risk, allocation of resources to vulnerable schools from the commissioning budget, development of school-to-school support and the deployment of the City of York partners, NLEs, LLEs and SLEs. The role of the Teaching Schools is being accommodated and adds value in this arrangement but the precise processes as to 'how' are still being explored.

> You do it through nudge; you do it through influence, you do it through clear moral purpose and shared vision; that is what we do here.

York is proud of its communication with both schools and chairs of governors. One Head remarked that it feels very much like a family – 'everybody knows everybody and is looking out for each other'. David Cameron talks of,

A real strong sense of 'York-ness' – at the first Headteachers conference in York, at times when Chief Exec or others spoke it was almost affectionate, at times almost poetic. A real pride – echoed throughout the conference. Also there is real tradition in York – from Rowntree/Cadbury culture that is built into their DNA – a sense of social responsibility and philanthropy that's almost built in and finally trust – high level of trust towards LA leadership team.[13]

Peter Dwyer reflected on what he described about adaptive leadership, leadership in a new world – in his words, 'you do it through nudge; you do it through influence, you do it through clear moral purpose and shared vision; that is what we do here'.[14]

Emerging lessons and conclusions on the development of successful networks

The principles that underlie successful networks are the same as for the individual school, as was noted earlier.[15] Therefore, the emerging lessons apply to all of the networks that have been identified in the studies, although the focus of some will be on delivery and others on helping create the conditions to support implementation. As might also be expected they complement David Hargreaves' conclusions[16] about the key requirements for mature partnerships, namely, having a narrative for the vision and strategy which can be evidenced and meet the four criteria: joint practice development, collective moral purpose, high social capital and evaluation and challenge. What has also become clear is a sense of the stages that networks go through as they become more self-enabling. This section indicates what some of these stages are drawing, mainly from the action research in the five case studies. There appear to be six closely intertwined key drivers: Relationship, Purpose, Adoption of a Long-term Strategy, Evaluation and Challenge, Systems and Implementation, and Sustainability as the Figure 11.1 illustrates which can be mapped against David Hargreaves' concept of developing 'Mature Partnerships',[17] underpinned by an approach to leadership or more 'adaptive' style which empowers and engages the wider workforce.

1 Relationships: This is placed first because it is the foundation on which everything else is built and is directly linked to the approach to leadership and leadership style required. It may include modelling being servant leaders and how to lead through influence. It is the key pre-condition. It is clear listening to those both providing and receiving services that the successful approach was one 'we are learning together', as one Hertfordshire primary Deputy working with

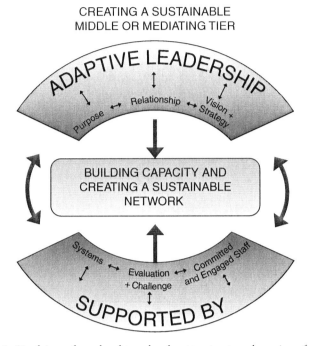

FIGURE 11.1 *Six drivers for school to school support networks - given force by good leadership and engaged staff*
©*Jonathan Crossley-Holland, David Crossley 2013.*

a failing school put it. Another important means of demonstrating this was looking for something good that the schools were doing that could be borrowed. All schools, however weak, have something to offer, it was said. It was clear, too, that with careful modelling by Heads and system leaders, in their own schools, as well as partner ones, underpinned by increasingly effective systems, especially for evaluation, for selection of mentors and coaches and for conducting peer to peer support, that the relationship can support increasingly effective evaluation and challenge. For Strategic Networks the big relationship shift was for the LAs to move from the 'master' to the 'servant relationship', as the LA role in the York Education Partnership was described. It is important for LAs not to think that this supporting role cannot be combined with facilitating leadership and challenge of under-performance. If they, or the School-led Partnership, abandon that, they have no role. In the end they are advocates for children.

2   Purpose – Collective moral purpose and more specific purpose or focus for the network: This moral purpose is defined as giving a commitment to all the children in an area and is widely acknowledged

equally by national and local leaders as absolutely key. What was apparent from all the five case study areas was that the sense of moral purpose was not just about making a difference for all the children but to serving the community in which their children grew up and from which they drew their identity. The big dividing line was between those schools who were prepared to commit resources to supporting other schools, even if not fully funded to do so. The picture was variable on the ground in all the areas.

The Specific Purpose is the reason for which something exists. Clarity about this was crucial for networks as for other organizations. Wigan LA put their success down, in significant part, to sticking to their focus on schools causing concern and not getting involved in other distractions, such as imposing cross-phase consortia on the schools. It was a demonstrable need and the LA could appeal to the view that if we do not sort ourselves out, someone else will. It was a brave place to start because many would have said that school-to-school support was not robust enough to tackle schools causing concern. What was equally clear was that an effective self-improving system, wherever it started, needed to make sure, through the collection of networks that it also paid attention to developing the number of outstanding schools, as well as tackling those causing concern, because outstanding schools were a key source of change capacity; provided, of course, they wanted to contribute to the wider system.

3 Adoption of a long-term strategy – Having a long-term vision and strategy for teaching and learning: All the school and stakeholder networks had a vision and strategy within which to pursue particular programmes, although, often, the focus was the particular programme. This makes a lot of sense as a starting point. The vision and strategy tended to be presented in terms of achieving Key Stage results and 'narrowing the attainment gap'. It seems to have been a consequence of the top-down nature of educational change over the last 20 years that many strategies produced by LAs and partnerships restrict themselves in this way. People talk about the bad effects that compliance can have on schools; LAs have been equally badly affected. One of the most disappointing experiences described was of a visit to a special school for children aged 2–11 with moderate and severe learning difficulties. The school was rated outstanding by Ofsted, yet staff at all levels were feeling semi-paralysed by the fact that they had not yet received details of the early years assessment for the new programme (they were one term into teaching it), by the prospect of a new national curriculum and

by excessive record keeping. The teachers felt that the programme was overly academic for the children and the staff were drained. If this school cannot feel it can adapt the curriculum in the way they felt best for the children, which one will? There is a need to have a long-term vision and strategy for teaching and learning, to build motivation and sustainability of the kind mentioned earlier, which will meet the short-term requirements and much more. This needs to look at the development of the systems to improve individual schools as an integral part of those in partnerships. This clearly, also needs to cover teacher recruitment and induction, leadership and succession planning and how to increase the 'professional capital' by increasing the number of outstanding schools with a collective sense of moral purpose.

4   Evaluation and Challenge: David Hargreaves acknowledges that 'Evaluation and Challenge at every level' has proved the most difficult of his four 'Maturity'[18] criteria to satisfy and often the last to be achieved. In this research it was very patchy, according to interviewees, both from schools and the LAs, in many of the networks in the case study areas. Ironically, Wigan's networks (the eight consortia) which had the most challenging agenda, namely, to take on the LAs statutory responsibilities, had the clearest solution; that is, to embed it in the whole system and provide funding for quality-assured consultants to come in from outside to support the challenge function and, failing that, the LA. Other networks were developing their capability, supported by training. Some were training to be Ofsted Inspectors and others as in Brighton and Hove were receiving School Improvement Partner training. Oddly, given its importance, it was rare to see evaluation and challenge as an explicit objective or a key feature that needed to be carried through all the key drivers, purpose, relationships, leadership, systems, workforce and underpin sustainability. Sometimes, doubts expressed by the LA, of schools ever being able to challenge colleagues effectively, can sound self-serving and a justification for the LAs continued role. It is often quoted that one Head is not going to tell another that it is time to go. However, for most evaluation and challenge purposes a combination of clarity about roles, training, working to embed evaluation, peer to peer support and challenge throughout the school, as many outstanding schools have done, was showing the way forward and increasing confidence. The LA was still seen as a key backstop.

5   Systems and implementation: Establishing the key systems and abandoning ways of doing things that are no longer fit for purpose to

ensure good practice becomes embedded. Systems are the way to ensure that outstanding practice becomes embedded, reducing the need for day-to-day leadership and includes quality-assuring inputs from leadership to teaching and making sure that there is sufficient capacity to engage in support. One of the underrated tasks for school communities is to create room for more important priorities by stopping doing things. This is linked to sustainability. The system has had a long period of receiving additional money to fund anything new. This has been a mixed blessing as schools have tended to be swamped by too many innovations and been able to avoid prioritizing. This has never been more important as resources become much tighter. Abandonment is crucial to creating the necessary capacity to do the important things.

6   Sustainability: This is the sixth driver and depends in part upon embedding the other the five drivers above, operating effectively and ensuring there is adequate capacity. In addition, it requires proper funding either from external sources or those involved in the partnerships themselves – Head after Head was clear about that – and a supportive national environment by reducing the costs of brokerage and commissioning to invest in schools which, in effect, become the new middle level of management as Wigan and Hertfordshire have done.

Conclusion

The national environment is mixed. The principle of school-to-school support is seen by school leaders as the best way of supporting and improving schools. It has succeeded in part because of very generous funding via previous government programmes, the National College and powerful national support. The National College programmes are still there but questions were being raised in all the areas about how far they will be able to meet the gaps in need. Schools fear reductions in their own funding. There is a fear, too, that the accountability requirements, on top of curriculum and assessment changes, will have the effect of causing schools to turn in on themselves.

School-to-school support judged by these five areas is developing strongly, although still in its early days, as the main source of support for an all-schools system. It is most likely to develop rapidly and look very different in England over the next two to three years and result in schools being engaged as never before in a collaborative endeavour to drive improvement. Networks are vital. However, it is worth recording that unless there is effective and appropriate leadership at all levels, we may look back on this period as the high watermark of school-to-school support when it is only just beginning to release the capacity and excitement in schools to collaborate real improvements in children and young people's performance.

Given that local jurisdictions are the key way of managing schools there are clear lessons for other countries and systems to learn from and consider here, seeds of similarity of approach with Finland and Alberta too. In closing, the one thing of most importance is the need for a vision for and focus on teaching and learning.

Case study – Cabot Learning Federation – motivation for change

DAVID CARTER

The Cabot Learning Federation (CLF) is an impressive example of a locality-based academy chain which is currently the sponsor of the ten Academies in Bristol, Weston-super-Mare and Bath in South West England. The chain is responsible and accountable for the education of 5,000 students between the ages of 4 and 19 and for the employment and support of nearly 700 staff. The chain has been led by David Carter, a successful school and system leader. In this reflection piece he describes their motivation, concludes with their vision and ten ways this federated approach is in their view working and benefiting both staff and students. This is a clear example of another taken-to-scale approach to what is a school-led middle tier. It also allows us to reflect on the advantages from his perspective of a hard federation with formal governance and control mechanisms and the similarities and differences between less formal networks we have studied.

> I wanted to find a way to develop a meaningful partnership with other schools to see if through collaboration we could maintain Cabot's profile but help the other schools to become outstanding.

History shows us that the motivations for radical change and development are varied and diverse. The journey of the CLF was no different. The first motivation for change occurred to me when I became Principal of John Cabot City Technology College (CTC) in April 2004. I was immediately struck by the vast number of parents seeking places for their children in year 7. For the 160 available places, it was not unusual for there to be in excess of 900 applications. In the late 1990s and early part of the twenty-first century, the CTC was a good school and performing better than many of the other secondary schools in the city of Bristol. It was this factor allied to the parental perception, not true in every case, that the alternative should they not gain a place at the CTC was a deficit option. For me in my second headship, I wrestled with this as every community and parent within it should have a range of good schools on their doorstep from which they could make an informed choice of the correct one for their son or daughter. This was not the case. I wanted to find a way to develop a meaningful partnership with other schools to see if through collaboration we could maintain Cabot's profile but help the other schools to become outstanding.

> I wanted to understand how I could change the culture of the relationship so that the reception class teacher in one of our partner schools would recognize the contribution that they made to an A-level student's success and the A-level teacher would acknowledge the work of that student's first teacher.

The second motivation concerned the way that our Academies worked with primary schools. The landscape in Bristol had been bleak for secondary but it was not a lot better in primary. I wanted to understand how I could change the culture of the relationship so that the reception class teacher in one of our partner schools would recognize the contribution that they made to an A-level student's success and the A-level teacher would acknowledge the work of that student's first teacher. In 2007 I had no idea how we would do this but since the introduction of primary academies following the 2010 general election and the establishment of the current model of CLF, this became possible.

Growing the federation

The CLF has had two phases to its development. In 2007, John Cabot Academy converted from its status as a CTC to become an academy and in doing so, became the sponsor of Bristol Brunel Academy, the former Speedwell Technology College in East Bristol, and located about a mile from John Cabot. This was an exciting opportunity but one that brought a number of challenges. The CTC and Speedwell had had minimal interaction and the view of staff was that students who would otherwise have attended Speedwell were admitted to the CTC. The labour government had introduced in 2006 a policy that enabled high performing schools to become sponsors of schools in more 'challenging circumstances'. This was the origin of the soft federation that has grown into the model we have today in 2012.

The reasons for the Cabot and Brunel partnership could not be further from the collaborative culture we have now. Understandably it took time to build trust and confidence between the staff but by 2008–9 there were a number of positive interactions that were moving us in the right direction. For me personally, it was a restless period as I worked on the transition from being the leader of one school, a role I had held in two schools since 1997, to that of working as an executive leader. I wanted to keep my contact with staff and students as for me that was the main reason for feeling so passionate about headship and it took time for me to work out the way to do this in my new role.

In September 2009, Bristol Metropolitan College, the former Whitefield Fishponds Community School became an Academy and joined Cabot and Brunel. At the same time, we moved from the soft federation where both Academies had retained their own trust governance arrangements to a hard federation where there was a single governing body with all staff centrally employed by the newly created CLF. It was at this point that we looked again at our governance and sponsor arrangements. Rolls Royce PLC had been the sponsor of the CTC and had retained this when the school moved from CTC status to Academy. In 2009 they agreed to continue to be sponsors but this time of the CLF and not just John Cabot. We had also had a productive relationship with the University of the West of England (UWE) for several years and they agreed to become co-sponsors of the federation with Rolls Royce PLC in 2009.

By September 2011 we had grown by a further two Academies as Wyvern Community School in Weston-super-Mare joined us as Hans Price Academy and Kingsfield School in South Gloucestershire joined us as King's Oak Academy. In September 2012, the family was brought up to date when Culverhay School in Bath became a co-educational Academy and Bath Community Academy was created. The earlier vision described above to take responsibility for the education of young people from the age of 4 years old was completed when our four Primary Academies in East Bristol joined us in September 2012.

Collaboration for outstanding achievement

What follows are the aims of the Federation which the commitments to children, their families, the development of staff and the the benefits and importance of collaboration.

Our Promise is to deliver an outstanding education to every child who attends one of our Academies. To achieve this, every student will be taught by a well-trained and well-supported teacher, in an Academy that is led at every level by an inspirational leader, with parents and carers who are partners in their children's education. As a result, we will create a federated learning community that, through collaboration and partnership, delivers outstanding achievement for all.

Our Belief is that through collaboration we can accelerate our vision of every CLF Academy being judged to be at least 'good' and on the path to 'outstanding' by 2013–14. Students come first, and we judge ourselves on how successful we are in supporting our most vulnerable children as well as those who are gifted and talented. Many of our students are the first in their family to attend University, and by placing learning and leadership at the heart of the federation, we can create a culture of success that supports them as they move into adulthood and employment, while becoming aware of the role they can play in the communities in which they live.

Our Goal is to share the effective practice that is developed by staff in one Academy so that students in another can benefit from federation-wide strategies. We embrace the uniqueness of our schools and the communities they serve. We want our Academies to have their own identities, but in the same way that families recognize the differences between 'siblings' and allow personal growth to take place within the family unit; the federation is the sum of the quality of the parts. It is our collective belief, that our shared abilities to deliver outstanding educational outcomes will make a difference to the communities we serve.

Where are we in November 2012?

The simple answer is we are a long way from where we were in 2007! I believe we have a genuine collaborative culture across our Academies. Seeing our secondary schools improve so that more families are willing to send their children to them and welcoming our primary colleagues have been two hugely satisfying and rewarding outcomes. The impact has to continue, but the final section of our reflection section should hopefully give you a flavour of where our developments have taken us.

Ten indicators that the federated approach is working for us

1   Our Academies are improving! In 2012, Hans Price increased its 5 A*–C with English and Maths from 23 per cent to 45 per cent in one year. King's Oak Academy moved from 32 per cent to 52 per cent. John Cabot Academy has sustained its performance in the mid 70 per cent for the past four years and Brunel and Bristol Met are both consistently above floor targets.

2   Ofsted has visited us regularly! Cabot was judged to be outstanding for the second time in 2009. Bristol Met was judged to be 'good' in June 2012. Brunel and Hans Price were both judged to be making 'good progress'. We are on the way to meeting our goal of all of our Academies being judged to be good or outstanding by 2014.

3   More children want to attend our Academies. Bristol Brunel opened in 2007 with 92 students in year 7. Since 2009, year 7 has been never less than 95 per cent full. Bristol Metropolitan Academy started with 60 students in year 7 in 2009. In September 2012 we had 157 students in roll in year 7. 511 young people are in our CLF Post 16. Our

communities have seen confidence in CLF Academies grow. In total, we now have 5,600 students attending one of our ten academies.

4   We have some brilliant leaders who are creating a sustainable future for the CLF. Two of the Principals in our secondary academies are on their second headship within the federation and we have promoted five colleagues to Vice Principal posts in the CLF and have a talent 'pool' of 35 assistant principals in waiting following an internal process we created in the summer term of 2012.

5   More staff are spending their working week in more than one Academy. The fact that all staff are employed centrally makes this possible. Colleagues wanting to experience a different Academy for professional development reasons or because they have a skillset that we urgently need to impact more widely have the chance to take advantage of this.

6   Our CLF post-16 is built around a collaborative structure where the 500 students access the courses that they want to study across the four Bristol Academy sites. Recruitment has never been higher and results are improving but not as quickly as we would like. For this reason, we are about to submit a bid for a 16–19 Academy Free School that will consolidate the post-16 work under one roof, with one leadership team and one collaborative culture.

7   We have become a Teaching School which is the glue that binds a lot of our work in the CLF together. We have a team of 40 Specialist Leaders in Education who lead and develop our school-to-school support plans. We have launched in partnership with the UWE a new model of school-based ITT and have 28 school direct and Postgraduate Certificate in Education (PGCE) students training in our Academies. In 2012, the CLF was awarded one of the 32 national licenses by the National College for School Leadership so that we are delivering National Professional Qualification for Headship (NPQH) and Senior and Middle Leader training across the South West.

8   Our relationship with our sponsors is a massive strength. Rolls Royce PLC and UWE have been partners in the deepest sense. They lead our governance structures and hold the Academies and the Executive Principal to account in an intelligent way but also ensure that they create opportunities for staff and students to benefit from their discrete areas of expertise. UWE also made me a visiting professor of education, which was a wonderful accolade but one that also cements the partnership.

9   Over the past three years we have developed a high-calibre central team that supports the Academies with financial management, human resource, ICT network management, public relations and project management. This in turn builds capacity for the Academies to focus more than ever on educational outcomes. As a single employer of 800 staff, it is vital that we earn and retain the reputation of being one of the best employers in the South West and this team is helping us to achieve this.

10 We understand better than before how the journey from 4 to 19 unfolds for young people. We have more to do in this area but seeing literacy and English teachers who work with Year 5 to Year 8 students at a recent training event, moderating children's writing to gain a better understanding of transition suggests to me that we are on the right lines.

Notes

1   McKinsey and Company 2010.

2   McKinsey and Company 2010, 82.

3   Robert Hill 2011.

4   NFER with David Crossley and Jonathan Crossley-Holland 2013.

5   Fullan and Hargreaves.

6   Crossley-Holland 2013.

7   Barber M et al. 2012, 45–50.

8   Comment from Nick Hudson, DCS of Wigan until December 2012, in an interview with David Crossley, November 2012.

9   Comment from Kirston Nelson, Head of Education in Wigan until December 2012, in an interview with David Crossley, November 2012.

10 NFER Enabling School Led System Leadership – locality report compiled by David Crossley.

11 Hargreaves 2012.

12 Comment from Peter Dwyer, DCS of York until December 2012, in an interview with David Crossley, November 2012.

13 Comment from David Cameron, Chair of York until December 2012, in an interview with David Crossley, November 2012.

14 Comment from Peter Dwyer, DCS of York until December 2012, in an interview with David Crossley, November 2012.

15 Hargreaves and Fullan 2012, 146.

16 Hargreaves 2012.
17 Hargreaves 2012.
18 Hargreaves 2012.

References and further reading

Barber, M., Rizvi, S., Donnelly, K. and Barber, M., *Oceans of Innovation – The Atlantic, The Pacific, Global Leadership and the Future of Education for IPPR* (London: IPPR, 2012), 45–50.

Crossley-Holland, J., Case Study of the Southend Education Trust (London: NFER, 2013).

Fullan, M. and Hargreaves, A., *Professional Capital* (USA: Teachers College Press, 2012).

Hargreaves, D., 'A Self Improving School System: Towards Maturity', National College for School Leadership (Nottingham: 2012).

Hill, R., *Chain Reactions* (England: National College, 2011).

McKinsey and Company, *How the World's Most Improved Systems Keep Getting Better* (London: McKinsey and Company, 2010).

NFER with Crossley, D. and Crossley-Holland, J., 'Enabling School Driven Systems', Research based on five Case Studies; Wigan, Hertfordshire, York, Brighton and Hove and Southend Educational Trust (Forthcoming, March 2013).

12

Making the Most of the Teachers We Have: A Case Study

Chris Holmwood

I have thought for some time that schools are very much like countries. Countries have their own history. They each have their own language. They build their own customs and traditions. They have their own prominent figures. They have their own annual calendar; they each use their time each day in a different way. Hence each school has its own culture, and it has come as a heart-warming surprise to discover that much of the international research and developing thinking across so many actual countries can be reflected in aspects of the story of an individual school and its journey through cultural change.

Shenley Brook End School opened in September 1997 with 120 pupils aged 12 and eight full-time teachers. It has grown into a large, oversubscribed, secondary school with 1,500 pupils aged 11 to 19. This is a fairly usual process in Milton Keynes, which itself is a new city which started in 1967 and where five large new secondary schools have been opened in the last 15 years. The school became a convertor academy in 2011 and a National Teaching School in 2012. Since it opened, the school has gradually established and sustained an excellent reputation through the high quality of its examination results and the fact that it has twice been rated Outstanding by the Office for Standards in Education (Ofsted). It would be tempting to presume that with a new build and fresh start this was always going to be the case. However, within the relatively short lifetime of the school we reached a point where it became apparent that its vision and culture would need to change if it was going to continue to raise the quality of teaching and learning and to achieve sustainable school improvement. In June 2006 we were inspected by Ofsted and adjudged to be an 'Outstanding' School but rated only as 'Good' for our Teaching and Learning. We took the opportunity to ask the Lead Inspector for some advice, hoping that an informal observation might prove more of a catalyst for improvement than the fairly standardized report we knew we would receive. The advice given proved to be the start of a new journey for the school. It was both simple and profound. The Inspector said, 'It's time to lift the lid on this place'.

It's time to lift the lid on this place.

That phrase truly resonated with us. When we walk along the central area of our school we continually see a huge glass ceiling. We therefore have a very visible, physical lid on the building and one through which we can see. This added to the strength and relevance of the metaphor. To be encouraged in the lifting of the lid and the unleashing of the school's potential was a dynamic moment which provided an overarching clarity of purpose and the language and symbolism with which to move forward.

However, before we could lift the lid on the school in the way we had been advised, there was another kind of lid lifting that had to occur. This meant re-examining our existing culture and discovering what there was within it that had allowed the lid to exist in the first place, as well as understanding what had subsequently kept it there, especially given all of the potential that had existed with the opening of a new school. This made for some uncomfortable but necessary reflection and analysis. I began to see the extent to which as a new school we were very much a child of our time, and how crucial our response to this advice would be in our future development as a young school as we grew into maturity. At that point, Mike Hughes, the educational consultant, became influential in our thinking. In his book *Tweak to Transform* he makes the following observation about pedagogy which seemed to describe what our classroom practice had become, and how it was symptomatic of a wider culture.

In recent years, teachers have faced the twinned pressures of ever increasing accountability and a content-heavy curriculum, with content rather than pedagogy often assuming centre stage. Not surprisingly the emphasis in many classrooms has been on delivering, as opposed to exploring, the curriculum.[1]

We were delivering to children and not enabling them to explore their learning for themselves.

This articulated why we were graded as 'Good' in Teaching and Learning; we were delivering *to* children and not enabling them to explore their learning for themselves. As we lifted the lid in this way, peering into the school's priorities and practices, we had to ask ourselves why that had become the case and to re-examine a wide range of aspects that had combined to create the school's culture.

The logical starting point in this process seemed to be that we consult key members of staff, and this was done at our annual Team Leaders conference. We explored the inspection report with them and shared the advice about 'Lifting the Lid'. We then asked them one simple question; 'What holds us back?' Individuals were asked to write their own responses on a post-it note and come forward to stick it on a flipchart. As people came up one by one an astonishing pattern emerged. Every single person had chosen to commence their response with the word 'Fear'. This had not been talked about at all; the question was 'What holds us back?' not 'What are you afraid of?'

How could we not respond to all this fear?

The post-it notes said; Fear of failing, Fear of falling results, Fear of change, Fear of losing structure, Fear that pupils will not go with it, Fear of getting it wrong, Fear of accountability and Fear of losing control of behaviour. I can only describe this session as having something like the atmosphere of a confessional. And it was a transforming moment in the school's journey. How could we not respond to all this fear? It taught us a lot about the legacy of a particular culture and that if we were to lift the lid there was much to be done to give people the sense of permission and confidence to innovate and to become more creative.

We found a similar theme emerging from discussions with students. We asked our eldest students what they most wished had been different about their education. They said that they wished they had had more choice, more independence, been more challenged and had had more fun. To refer back to Mike Hughes, this seemed to be the language of young people who had been delivered to, and had yearned to explore.

It is worth pointing out at this stage that the school was highly successful on a range of external accountability measures; examination results, league table positions, specialist status applications and Ofsted ratings had all been extremely favourable. As a new school we had focused upon these very criteria in order to secure our reputation. Yet at what price?

> 'Lifting the lid' meant that it was time for our accountability measures to become the by-product of what we did rather than our sole focus.

We seemed to have created a culture of fear among our teachers and had students who felt they were not given the opportunity to fulfil their potential; all while being publicly acknowledged as a highly successful school. This paradox called into question what our own vision of being a highly successful school should be. We felt we had been inadvertently complicit in the wider negative educational culture, driven by our response to the external accountability that we faced. It became clear that if we were genuinely committed to creating deep learning in our school then there would be strategic implications at leadership level that would require a significant change in our own culture within the school. 'Lifting the lid' meant that it was time for our accountability measures to become the by-product of what we did rather than our sole focus. The result of this decision was the creation of a powerfully positive culture which transformed the school.

Teaching and learning improved from good to outstanding in our 2009 Ofsted inspection and we moved to the top 3 per cent of RAISEonline for our value-added data in 2011. The number of students who attain five General Certificate of Secondary Education (GCSEs) at A*–C with English and Maths has steadily risen from 51 per cent to 76 per cent in the last five years. We are also delighted that we have become a highly creative school, where vibrant learning takes place and where our 'staff development culture has been enhanced greatly by a philosophy of building a school of leaders'.[2]

> The problem is that the lid is so very heavy.

It would be foolish to pretend that this transformation has been easy. The problem is that the lid is so very heavy. It has the weight of the entire wider system behind it. However, it is made heavier when a school pulls it down further upon itself, allowing the external accountability culture to pervade its very classrooms and frame its every priority. In order to lift it requires a fundamental realignment of values, the creation of confidence, the desire to change and the focused unleashing of the innovation and creativity of its staff. It requires an understanding that school improvement is essentially about self-improvement, which means that creating a reflective and collaborative culture and commitment to high-quality staff development is key. This in turn requires the courage to accept that in seeking to improve a system we need to understand that this is about growing people, both professionals and students; and that growing successful people is the fundamental purpose of education itself, not just about creating systems that measure them. It requires an acceptance that in focusing upon the importance of teaching we must focus upon the importance of teachers and that this is as much about people as it is about process. If we are to truly bring about sustainable school transformation, then that surely requires developing a culture which makes the utmost of the teachers we have.

> Some schools have chosen to be bold and are proving that you can be innovative and forward looking and still be designated outstanding by Ofsted.

That communicates a little about our school's turning point and something of where we have currently arrived in our journey. I would like to think that we are well described by David Crossley when he writes 'Some schools have chosen to be bold and are proving that you can be innovative and forward looking and still be designated outstanding by Ofsted'.[3] I feel this general explanation fits our situation fairly well, but this description also raises a compelling question; 'How on earth did we end up here?' That despite being bold, innovative and forward looking a school can *still*, *somehow*, *against the odds*, become outstanding?! Schools should be outstanding because they have those very qualities, and the problem lies in the fact that this approach is undertaken too often in spite of the system rather than because of it. This unfortunate contradiction is described by Michael Barber in his thoughts about the education system of the future. He identifies;

> We need to find ways of integrating into it a systemic capacity to innovate. Unfortunately, much of the education reform debate in recent decades has set up whole system reform and innovation in opposition to each other.[4]

Wider implications of our experience

It would therefore be interesting to explore the degree to which our own experience of cultural change could translate more widely and whether or not aspects of our innovations are replicable within the wider system. Our initial response to the mandate to lift the lid in 2006 is appropriately articulated in the phrase 'The inspiring future of school improvement lies in the fear factor giving way to the peer factor'.[5] That was precisely our challenge, and then our journey, and is in essence what so much of the international research is coming to support.

> Middle Leaders told us that the relationship between teachers and pupils had to change.

It was important for us to ask our Middle Leaders what needed to be done in order to remove the fears they had so unanimously expressed. They told us that the relationship between teachers and pupils had to change. They added that there was a growing feeling that we need a common language of learning. This provided an opportunity for the collaborative creation of a language that could truly reflect our values, inform our pedagogy, promote reflective practice and relate to both assessment and target setting. We therefore developed a framework called ASK, which as an acronym relates to the skill of questioning at the heart of both successful learning and teaching, and is designed to support the development of the Attitudes, Skills and Knowledge of a successful learner.

Measuring what we value

Five key attitudes were agreed as standard across the school, with skills and knowledge designed as subject specific. Initially these were used for self-assessment and target setting, but over time have become more embedded; some teams choosing to design their own lesson planning and observation forms around them. These five attitudes have developed to become Curiosity, Creativity, Cooperation, Commitment and Consistency.

Our skills development framework has focused upon Teamwork, Expression, Numeracy, Solving problems, Independence, Literacy and Enquiry – under the acronym TENSILE, a word which means 'to be capable of being stretched' and which has entered the language of the school as an adjective in which students discuss how tensile they have been. It should be said that the driving forces behind these innovations have not been at senior leadership level, which says something about the change in our school's culture from one characterized by fear to one of creativity and collaboration; two words which appear as our aims in our School Improvement Plan.

It is worth pointing out that many other schools can and do use other successful frameworks that introduce a common language of learning such as Opening Minds and Building Learning Power. I have seen both of these in action and admire their values and structures greatly. Yet it seemed important that we created our own language if we were to lift our lid. It was more about the process than about a package, and about transforming the school from the inside out in order to change relationships, create dialogue, encourage collaboration and give confidence in the use of creativity at every level of school improvement. I would argue that if something like ASK were to be replicated more widely it should engage with the values and creativity of the teachers and students in each school, and be a process through which they create their own language of learning.

This is also reflected in the development of our student leadership culture across the school and the introduction of our Leadership Trail and Graduation Certificate in our Sixth Form.

Our journey in developing this area has therefore been undertaken slightly ahead of the more public debate and international focus upon skills and knowledge. Cridland quotes the Organisation for Economic Co-operation and Development (OECD) 2012 strategy report in the Confederation of British Industry (CBI) report;

> Skills have become the global currency of the 21st century. Without proper investment in skills people languish on the margins of society, technological progress does not translate into economic growth, and countries can no longer compete in an increasingly knowledge-based global society.[6]

He goes on to write,

> The CBI would go further than this. We believe the attitudes and aptitudes of the British workforce, underpinned by skills, are the most critical factors in determining the UK's ability to grow the economy and strengthen its society over the years ahead.[7]

In creating our own ASK language of learning and assessment framework we appear to be in tune with these aspirations, and have therefore interestingly sidestepped the current national debate, mainly prompted by the Secretary of State for Education Michael Gove in his approach to examination reform, in which skills and knowledge have become polarized and with a growing emphasis upon knowledge.

There were, however, two other important areas in which establishing a common language of learning was to become significant in transforming the school. These were in the areas of how we encouraged both learners and teachers to reflect upon their practice and how we might challenge and support them to improve; separately and together.

We introduced a Learning to Learn curriculum in year 7 which over time has developed into our wider Lifeskills curriculum. Many schools have adopted this approach; we felt that it would assist us in Lifting the Lid by contributing to a more reflective and creative learning culture. We knew, however, that this had to become more central to the learners' experience as it is not uncommon for learning styles related work to remain on the margins of students' education in schools and not be seen as central. We had been guilty of that ourselves by using an education consultant named Tom Barwood with our year 11 students every year in the run up towards their final exams; and it was he who challenged us to embed this practice from the start and not to use it as some kind of last minute booster. We therefore developed a cross-curricular project called Brainstation in which students were off timetable in teams in which they were challenged to see how well they could use their 'smarts'; terminology used by Jackie Beere.[8] These are described as Word Smart, Picture Smart, Music Smart, Self Smart, People Smart, Number Smart, Body Smart and Nature Smart. The challenges staff have devised include learning to count to 10 in Japanese (Word), learning the Haka (Body), balloon modelling (Picture), encouraging maggots to move towards light (Nature), African Drumming (Music), working as a team to escape a shipwreck (People) and resisting the temptation to eat chocolate in order to gain more later (Self).

This was essentially a multiple intelligences challenge, for which students had prepared by exploring how they prefer to learn and by developing an understanding of how to use their strengths and to develop their weaknesses. This event now involves over 30 teachers in its planning and delivery each year and that in itself has done much to encourage creativity across the staff. After the event students are presented with a 'Smart Card' and have two weeks in which to use it to demonstrate how they have used each of their 'smarts' in both an obvious curriculum area and one that is less obviously associated with that type of 'smart'. The students have to justify to their teachers that they have used them successfully, and this has initiated much creative dialogue and reflection between teachers and students on how they like to learn, how they are transferring their 'smarts' across curriculum areas and how they are developing as learners. The project is underpinned by the phrase, 'It's not how smart you are, but *how* you're smart that counts'. We share this in a presentation to parents which involves them considering their own preferred learning styles and this has increased their support and interest in this approach and also raised the quality of debate about learning at home;

conversations can shift from the usual 'What did you do at school today?' to 'How?' It has therefore promoted an enthusiastic approach to learning early on in students' secondary school career, and engaged them creatively and reflectively with their learning. It has contributed significantly to moving our culture away from delivery and towards exploration and this way of working has done much to ensure our students can no longer say they wish they had had more challenge, choice, independence and enjoyment.

This is also introducing these students to some of those very skills that were earlier described by OECD as 'the global currency of the 21st Century'. Professor Guy Claxton spoke at the Specialist Schools and Academies Trust (SSAT) Conference in Liverpool in December 2012 about the reaction of major nations to the Programme for International Student Assessment (PISA) report and gave examples of how these skills are being debated and agreed upon in countries around the world. He cited Hong Kong's decisions to ensure students learn to communicate, adapt to change, solve problems, analyse, conceptualize, reflect on how to improve, manage oneself and then explained how this approach is more sophisticated as it is essentially about 'cultivating mindsets'.

> It is easier to help teachers act their way into new ways of thinking than think their way into new ways of acting.

Could the Brainstation and links with our ASK framework be replicated more widely? Again I would argue that it is the process of collaboratively creating these experiences and the debate which lies behind them that is instrumental in bringing about a cultural change that enables both the teacher and learner to grow. At the same conference Professor Dylan Wiliam said that 'it is easier to help teachers act their way into new ways of thinking than think their way into new ways of acting'. This is where cultivating an overlap between strategy and implementation becomes powerful. Michael Barber writes in *Oceans of Innovation* of the 'false dichotomies' that exist in educational policy and suggests that they should become 'combinations', citing strategy and implementation as one such present dichotomy but potential combination. He says that 'The key questions are how to create structures and relationships within systems where information and ideas flow in all directions and leaders at all levels rise above the increasingly sterile debates of recent years.' Teachers can be gradually encouraged in taking ownership and shaping the initial strategic ideas with their own creativity. They can then use these in collaboration with the students who then challenge the staff themselves to reflect further upon their practice. In looking at system-wide improvement it is easy to overlook the impact that the synergy between teachers and students can create in achieving sustainable school improvement from inside the classroom and how it can then be spread at scale across a school or even beyond.

The other strategy through which we sought to develop a common language of learning was pedagogy itself, and this was another area through which we moved away from the culture of fear through a peer approach. We initiated Lesson Focus weeks in which teachers across the school trialled new approaches to lesson planning, teaching or evaluation on a common project. Teachers shared this within their teams and the results and feedback were passed on to senior leaders with oversight of staff development who then analysed, collated and shared an overview of what had been learned at teacher, team and school level.

> An external accountability measure was positively met as a by-product of our vision and not as an accountability driven focus in itself.

Sharing the details of all of these projects would be a book in itself so I will give brief examples. The interesting thing about these activities and projects were that they were deliberately 'unOfsted'. They did not relate to delivering to a criteria but were about exploring best practice together. So it is good to share that Ofsted remarked during their inspection of 2009 that 'the quality of debate about pedagogy in this school is quite exceptional'. The report itself stated,

> Teaching and learning are outstanding because the school focuses so strongly and effectively on improving the students' ability to learn. The school encourages creativity and is keen for students and teachers to try out new ideas and make them work. Questioning is excellent and students enjoy being challenged . . . Students are very good at reflecting on the strengths and weaknesses of their own performance.[9]

To return to an earlier theme I would say that this report is a good example of how an external accountability measure was positively met as a by-product of our vision and not as an accountability driven focus in itself. This progress from Good to Outstanding in Teaching and Learning was not made by constant use of the Ofsted framework in school. I believe that this approach can be counter-productive in moving towards outstanding; if teachers are essentially teaching to a prescribed criteria then they will not become the reflective and creative practitioners who encourage the same qualities in their students. They are in danger of becoming the conduit between the external accountability culture and the classroom itself.

In achieving this we started with some imaginative approaches to lesson planning and evaluation that we had learned from elsewhere and then began to refine them and make them work well for us. Often it was less-experienced teachers who were instrumental through their questions, ideas or initiative in shaping and improving these approaches further. Examples of projects include 'Eureka!', originally designed by Kevin Crossley at Edison Learning as a process through which teachers and students simply record the eureka moment; the moment the penny drops or the light comes on; the moment that the learning happens! This resulted in a wonderful dialogue between staff and between staff and students about how this took place; when it occurred; why it occurred, and crucially, how more of such moments could be created. It created reflection about the nature of different subject disciplines and led to small changes in practice such as in Physical Education (PE), where students now discuss a question or solve a problem while getting changed in order to move towards a key learning moment sooner in the lesson.

> One school we have supported with these approaches has seen their Ofsted grading for both Teaching and Learning and their whole school grading rise from 'Inadequate' to 'Good'.

But can these types of approaches be replicated more widely? They already are, inasmuch as these tools exist and are promoted by their creators in schools across the country. Again, it is the process, and not the package, which has had significant impact; not only within our own school but in our work with other schools. It requires the integration of a number of approaches developed with a range of support; multi faceted to meet a complex need and strategically managed so as to feed off each other successfully. One school we have supported with these approaches has seen their Ofsted grading for both Teaching and Learning and their whole school grading rise from 'Inadequate' to 'Good'.

This work has involved 15 of our own teachers in collaboration with the staff from the other school and has in turn increased confidence in the leading of strategic teaching and learning initiatives within the school. We have restructured the school's use of directed time to include meetings for Teaching and Learning Development Groups. Each has two leaders, and the groups are cross-curricular to encourage the spreading of best practice across the school. The groups are Literacy across the curriculum; Numeracy across the curriculum; Developing Independent Learners; Effective Feedback; Creative Information and Communications Technology (ICT); Learning Strategy, Support for Learning – Special Educational Need (SEN); Support for Learning – More Able; Questioning for Deep Learning. The work of the groups is shared through a newsletter and through Learning Conversations which are scheduled throughout the year. In raising the quality of debate about pedagogy the school also invested in 27 staff who undertook a Postgraduate Certificate in Advanced Pedagogical Practice, some who have continued on to complete the full Masters programme. This has introduced action-based research practice across the school, much of which is continuing to underpin the work of these new groups.

Our ambition to lift the lid was unleashing the creativity of our staff and impacting demonstrably upon the culture of the school and the quality of teaching and learning. However, middle leaders had initially expressed their 'fear of falling results' as a potential barrier to school improvement and it was clear that we would require an accountability structure which supports the transition towards more innovative teaching whilst challenging teachers to raise their aspirations for their students attainment. It was important that we ensured lifting the lid on the school also meant raising attainment.

Our own accountability structure

The accountability structure we introduced reflected our new values by focussing with equal emphasis upon the progress made by all students and not just those who happened to directly relate to external measurements upon which the school was judged, such as those students on the GCSE C/D borderline. We developed a system that measures performance by the value that it added and we linked it to the performance management and professional development culture of the school. Every teacher agreed a value added base measurement target as part of their performance management, which was also related to a teaching and learning target and a leadership development target. This moved the school from discussions about individual children and specific grades towards discussions about whether every student is reaching the potential of which we believe they are capable. This was deliberately challenging, and it was strategically important to implement this alongside the work on innovation and creativity and also within a new leadership culture. It was essentially saying that with senior leadership support teachers could use innovative strategies to improve students experience and attainment. As mentioned previously, one of the by-products of this was that the school moved into the top 3 per cent on RAISEonline for our value-added data in 2011.

It was important that this be supported by a move towards a more democratic style of leadership at senior level. We soon began to see the strong connection that had previously existed between top-down management that delivered to staff and the didactic teaching that they then delivered to children. We saw how a more democratic style of leadership resulted in a large increase in facilitative teaching. This encouraged exploration and innovation; not only by teachers but also by their students. This shift occurred through what Hargreaves and Fullan have described as 'effective and empowered collaboration' and creating an aspirational and highly supportive culture which was working towards challenging targets through a shared sense of vision. Our leadership journey as a school moved from having a culture which created dependency to one which was now developing capacity. The transformation from 'done to' into 'done by' was underway.

There is much to tease out from this story which is of relevance to the wider issues and opportunities debated in current educational thinking, and I have tried to do some of this along the way. In conclusion I have three observations that relate our own journey to the wider concepts about system-wide improvement.

The first is about the McKinsey report of 2010 and how it seems to relate well to many aspects of our own journey. 'Systems moving from good to great . . . provide only loose guidelines on teaching and learning processes because peer-led creativity and innovation inside schools becomes the core driver for raising performance at this level.'[10] The professional responsibility with which our teachers have embraced this is a case in point.

The report also chronicles the introduction of a new education body in Singapore; TSLN – 'Thinking Schools, Learning Nation'. This was used from 1997 to change the national school inspection model, 'replacing the previous highly centralized model with a more collaborative one focused on self-assessment and quality assurance'.[11] This is where the accountability system could do more to invigorate rather than to inhibit. The report explains how 'In the final frontier of school improvement, the journey from great to excellent, systems focus on creating an environment that will unleash the creativity and innovation of its educators and other stakeholder groups.' We have been able to achieve that within our own environment, but that was greatly helped by Ofsted's role in encouraging us; not merely assessing us. On the whole, though individual schools may create this environment, the system does not. It will be interesting to see whether the new policy of Teaching Schools, outstanding schools with experience of established innovative practice, can contribute to this transformation of the climate. We are one of them, and that would be my aspiration.

My second observation is that our reflection and indeed our understanding about the components that have created our journey have been much enhanced by becoming more outward-looking as a school. It is this which has enabled us to reflect upon how our recent journey coincides with current educational thinking. The school has opened a Leadership and Training Centre as part of its Teaching School work and has had the opportunity to join various networks through which to share and develop its work. Whole Education have become a key network for us in finding likeminded schools who are keen to share innovative practice and contribute to the changing of the climate of which I wrote; emphasizing the need for young people to experience a holistic education and encouraging each other and sharing best practice in doing so.

It is through Whole Education that I have encountered the 'Fourth Way Framework' from Hargreaves and Shirley, *The Fourth Way*[13]. This framework has a particular emphasis upon 'the things to retain and abandon' in bringing about sustainable school transformation. Our story models this well, if not boldly, when one considers the changes that have occurred before our school has reached its fifteenth year. We have done much to abandon 'autocracy and imposed targets' and have sought to work collaboratively and to challenge ourselves by measuring what we value. This has led to significant resource implications, especially in terms of our large investment in our staff-development culture, and also in the creation of roles which are fairly unique to us. These include an investment in an Extended Leadership Group, the role of a Director of Extended Learning, who coordinates and evaluates the learning that goes on across the school outside of the classroom, and another role which includes responsibility for whole-school, off-timetable, cross-curricular themed days. My own role is an investment by the Governing Body in both further developing our own leadership culture and a commitment to sharing that more widely in support of other schools. Our school's fitness suite has therefore been moved elsewhere in order to create a renovated space which operates well as a professional training environment within a school; a physical embodiment of the abandonment and redeployment characterized by the Fourth Way Framework which supports the strategic one in entirely reframing my previous role for this purpose.

Crossley suggests in *Learn to Transform*[13] that 'the time is right . . .'

- for an innovative approach to school improvement;
- for something that wins hearts and minds and is genuinely inspirational;
- to enable and empower schools to take charge of their transformation agenda;
- to commit to optimizing opportunities for all.

I think it is fair to say that we may not have articulated our journey with this clarity in advance, but that it describes our destination very well. We have perhaps modelled the 'Alternative Inside Out Model' moving from an entire structure built upon the implementation of a 'defined top down policy' to transforming the school from the inside out. No one else was going to lift the lid!

If countries are failing to improve their schools, is it time to allow schools to improve their countries?

It saddens me that much of this has been done despite the system rather than because of it. It frustrates me that outstanding schools earn the freedom to innovate in this way whereas less successful schools are subject to tighter control and accountability which means these successful strategies are less likely to be used where they could have most impact. It excites me that my own school's story reveals many aspects of wider thinking; that our instincts are being articulated with such intelligence by key figures at an international level. So if we are willing to consider an inside-out approach to sustainable school transformation, perhaps it is worth concluding with this question. If countries are failing to improve their schools, is it time to allow schools to improve their countries?

Notes

1 Hughes 2002, 53.
2 Cobbett 2012.
3 Crossley 2012.
4 Barber 2012, 61.
5 Hargreaves and Shirley 2009.
6 CBI 2012.
7 CBI 2012.
8 The Learner's Toolkit 2007.
9 Crown copyright 2009.
10 McKinsey & Company 2010, 26.
11 McKinsey & Company 2010, 60.
12 Hargreaves and Shirley 2009.
13 Crossley and Corbyn 2010, 1.

References and further reading

Barber, M., Oceans of Innovation (London: IPPR, 2012), 61.
Beere, J. The Learner's Toolkit (Camarthen: Crown House Publishing, 2007).
CBI, First Steps; A New Approach to Schools London, 2012. www.cbi.org.uk.
Cobbett, R., Inspiring Business Performance Ltd (2012).

Crossley, D., *Five Approaches that will make our Schools World Class*, SecED, 24 October 2012. www.sec-ed.co.uk.

Crossley, D. and Corbyn, G., *Learn to Transform*, (London: Continuum, 2010).

Hargreaves, A. and Shirley, D., *The Fourth Way. The Inspiring Future of Educational Change* (Thousand Oaks, CA: Corwin, 2009).

Hughes, M., *Tweak to Transform – Improving Teaching: A Practical Handbook for School Leaders* (London: Continuum, 2002), 53.

McKinsey and Company, *How the World's Most Improved School Systems Keep Getting Better* (Mckinsey and Company, 2010).

13

Making Sure Every Person Matters

Alan Yellup

Introductory remarks

Wakefield City High School at the end of the 1995 academic year bore every hallmark of a failing school so along with over 200 leaders of similarly performing schools I was invited to a 'Raising Standards' conference. I vividly recall travelling south to London imbued with optimism at the prospect of listening to colleagues who had successfully overcome significant challenges, similar to mine; discovering new initiatives, and returning armed with a toolkit and repair manual for school improvement. How wrong I was! That day however, was to prove a seminal moment in my career for it provided me with the unshakable conviction 'That there really is another way' to raise standards and improve schools. We were unceremoniously lectured on our individual and collective shortcomings in failing to deliver acceptable standards of attainment – the raw negativity and accompanying demotivating effect of that experience did serve to crystallize in many of us a philosophy, approach and firm conviction diametrically opposed to this *unholy trinity of naming, blaming and shaming* whatever the circumstances as a key driver to raising standards. This I decided would be an approach in which *positivity*, *encouragement*, *sharing of ideas resources and strategies* would be the cornerstones of strong collaborative networks operating under the aegis of 'Raising standards with dignity'. Central to this approach I decided would be that 'Every Person in a school community Matters' (EPM) – I believed it too simplistic to focus solely on 'Every Child Matters' (ECM) not least because it delivered a message that other members of the school community did not matter. So EPM not ECM became one of our mantras.

A number of colleagues present at that event subsequently became key drivers of the Specialist Schools and Academies Trust's hugely influential and successful Raising Achievement and Transforming Learning (RATL) programme. It could therefore be argued the event achieved its objective of serving as a catalyst of raising standards. Standards did indeed rise, but not in the heavy-handed, 'top-down' way the government intended

Wakefield city high school's journey from failing to outstanding

This is the story of Wakefield City High School's challenging journey from being one of England's lowest-performing secondary schools, to becoming judged outstanding by the Office for Standards in Education, Children's Services and Skills (Ofsted) in successive inspections in 2004/5 and 2007 and March 2013, recognized as high-performing by the government and now a National Teaching School. To fully appreciate the magnitude of this achievement it is necessary to have a brief glimpse at the school's context, much of which remains substantially unchanged.

Context

The school is located in the centre of a large council housing estate close to the centre of Wakefield. Formerly the West Riding of Yorkshire's county town and the centre of coal mining, engineering and textile industries all of which have disappeared and been replaced by service and light industries, employing a much smaller percentage of the population. Social deprivation statistics place the school's catchment area among the most deprived areas in England, with 85 per cent of the current 700 students on roll coming from families which are classified as hard-pressed or living within difficult means.[1] Students' low levels of prior attainment on entry to school are compounded further with 30 per cent of students having English as a second language.[2]

Beginning the journey: Staring into an abyss

Notwithstanding the context presenting significant challenges, I inherited a school with the lowest standards of all 18 local authority (LA) secondary schools and among the poorest standards nationally. Staff morale was low:

they felt badly served by my predecessor; confidence in the Senior Leadership team was at a low ebb and was accompanied by equally low expectations for students' achievement and behaviour. Graphically illustrated when asking the deputy heads why there was little display of students' work or information around the school and being informed, 'It's a waste of time putting it up, because the students will rip it down'. At this early stage I was receiving a clear message with respect to their expectations. Would it be a widely held view? These views were widespread and by no means confined to members of staff, but manifested in the attitudes of parents, governors, the local community and not least the LA. A parent rang up on exam results day at the end of my first term and enquired, 'Hello love did our Lucy sit any exams and if so did she pass owt?' The LA though had already given me a foretaste of what to expect. I experienced on my appointment as Headteacher a moment of sheer incredulity, but nevertheless a strong pointer as to their future plans and investment for the school, in the form of words used by the Deputy Chief Education Officer: 'congratulations Alan: well done; a strong and powerful interview – now do three years there and then get yourself a decent school.'

Lack of trust was visible at most levels and certainly not helped by a closed leadership style. I was told in no uncertain terms 'There was no point in putting ideas forward, leaders decide in advance what's going to happen'.

An evening which still haunts me is my first experience of the 'Annual Awards Evening' for its combination of apathy, anomie and absence of customary social graces – attended by fewer than 30 people including a dog tethered to a chair leg and three or four babies who made their presence felt in a number of ways, some distinctly more anti-social than others!

I fixed deep in my psyche three intentions: *first*, things would never again be so bad; *second*, a speedy and decisive positive cultural and ethos shift was critical to underpin any successful and sustainable improvement programme and *third*, not to leave until the school had been transformed.

Life in such multi-ethnic inner-city schools therefore presented a daunting prospect – a cocktail of socio-economic, psychological, educational and material deprivation producing a near perfect state of anomie. A prospect which in today's climate of continuing, unrelenting political emphasis on short-term system achievement, an over-reliance on a narrow range of quantifiable data, leadership styles where it seems emotional intelligence is considered pathological, policed by a pernicious Ofsted inspection system, hardly represents a beckoning call to inner-city headship.

Overcoming challenge and sustaining momentum

If pressed to single out the critical factor in bringing about this remarkable transformation then unequivocally it would be creating a cultural and ethos paradigm shift (Figure 13.1).

I sought to change a school and community culture clouded by anomie, lack of self-belief, trust, confidence, energy, urgency and with low expectations to one in which the very opposite characteristics prevailed. Culture, ethos and leadership lie at the heart of all sustainable school improvement. First-class teachers and able students combined provide no absolute guarantee of maximizing success; however when they operate within a vibrant, positive culture, encouraged and supported by perceptive, emotionally intelligent leadership then their success knows no limits – they become unstoppable.

Our transformational continuum

Our journey along the transformational continuum however followed a classical sigmoid curve pattern and is best described by four distinct phases (see also Table 13.1):

1   Culture and ethos change (1996–7);

2   Overcoming inertia and liberating talent (1997–2006);

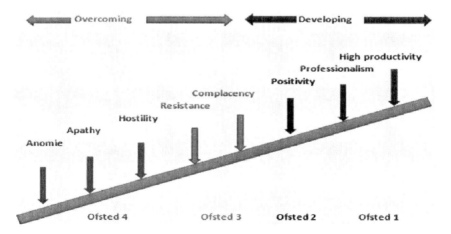

FIGURE 13.1 *The transformational continuum*

TABLE 13.1 Some key data

Measure	1996	2002	2007	2011
5A-C	12%	36%	72%	90%
5A-C inc English and maths	9%	16%	49%	62%
Attendance-students	88%	90%	93%	94%

3 Ordinary people doing extraordinary things (2006–11)

4 Where next and lessons learned (2011 onwards)

Phase 1: Culture and ethos change

This initial phase involved establishing core values, sharing a positive vision of the future, defining clear learning and achievement priorities, building confidence and self-esteem, conducting a frontal assault on negativity, raising expectations and fostering a culture of mutual trust – in short shifting the culture from *can't do to can do.*

Aware people almost always buy-in to leaders first, then into their philosophy, vision and practice I knew winning the hearts and minds of staff and students would be crucial to future success. I avoided an overnight introduction of 'death by a thousand new policies' and any belittling of past standards – an alternative approach to the advocates and devotees of an educational 'Blitzkrieg'. The initial whole-school assembly enabled me to deliver a vision for a school in which everyone worked hard, developed the necessary knowledge skills and attitudes for a successful and happy life, but also played hard and had fun along the way. I am convinced neither staff nor students perform at their best for leaders they do not like or respect. Adversarial approaches prove largely ineffective in the long term with potential limited to some ephemeral short-term gains – hostility, conflict and the passive respect of the coward for the bully are not uncommon side effects.

From the outset I began the process of building confidence and esteem declaring that it was to become a 'staff first' school. They were, I assured them, my most prized asset and would be well supported and provided with a professional working environment. I adopted a high personal profile with students and staff, making myself accessible to all, introducing a concept hitherto alien to the school – humour; seeking out and praising good practice and performance. Staff briefings provided the barometer of staff attitudes and levels of commitment and were changed to highlight and focus on positive information – a ban having been placed on the customary daily diet of negativity which satiated the needs of staffroom 'pedlars of doom and gloom' – those energy sappers who, if offered a blood transfusion would doubtless argue over the shade of red or seek some official rubric.

Humour used judiciously alongside praise sent staff to their teaching commitments with a feeling of well-being rather than harbouring resentment, feeling undervalued or peripheral to the school's leadership. Briefing meetings also served to combat what seemed then and remains today an incessant flow of criticism stemming from the media (not exclusively right wing in orientation), Ofsted and government sources. Members of staff were constantly reminded in those early days to focus on the quality of work they were doing and not to waste precious nervous energy on these often ill-informed views.

Impending Ofsted visits were a frequent source of concern for staff. From the outset it was established that the outcome of any inspection should be a by-product of a continuous improving process, so necessary to deliver a high-quality education entitlement for students coming from some of the most disadvantaged backgrounds and not for the benefits of an inspection team. And certainly not the result of a temporary spell of enhanced planning, more active and engaging teaching and pristine classroom display. Our moral purpose was made clear, in condemning the view expressed by the principal of one nationally recognized school that 'we play to the gallery when Ofsted are in'. Staff confidence was built too by reminding them that few Ofsted Inspectors would cope with the daily challenges they faced. In retrospect those morning briefings, which still continue, were highly influential for raising morale, building confidence and self-belief and instilling the core values of trust and emotionally intelligent professionalism.

Why a staff first policy?

Why espouse a staff first policy? It ran and still runs counter to all accepted wisdom. Endless policies and documents stressed the importance of students: almost it seemed to the expense of any feeling for, or acknowledgement of teachers' professionalism, pride and self-esteem. It continues to puzzle me that the focus remains on the exclusive concept 'every child matters' rather than on an inclusive and higher-level emotionally intelligent concept of 'every person connected with the school and in the community matters'. My rational was based on a belief that teachers held the key to raising students' aspirations and if their morale or their own aspirations and expectations for their students' achievements were low, then both students and the school were effectively shackled in a perpetuating low-performance straightjacket. If *teachers believed* then I was convinced *students achieved* – a point I constantly stressed.

Every person connected with the school and in the community matters.

I also calculated that the self-interested and constraining influence of unions would be weakened by a high-profile 'staff first' policy and approach and help combat the restrictive and inflexible approach to 'one meeting per week', and indeed it did. Meetings continued, with no pressure applied to attend beyond the one hour. But, I did point out that most successful countries operate under a flexible constitution and in so doing reinforced another maxim – we should 'work in order to live and not live for work'. I guaranteed any unnecessary meetings would be cancelled. My view was that if a domestic crisis occurred or they requested attendance at a funeral not designated for paid leave, then staff should be free to deal with the problem or to pay their respects to a close friend without bureaucratic recourse to close scrutiny of pay and conditions of service documents. I stressed that flexibility, based on a high level of trust, would not only provide a higher quality working environment, but improve our performance and effectiveness. But there had to be a buy-in by the staff. Flexibility has to be reciprocal. Within three weeks staff stopped leaving meetings after one hour, particularly when they realized decisions would sometimes be made in their absence.

What are the prospects of attracting, recruiting and retaining able and enthusiastic teachers, so necessary to raise the standards of students with very low prior attainment and from the most challenging of backgrounds, if the predominant culture is one of blame, high accountability with an absence of support (emotional or material) or where people feel undervalued and not trusted? In lifting the appearance of social areas out went chipped and tannin stained mugs, threadbare curtains to be replaced by good quality crockery, curtains, carpeting and furniture – small wonder we are sometimes classified as a quasi-profession. Similar changes were made in the classrooms and to the students' social areas to illustrate that they too, were valued and entitled to better facilities and working conditions.

So the shift along the transformation continuum was underway. In addressing the absence of display I suggested we make displays of students' work a prominent feature of corridors and classrooms. If it was damaged it would be replaced until they (the students!) tired of damaging it. I have no recollection of any damage. Not unsurprising really given a noticeable absence of graffiti around school. With regard to lack of trust, whatever I promised, I tried hard to deliver in order to build up confidence between the staff and Senior Management Team (SMT).

Classrooms, previously secret silos, were opened up through walking the school and daily 'drop in visits'. Teachers were informed the prime object for such visits was to search out and share best practice, meet students and discuss their work. If things were going wrong then we would have a conversation to discuss support. I explained that when I became infallible, I would expect the same exacting standards of others – a policy which cut a swathe through the unions' 'classroom exclusion zone' where practice shall be 'neither seen, nor heard', except on those one or two formal occasions for appraisal purposes preceded by atypical attention to planning and preparation presenting a wholly unrealistic view of their current practice. My primary aim was to leave as many classrooms as possible with the students and staff feeling valued or, if necessary, supported in times of difficulty. Praise and rewards were used at every opportunity both with staff and students.

Tense, nervous members of staff do not deliver effective lessons; rarely do they try out new ideas and almost never engage powerfully with students in their learning. It is not surprising that we find very able teachers inaccurately judged by inspectors who intimidate by their very presence in the classroom, armed with the classic hall marks of their trade – the inspectors' clipboard.

The school's public face required drastic changes. The entrance hall was tidied and livened by display; written communications were vetted for tone, tenor and accuracy – we had to present a more professional front. Regular newsletters were sent home and a constant flow of items sent to the local press highlighting any successes. My Personal Assistant (PA) who had taken the art of gatekeeping to new levels was required to open up access and parents were no longer required to wait for an appointment. If an urgent problem or concern arose they were guaranteed immediate access. What I could not guarantee was that parents could turn up impromptu and see exactly who they required, but they would see a member of the school leadership team who would either deal directly with the issue or take the necessary information. This open school approach instantly reduced the opportunity for feelings of anxiety, frustration, anger or mistrust to fester and improved our public image.

Feedback, both verbal and written received from a wide range of stakeholders – staff; students; parents; governors; the LA and the local community – proved extremely positive and provided the firm foundation on which to begin constructing a sustainable programme of improvement.

Phase 2: Overcoming inertia and liberating talent

This phase was characterized by a programme of structural and organizational overhaul only made possible by shifting the school's culture and ethos. This led to a rapid rise in standards – among the top six most improved schools in England – and culminated in becoming the first high school in the Wakefield Local Authority area to achieve an outstanding Ofsted report academic year 2004/5 and gaining Beacon, Leading Edge and specialist maths and computing college status. It was to mark the beginning of our longstanding commitment to school-to-school support.

Leadership development school-wide formed an important part of our agenda. First, a distinction was drawn between leadership (Doing the right things) and management (Doing things right). Second, leadership was pointed up as an all-pervasive presence across the school and not the exclusive preserve of the SMT, a deliberate tactic to encourage initiative and ideas from the whole community to break the stranglehold and monopoly over new ideas and initiatives of the SMT and faculty leaders, and to encourage the winning over and using ideas of a much and often-neglected resource – influential student leaders. The fundamental principles of leadership I asserted are the same, irrespective of rank, with leadership in the classroom critical to improving standards of student learning and well-being. It was also made explicit that successful leadership is based on 'influence' not upon 'power'. Influence being the higher level concept as exemplified by King Charles I, Adolph Hitler and Benito Mussolini who all acquired immense powers, but came to rather sticky ends as their influence waned.

The focus on leadership styles proved instrumental in embedding the changing culture and ethos driving progress along the transformational continuum. Having overcome the anomie apathy, hostility and complacency of the early phase and established positivity as a key feature of our daily work, we began to dig deep into the roots of professionalism which would lead us to high standards. A starting point involved drawing on the wisdom espoused by a rich mixture of philosophers, world leaders and renowned educationalists and forming the link between their principles and our everyday work in school wherever located in the system. Relevant quotations were posted around the building and used to guide us on our mission. Hence reference was made to Newton and his third law of motion 'to every action there is an equal and opposite reaction' as applicable in social science as in natural science. Treat people with respect and you are more likely to receive it back in equal measures. In carrying out classroom observation or when listening to other peoples' opinions, Disraeli's words seemed pertinent, 'how much easier it is to be critical than correct'.

For staff striving in challenging circumstances, while laying solid foundations to future improvement, Winston Churchill provided reassurance 'success is the ability to go from one failure to another with no loss of enthusiasm'. School improvement is not and never will be a simple input-output model with tidy dependent variables, but is bedevilled by independent variables manifesting varying degrees of complexity.

For those seeking tidy solutions with secure assured futures, the American educationist Willard Waller's cautionary reminder was and is still used in school as a guard against another potent enemy of school improvement – complacency. Waller advised us 'education always exists in a state of perilous equilibrium'. Cue EBacc, ABacc, VBacc and a plethora of current reforms.

Two key organizational and structural changes took place early in this phase: dismantling the faculty structure and appointing two Heads of school. The secret garden of an all-male SMT was opened up and extended to infuse new energy and life with the inclusion of two newly designated female 'heads of school' who had been identified as possessing the creative flair, high energy and vision to guide an improvement programme.

The need to dismantle the faculty structure came to light following a brief curriculum discussion with a newly appointed head of technology who privately voiced opposition to an initiative which I had believed to be fully supported by the whole science and technology faculty. I quickly realized that in fact a majority of heads of departments had concerns opposed to the initiative, but nevertheless the head of faculty's view prevailed. I also quickly realized that this was not an isolated case and the modus operandi in other faculties was remarkably similar. The school had in effect been run with power concentrated in a small, remote and inward-looking leadership team who rarely if ever walked the school, led by a deputy head with responsibility for curriculum who proved resistant to change and would often prefix discussions suggesting viable alternatives with the phrase 'if it ain't broke don't mend it' and three faculty leaders (one a senior teacher also doubled as head of faculty) equally inward-looking and reactionary. Heads of department were thus liberated and encouraged to take calculated risks without the fear of failure having been reminded that in reality 'great minds don't think alike, they think differently' and freed from autocratic senior level constraint.

A third organizational structure followed with the formation of a Curriculum Advisory Group (CAG) comprising Heads of Departments and year group leaders, chaired by the Heads of school. A forum had now been established for a much wider staff involvement in curriculum development. By the end of this phase the Senior Management Team had become the Senior Leadership Team and a shadow Extended Senior Leadership Team had been created – an entry into the field of succession planning long before it had become a fashionable concept.

Having laid the foundation stones of a positive achievement culture and ethos, without which the whole superstructure of the school is vulnerable and in danger of collapse, I turned to teaching and learning. The initial focus was on teaching and learning styles. Another key object was to get away from my mother's view of medicine which seems to me to pervade much of education thought and practice at times 'if it doesn't taste nice then it must be doing you good'. I wanted everyone in school to work hard and effectively, but also to enjoy the work and to have fun along the way. Just as Stephen M. R. Covey talks of the speed of trust making businesses more productive[3] then we can justifiably add 'the speed of fun' in making schools better places in which to work, thrive and help deliver results which are better than could ever be imagined.

> The curriculum on close inspection resembled that of 1902 with Latin replaced by Information Technology.

Next, attention turned to curriculum provision. This involved an in-depth scrutiny of formal and informal elements. The curriculum deputy was the main resistor to change and thus the curriculum on close inspection resembled that of 1902 with Latin replaced by Information Technology. Few vocational courses were offered and delivery was by way of eight, 40-minute lessons each day. A number of practical subjects did have double periods of 80 minutes. However eight changes of lessons with no allowance for changeover time meant a loss of 40 minutes each day. In addition pastoral periods of 25 minutes preceded lessons each day with variable quality of tutoring. One day per week for each year group was taken for assembly and these sessions would regularly run into the first lesson thus eroding more teaching and learning time.

Three issues for attention emerged. First, the balance of the curriculum needed to be addressed; second, the structure of the day required changing to reduce the loss of time and third, having seen too many students following optional courses which they had either not chosen or to which they were not suited, the curriculum needed to be student-led and not teacher-led. A complete overhaul saw vocational elements and offsite learning introduced and then an option choice system for elective subjects built around student choice. Unpopular subjects withered on the vine. Standards in English were very low and provoked the whole-school push on literacy by every department, combined with reducing science provision to accommodate an English Enrichment period across the entire Key Stage 3. Sessions would involve spelling practice, grammar, use of mnemonics to recall key facts, reading practice and much more, including the DEAR project (Drop Everything And Read). On given days and times the school bell would herald a period of 20 minutes private reading for staff and students. I felt from the outset that unless our students mastered English they were always prone to achieve nothing other than modest success in any examination which required the ability to read, interpret, convey understanding and demonstrate their skills through externalizing thoughts verbally or in written form. It was interesting to note the improvements in maths results that accompanied the rise in English standards and reading age scores. Standard Assessment Tests (SATs) results were complemented by the introduction of Cognitive Ability Tests (CATs) and Suffolk Reading Age tests administered initially on entry to the school due to an aversion to testing in two main feeder primary schools, but later in Year 6 to inform student grouping.

The innovative aspects to the curriculum at Key Stage 4 were designed by one of the two newly appointed heads of school who eventually designed the Young Fire-fighters Award and had it accredited by Edexcel at A*-G level. Originally designed for middle to lower ability students it now attracts students of all abilities and culminates in a passing-out parade which demonstrates rescues using breathing apparatus from a burning building, use of high pressure hoses to extinguish fires and the use of chemicals to extinguish chemical-based fires – all carried out in the presence of West Yorkshire's Fire Chief.

The structure of the school day changed to five periods of one hour duration. Other additions included: Certificate of Personal Effectiveness (COPE), Award Scheme Development and Accreditation Network (ASDAN), community-based projects, business mentoring, use of inspirational performers such as the 'dreadlock alien', the Aim Higher project which took students from deprived backgrounds into some of England's most prestigious universities as part of a process of demystification and to raise awareness and ambitions, Bumpy-course involving the construction and repair of go-karts as part of an alternative, flexible curriculum offering. The day was divided up 2–2–1 with break at the end of period 2 and lunch at the end of period 4. Thus the bulk of work was carried out in the morning sessions with only one period in the afternoon along with the pastoral period which had been moved from the morning.

The 6Ps

The 6Ps (preparation, planning and presentation prevents poor performance) was constantly reinforced and became a rallying call. Seeking out stimulating material, cultivating a strong culture of powerful starters to inject pace at the beginning of a lesson so as to maximize use of the full one-hour session and whole-class involvement in plenary sessions which teased out exactly what had been learned and understood. New technologies were the subject of a major investment to not only aid such teaching and learning, but to support administration at all levels. Lessons were enhanced through the introduction of smart boards and visualizers in each classroom and the use of software packages and access to the internet in dedicated PC suites. The tracking of student progress, attendance and the production of progress reports was made easier by the purchase of a management information system.

Raising the aspirations of students began by first raising the aspirations that staff had for their students.

Raising the aspirations of students began by first raising the aspirations that staff had for their students. Once this hurdle is cleared then a significant barrier has been removed. Higher expectations lead to more stretching lessons, often accompanied by more engaging teaching and learning opportunities. Comparative data used judiciously and positively showed staff and students what was possible and involved both parties in a shared target-setting process aligned with regular monitoring and evaluation of progress. At no stage was Red/Amber/Green (RAG) rating used following a moment of enlightenment. The school adopted a 'red free zone' early on when RAG rating spread in epidemic proportions fuelled by governments' and LAs and subsequently demotivated students and staff alike in droves. The lesson was learned early in the Maths department where the first tracking sheets of three members of staff led to a Red sea of a different kind – one causing much distress, feelings of inadequacy and indeed humiliation. Deservedly, so I hear, the advocates of tough top-down high accountability cry. Having seen at first hand the distress caused the Head of Maths took a brave decision and decided to erase the red and to focus on the green (representing those students making good progress). He did two things: he found out what was special about this group of students and also looked at how many students were within 4–5 marks of becoming green and produced a new class monitoring sheet – it had a totally different feel and more importantly so did the staff involved. Subsequently the next two tracking sheets produced substantially more patches of green until eventually most students in the class achieved in excess of their targets. Had the red remained with customary accusatorial way of holding-to-account I fear that they would not. The member of staff who cried at the 'red sea' eventually produced the first level 8 Key Stage 3 results and became part of a team which produced Contextual Value Added (CVA) and Value Added (VA) results among the highest in England.

Close liaison with the primary schools was viewed as an important investment for our school, not only protecting the school from the predatory approaches by competitor high schools (seven within a three-mile radius and all located in more attractive middle-class housing areas and not in the middle of the largest council housing estate in the city) but to provide a coordinated programme of support to improve performance in the core subjects so that students arrived with higher levels of prior attainment and were better placed to achieve higher grades at the end of Key Stage 4. With the acquisition of maths and computing specialist college status technology to the value of £30 000 was put into the feeder primary schools by way of trolleys of laptop computers. In addition Information and Communications Technology (ICT) technicians were released to support staff in the use of ICT and leading maths, English and ICT teachers were timetabled to work on a weekly basis with primary colleagues. High school students in Year 7 assisted students in Year 6 with reading programmes and a rota of Year 5 and 6 primary students visited the academy on a weekly basis experiencing a full range of curriculum experiences over a two-year period.

This phase drew to a close with the school achieving CVA scores in the top 1 per cent nationally and attainment rising to national average from the lowest of starting points.

Phase 3: Ordinary people doing extraordinary things

This phase was marked by significantly raised levels of attainment and high value-added measures continuing on a steep upward trajectory with results far above expectations and CVA and VA results for overall performance never outside the top 10 per cent of England's schools with maths rarely outside the top 1 per cent. We gained prestigious awards and statuses and were supporting schools in challenging circumstances nationwide. Following a second outstanding Ofsted inspection in 2007 the school became a fast tracked converter academy at the end of December 2010.

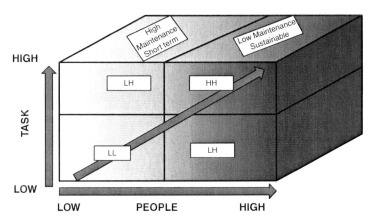

FIGURE 13.2 *Task/people cube*

Raw attainment overtook national averages on most key performance indicators, attainment was better than expected by 50 percentile ranks and progress 93 ranks higher.[4] Evidence therefore that if the culture is right and teachers believe then students can not only achieve, but do so impressively.

The model of leadership we had adopted and coached across the school is shown in Figure 13.2. Although a high emphasis on task, providing those tasks are effective, will bring about improved results irrespective of whether or not the approach is people-centred, sustainable long-term success is a more likely outcome if strongly people-centred. By adopting this approach and combining it with professional development and career advancement a highly skilled workforce, so necessary to raise the standards of students with previous low attainment and motivation, remained at the school and continued to raise standards. People-centred approaches are often confused as synonymous with a 'soft style' of leadership – an erroneous assumption, for it merely points up that what is really important is 'not what you say or do but the way you say or do it'.

'If teachers believe the students will achieve' became and remains an underpinning mantra for the school.

Our leadership of the learning programme constantly reinforced the views of leading educationists. We had to address the fact that the pathology of failure and low standards always accrued to the shortcomings of students and their families, very rarely did it point to staff shortcomings. Comparative data, from sources such as the Fischer Family Trust and Professor David Jesson highlighting significantly better performance, by students in similar schools, however backed Sir John Jones' view that 'if teachers are good enough then students are smart enough'[5] and that they are less likely to work for teachers they do not like or respect. I took this analysis a stage further by positing that members of staff are unlikely to work for leaders they do not like or respect, whatever the level. My conviction that 'if teachers believe the students will achieve' became and remains an underpinning mantra for the school along with an equally firm conviction that standards are rarely raised when students, schools or staff are stripped of their dignity-something at which the Ofsted inspection regime with its current pernicious approach is particularly adept.

A modification of a formula developed by Hopkins (see diagram) was used with senior and middle leaders to reinforce the need to provide a work setting and a work environment which further supports their motivation of teachers. Again the essential feature of teacher motivation was based on a positivistic approach and every opportunity exploited to minimize any disconnect between leaders and their teams – at all levels. 'Top-down' high accountability models, the preferred leadership styles of government and much favoured by organizations such as the National Center for School Leadership (NCSL), may work well in the short term, but are structurally weak in the sustainable long term where staff either burn out or leave.

$$TP = f\{m+a+w.s+e\}$$

Teacher Performance is a function of motivation, ability, the work setting and the ethos.

Staff meetings often held because of tradition and regurgitating information, better circulated electronically and inevitably top-down in orientation were disbanded and replaced by weekly professional development (PD) sessions run by the INSET (PD) committee. Learning communities were formed and developed quickly comprising a rich blend of youth, experience and subject expertise and combined with confidence to innovate and pioneer new methods free from fear of failure and a 'one-size-fits-all' mentality characteristic of those leaders dominated by control theory.

With positive cultural change now firmly embedded and key structural and organizational changes completed, that is, staffing, timing of the school day, curriculum provision, I felt it was time to delve deeper into staffing structures, recruitment, deployment, development and retention and to carry out further organizational structures which would support core subjects, especially maths and English – a farsighted move at a time when many other schools were casting around for and introducing courses which would give a quick yield of five or more level 2 passes. Schools who had rocketed up the league tables on multi-4 level award General National Vocational Qualifications (GNVQ) courses in either science or ICT and permed one from any of the remaining courses to complete their 5+ level 2 percentage passes, suddenly fell below the new floor target of 25 per cent 5+ level 2 passes including English and maths – something we have never done despite the inexorable raising of the bar to the current 40 per cent.

Curriculum enrichment became a permanent feature of our work. Poetry days, for example, were held when staff shared their favourite poems with students during pastoral periods and photographs of staff with their favourite books were mounted and displayed prominently along corridors. At that time the school had few Learning Support Assistants (LSAs) and those that were employed were well-intentioned, but untrained, additional pairs of hands. A visit to the chief executive officer (CEO) of Wakefield delivered the unequivocal message that students of such low ability (among the lowest 125 of secondary schools nationally) combined with all the other disadvantages of inner-city location could not be successfully moved on to higher levels without a low pupil teacher ratio (PTR) and quality teaching and learning support.

The key to raising standards irrespective of the wonderful developments of new technologies nevertheless boils down to the most powerful influence of all – well-supported, able, enthusiastic, dedicated and optimistic teachers. The timetable was collapsed periodically to accommodate English and maths coursework revision days, moderation days and for master classes – in the case of English delivered by the chief examiner of one of the main examination boards. This was supplemented by in-house master classes taken by staff with particular expertise in an aspect of English or maths. The modular approach to examination preparation maintained students' interests and kept them motivated and keen.

Collaboration between departments with respect to student attainment and progress ensured that students confident of securing a higher level pass in one subject but not the other were identified early and able to receive additional support from the LSAs – usually on a 1:1 or small group basis which varied between withdrawal from class, pastoral period, breakfast pre-school session or twilight session at the end of the school day. Eventually few if any students able to achieve higher level passes in English and in maths failed to do so, thus keeping the school well above the floor targets and securing impressive value-added scores and three levels of progress percentages usually in the top few per cent of schools nationally. Eventually the two departments were located next to each other in a separate block now known as the AIME (Achievement In Maths and English) building. The departments which now work in tandem are often referred to as the ' Manglish' department.

In any position of leadership it is prudent to temper 'idealism' with 'realism' and the undue focus on English and maths at a cost to other curriculum areas is such an example. The reality being a schools' future is dependent on staying well above the floor target and thus avoiding intervention by another unholy trinity: the Department for Education (DfE), the LA and Ofsted.

The career structure in school was widened beyond the narrow national frameworks and posts created sometimes with an honorarium attached and on other occasions with a new title, for example, Associate Assistant Headteacher. In the current structure which incorporates an Executive Headteacher post I focus on outreach support work, leading the Teaching School Alliance, Multi-Academy Trust and bespoke support to LAs and schools across the country. I am supported by two Co-Headteachers, who incidentally, were the initial two appointments, heads of upper and lower school, to strengthen the SMT in the dark days of the failing school.

Where recruitment has been difficult in shortage subject areas we have actively sought to grow our own. Maths provides a classic example where two LSAs have become Higher Level Teaching Assistants (HLTAs) and are now studying part-time for degrees to eventually achieve Qualified Teacher Status (QTS). Able Initial Teacher Training (ITT) students have been snapped up following periods of teaching practice whenever practicable to do so and where gender imbalances have occurred a creative approach to appointments has been adopted.

For staff requiring support, a programme of mentoring and coaching was established. Coaches underwent a course of training as part of quality assurance to ensure consistency of coaching across the school. Care was taken that those staff struggling were not paired with outstanding teachers who we felt would only serve to highlight their shortcomings, but rather with those colleagues who consistently produced engaging lessons and had a sound track record for producing good value-added material among their students and classes. As someone confident and predisposed towards the positive use of data to raise standards I led a number of sessions with senior and middle leaders to raise awareness of its huge potential if used constructively to inform planning of lessons, set targets with student involvement, monitor and track progress and to evaluate school, staff, class and individual achievement.

An innovative method for students tracking and plotting was developed in the maths department (Going Green incorporating the use of 'Flight Paths') which was later rolled out across other subject areas. This involved students plotting a straight line graph from their sub-level average point score on point of entry at age 11 to their Fischer Family Trust (FFT) D (top 25 per cent of the cohort of equivalent students nationally) estimate plus one sub-level, for example, 4a to 7c. Following any standardized assessment opportunity students would plot their level of attainment using fine grade descriptors on the graph. Any plot above the line represented achievement above already high expectations and resulted in 'Going Green', the students' names being recorded on publicly displayed 'Going Green charts' and letters sent home to parents. Student motivation was high, so too that of staff who encouraged students to reach or get above the line and it became not uncommon for whole classes to 'Go Green'!

Phase 3 drew to a close, having secured a second successive outstanding Ofsted report, designated among the first National Teaching Schools, granted converter academy and approved academy sponsor status and on the cusp of converting to become a multi-academy trust sponsoring two high schools and two primary schools. The curriculum has broadened to incorporate valuable vocational elements, with attainment and progress high in the core subjects of English, maths, separate sciences and modern languages. In maths, for example, a number of students now sit AS and A level exams as 16 and 24 per cent of students attained A* /A Grades at General Certificate of Secondary Education (GCSE) level – well above the national average.

If teachers believe then students will achieve – we are living proof. We do walk on water! But only when it is frozen!

Phase 4: Where next?

The next stage of our journey is aiming to develop and provide a world-class 'Whole Education' for truly disadvantaged school communities. It will be a difficult journey at a time when the educational landscape is fast changing and the architects of educational policy are, it seems to me, in direct conflict with the concept of a 'Whole Education'. How can a country with such a rich heritage in the arts suddenly marginalize these areas of experience? How can a country which preaches inclusivity marginalize students by declaring some qualifications more worthy and, worse, when they do achieve creditable results immediately question the efficacy of those examinations.

It promises to be a period of significant further expansion of school-to-school support and system leadership melded with an interesting juxtaposition of government-declared 'increased autonomy' and skilfully constructed 'prescription by stealth'. Wakefield City High school continues our journey as Wakefield City Academy, now a multi-academy trust sponsoring primary and secondary schools and leading a powerful regional teaching school alliance. Currently we are developing school-to-school support programmes and professional development programmes for teachers intended to provide world-class practices in our supported schools and alliance with the aim of producing well-educated, well-adjusted students fully equipped with all the skills to adapt and respond to life in the twenty-first century.

Liaison and joint working with our feeder primary schools is now developing further as a pathfinder school for Whole Education (which brings together the best practice and sharing of knowledge from all sectors of education), as the lead school of the Wakefield Regional Teaching School Alliance and the Wakefield City Academies trust. Having been approached by three primary schools seeking training and development for all their staff with a core and bespoke subject training experience, we have responded by providing a programme of coaching and support to primary school teachers, without removing them from their classes. This means children do not lose their class teachers for five or six whole days, staff do not have to exclusively sacrifice their free time, staff do not feel singled out and suffer further dents to their confidence and all staff receive training for five days with no cover costs, which at close to £200 per day would cost in the region of £10,000. Up to 40 teaching staff will initially receive high-quality 'on the job' training and coaching for two full days in school. In addition they will have the use of the latest IRIS Connect lesson observation technology to review their lessons and, if they wish, have a commentary overlay by their coach or an Ofsted inspector acting as an education consultant for our teaching school alliance.

Another exciting current development revolves around our innovative Continuing Professional Development (CPD) initiative developed through our teaching school activity. We have developed two teacher development programmes Going to Outstanding (G2O) and Securing Consistently Outstanding (20/20) which employ a theme-based, bespoke provision for EBacc subjects and are delivered over a five week period in five different school locations by quality assured lead practitioners from across the alliance.

What lessons have we learned?

Ignore culture and ethos at your peril

Positive culture, ethos and leadership lie at the heart of school improvement. No matter what structures are put in place, however able staff and students may be, there is no guarantee a school or academy will become outstanding. It is 'the shared beliefs and priorities which drive the thinking and actions of people within a school community'. The chemistry of social interaction is the influential determinant of a school's performance. How often do we see bright students put down by teachers whose perceived supremacy in the classroom is threatened? Conversely it is not uncommon for able and conscientious teachers to be shunned by able students, because they do not warm to the quality of interpersonal relations operational in the classroom

The critical nature of leadership

Without emotionally intelligent leadership and dogged determination fuelled by perpetual optimism and positivity distributed throughout the school sustainable improvement at the level achieved would not have proved possible. The cultural shift was achieved first by winning the hearts and minds of the staff and students and recognizing that ultimately 'influence' and not 'power' is the higher-level leadership concept. Adopting a high task-high people approach to leadership enabled the introduction of crucial developments without undue delay.

The speed of trust

A culture of trust, co-operation and responsibility lifts everyone in an organization. It lifted our school community from being demoralized to being proud and confident. Constant surveillance and endless interference is incompatible with sustainable improvement and played no part in our improvement journey as witnessed by our lesson observation and drop in visits. Responsibility before intelligent accountability has been one of our operational cornerstones. Trust sometimes brings the risk of being disappointed or let down, but it is still far better in the long run than taking for granted that everyone is incompetent.

Staff first policy

The school staff have proved our most valuable asset. Making them the top priority unlocked the doors to each and every component necessary to effect significant and sustainable change. Remember if teachers are good enough then students are smart enough.

Crucially it emasculated the unions with regard to the constraining and self-interested aspects of their work and enabled development to proceed apace.

Raising expectations

If teachers believe then students will achieve. The key to raising students' aspirations is to first raise the expectations teachers have for their students – a strong message arising from our gender- and ability-based approach to core subject teaching at Key Stage 4. Teachers then in turn will encourage, support and raise the aspirations of students.

Every person matters never simply every child matters

Every person in a school community matters and when they do not it is inevitably the students that are short changed.

Recruitment, development and retention of staff equally important

Retention of able staff is as important as recruitment and often dependent on ethos and culture. Why else would staff remain in an inner-city school, located in a seriously challenging multi-ethnic social environment in buildings more suited to the early part of the twentieth century? A declared staff-first policy which has at its heart an investment in their well-being and future with high quality pastoral support systems and professional development programmes, clear in-house career progression lines, financial incentives, a positive culture and ethos in which coercion and threat dressed up and rationalized as high accountability has absolutely no part to play, but where feelings of trust and being valued are paramount and where calculated risk-taking is positively encouraged. Success in the especially challenging landscape of inner-city schools serving disadvantaged communities often hinges on continuity provided by a stable staff and leadership team.

Target setting and data – always use data constructively not destructively

Data Driven Decision Making is important, but has to draw on more than a narrow student performance quantitative base and embrace qualitative social and relationship data. Short term deadlines with targets based on a narrow range of quantitative data with the prospect of dismissal does not allow for the embedding of sustainable long-term strategies – a point which has been slow to dawn on governments, LAs and especially the current breed of Ofsted inspectors. The key to success is to create the 'buy-in' and momentum which ultimately transforms the beliefs and attitudes within the school community. This normally takes between three to five years. Interestingly at least one year longer than most school leadership teams are given when faced with the task of turning a school around. Beware that targets only in basic subjects can plunge schools into a culture of presentism, short-term solutions and avoidance of long-term efforts to transform. Always use data constructively not destructively; we saw earlier the benefits accruing to our maths department by abandoning the Red from the RAG analysis.

Collaborative working

I still constantly remind staff that 'shared experience is the driver of change in teaching and learning and that "good ideas" come from people working together and learning from each other'. We have yet to support a school in challenging circumstances without bringing back some 'gold nugget' of practice or information useful to our academy. Be outward facing.

Combat the peddlers of doom

Poverty and deprivation can be overcome, we are living proof, but not by fear, coercion, a process of presentism or in the short-term. Confront negativity from government, media and Ofsted sources head on in the staffroom and through using the media to promote your positive messages.

Be optimistic and take risks

Be bold, and be different – 'Great minds don't think alike' they think differently and staff should be encouraged to push out the boundaries of teaching and learning freed from the constraints of fear of failure, to be themselves, to become unstoppable and put the fun back into learning.

In conclusion

It has been a long, sometimes difficult and arduous journey, but immensely satisfying in challenging the myths surrounding educational achievement of inner-city students, the effectiveness of high accountability 'top-down' leadership as a driver of improvement, the efficacy of a narrow focus on what determines outstanding preparation of our students for life in the twenty-first century.

There is another way

A system in which standards are raised with dignity, where the focus is on providing a 'whole education' which is inclusive and everyone matters, where planning for long-term sustainability predominates over a focus on short-term First Aid 'quick fix thinking' and a positive culture and ethos in our schools allows professionalism, trust and innovation to flourish for the benefit of our society.

Notes

1 Wakefield Council 2012, 2.

2 Wakefield Council 2012, 1.

3 Covey 2012, 20.

4 SSAT Educational Outcomes 2011, London.

5 Sir John Jones at a Leadership INSET session for Wakefield City Academy at Oulton Hall, Leeds, July 2011.

References and further reading

Covey, Stephen M. R., *The Speed of Trust* (UK: Simon & Schuster UK Ltd, 2012), 20.

SSAT Educational Outcomes 2011.

Wakefield Council, *Secondary School Profile* (Wakefield City Academy, 2012), 2.

14

Summary: Ten Key Ways Forward

David Crossley

Inspiring and encouraging teachers, aspiring leaders and school leaders to have the confidence to make a difference

The aim of the book was to offer a sustainable and inspiring approach to school change and transformation. It sought to inspire and encourage teachers, aspiring leaders and school leaders to have the confidence to make a difference. For locality and system leaders it sought to encourage them to build a school-led inside-out approach as the most sustainable and energizing means to change.

A once-in-a-generation opportunity to really change the way the education sector is led, works and thinks about itself and its role in society

The book encourages all to embrace the benefits and opportunities of autonomy and seize what many of our contributors illustrated and Dame Pat Collarbone argues is: 'a once in a generation opportunity to really change the way the education sector is led, works and thinks about itself and its role in society.' This we know is challenging, as the previous Second and Third ways that Hargreaves and Shirley describe and the resulting dependency culture have dominated the recent past with a focus on top-down done to initiatives. As we have argued throughout the book the time is right for educators to take a lead: what this involves is the same for the teacher in a classroom and leaders at all levels. If we embrace this opportunity, learn the lessons and build on the strengths of previous ways or approaches to school improvement, we have the potential to create and continue to build the very best opportunities for all the young people in our care.

Embedding and taking innovative practice to scale requires clarity about purpose and outcomes combined with rigour and a focus on implementation

Effective collaboration is the key to becoming world-class and this applies within schools, between schools and at a wider system level too. Embedding and taking-to-scale innovative practice within and between school levels requires clarity of purpose and outcomes combined with rigour and a focus on implementation. It is not about a return to an anything-goes First way. This is as demanding as some of our top-down initiatives but this time, in an inside-out model, the responsibility for it lies with educators and is part of their professional responsibility. At a system level and in a locality this requires a change from conventional command and control models. As David Jackson argues in his chapter on the New York iZone 'creativity requires us to abandon some of the traditional assumptions about schooling and about system relationships'.

The potential of wider community relationships is highlighted in the chapter on the transformation of Nashville and the reflections of Marc Hill from the Chamber of Commerce. They show how a deep partnership between schools and businesses can be a powerful force not only for improving education but for the transformation of the wider community too.

Sustainable transformation and being world-class is not about a one-size-fits-all

Successful sustainable transformation involves an approach to leadership that empowers at all levels, from those involved in system-wide leadership, to schoolwide leadership and team and classroom leadership too. Those who have been successful in sustaining and improving while being innovative and forward-looking focus on the quality of implementation and often use quite simple frameworks to support, embed and take to scale their innovations. Mark Lovatt described the approach at Cramlington Learning Village as involving *piloting the change* with a small group of advocates, learning lessons and *embedding the pilot*, then *taking to scale*. Of course taking to scale is the hardest part of the process. Further, the three simple underpinning principles of the iZone – leadership, empowerment and accountability – apply more generally too. Accountability matters; it need not be punitive and a cause for fear and, as we have shown, there is another way. Accountability can be both supportive and can empower as well as challenging and it is an important part of knowing where we are in relation to others, which in turn allows easy access to the knowledge we need to improve upon. Further, those in leadership who desire a true transformation of the education system must recognize that being world-class is not about a one-size-fits-all. Being world-class means being clear about core principles and the broad brush of design elements but then allowing and encouraging a range of responses. This creates empowerment, ownership and buy-in and is more likely to lead to quality and sustainability.

Ten key ways forward . . .

The diagram below summarizes the key elements underpinning successful sustainable transformation combining leadership that empowers with accountability that empowers.

FIGURE 14.1 *Being World Class involves. . .*

These ten key concluding points arise from the writings and vision of the forward-thinking educators who have informed or contributed directly to this book. The challenge for all of us is how to take their ideas forward to make education, in its widest sense, truly world-class.

Recognize that there is much to inspire us now

The first thing is that there is much to inspire us within our systems now. Interestingly the schools and locality areas that have been included, and there are many more, have been creative while at the same time having met or usually exceeded the accountability demands of their system. Further, part of the reason they have achieved what they have in the conventional ways in which they are judged is because of what they have done. That being said it is interesting to ponder what could be achieved if systems encouraged, enabled and empowered schools to be innovative, creative and forward-looking. An inside-out approach is about schools seizing the agenda as Chris Holmwood remarked earlier, 'If countries are failing to improve their schools, is it time to allow schools to improve their countries?'

Developing plans that move beyond narrow system demands is the most sustainable and motivating way forward for all schools and systems

This leads me to argue that taking risks, exploring where we might be carrying out Research and Development on behalf of the system, is almost a responsibility of our very best schools because it is easier for them to do it. However, this will not narrow the gap – it may well widen it. This is why this moral obligation to the system or locality sits alongside supporting other, less-successful schools and represents a continuum.

Recognize and utilize the fact that there are more good parts of schools than good schools as a key driver for change

There are more good parts of schools than good schools and there are pockets of greatness and great staff in all schools. I hope that what you have read will encourage staff in schools to unleash their creativity and encourage those who are system leaders to build and design their approach to system improvement around this notion. This approach both motivates and validates strengths throughout the system, not just those in our very best schools. I would also argue that looking beyond narrow government targets is a vital component for schools in challenging circumstances too as it enables all schools to move beyond the never-ending hamster wheel of trying to get above floor targets which are usually changed as soon as they reach them. Systems can help enable this sort of approach by designing accountability measures to recognize this and by moving beyond making judgements primarily at a school level.

Encourage innovation, creativity and longer term planning and thinking in all schools by simultaneously responding to the short term and focus on the medium and longer term too

The approach we argue for also encourages a simultaneous plan for both the immediate demands and the longer term. It avoids an undue and, in the end, debilitating focus on presentism. In addition, all the schools and localities we have studied began their innovative development before they became outstanding and it was part of why they are successful. In both New York and Nashville their inspirational and innovative approaches are seen as a lever for change and improvement despite the critical judgement they faced. Wakefield City High began its transformation journey in real adversity too. In schools like Westfield, Cramlington, Shireland and Shenley Brook End it was part of their journey to being judged as outstanding – not something they did when they became outstanding. This process can be aided by systems exploring smarter approaches to accountability that develop and foster professional responsibility and use data constructively rather than destructively.

Embrace technology but make sure it is your servant

Technology can create capacity and enable schools to do new things in new ways. Today's learners need to be digitally fluent but take the advice of Karine George, 'Like building blocks technology has transformed even the simplest of procedures and given a level of independence to our children not evident previously'; Sir Mark Grundy and Kirsty Tonks view it as a great leveller too. Never forget the reasons why we use technology and what it enables – it is not an end in itself. New technologies make a personalized, more customized, school experience possible and therefore are a key catalyst for transformation. Schools also need to deal with students and how they best learn and this links closely to student empowerment and responsibility for learning.

Focus on abandonment and redeployment of existing resources as it is both the most sustainable and most empowering approach to change

All the examples we studied did not simply add to what they did before. They all abandoned things and redeployed resources, including staff. They recognized they could do anything but not everything. They did not just rely on additional resources from governments either. They knew what they wanted to achieve and found ways of realizing their goals. In a time of recession this may appeal to governments and be our only choice but it empowers us and puts the choices where they best belong.

Focus on the quality of implementation

Remember most things fail not due to the quality of the idea but because of the quality of implementation. Focus on and plan for it more as it is especially important when undertaking significant change.

Effective collaboration is the key

As was indicated above, any school can do anything but not everything, so share the load first in day-to-day teaching by finding ways to reduce the isolation of teachers in individual classrooms; move away from the notion of the omni-capable single teachers isolated in a classroom on their own. Enable teachers to work in teams; give time to play to and utilize their different strengths, within teams and within schools, and thereby creating a better division of labour. This also avoids everyone creating their own version of a very similar wheel. Finally, develop effective co-operation between schools by always ensuring that when you collaborate you are clear about expected outcomes. Make sure collaboration results in less rather than more work.

Recognize that it is not easy to change but if you get the culture right anything is possible

Everyone knows and understands the old way of doing things. While change at its best is a combination of a top-down and bottom-up process so too is resistance to change. It is not just politicians and system leaders who can stand in the way of creating a truly world-class system, teachers can be blockers too. Abandonment often involves abandoning the things that give people security and status and can also undermine their confidence. So in the final analysis it is about creating a positive culture that is receptive to change and in which people feel supported and can play their part.

Focus on engagement and buy-in but also on progress

The approach that works best for young people in classrooms, works best for teachers in schools and also works best for systems as a whole. It is all about culture, engagement and buy-in. However a positive culture and engagement are not enough on their own as what is important is whether a student, teacher, school or system is moving forward and making progress.

And finally . . .

An inside-out approach is likely to yield the most for schools and school systems

So it is an inside-out approach that is likely to yield the most for systems, localities, schools and parts of schools too. An inside-out approach is also the most sustainable approach.

An inside-out approach does not rely on external, usually time-limited, resources and can be simply part of how you do things; it also empowers staff too.

However an inside-out needs a different approach to leadership as conventional concentrated executive power is unlikely to make the most of all the talents we have. Leaders need to focus on influence, inclusion, persuasion, coaching and support as well as generating broad buy-in to share goals which they act as the guardian for. So the most important lesson is *trust educators more and build a shared coalition of interest with them.* If the view is taken that it is not the right time to trust educators it never will be the right time; and this in turn dramatically limits system-wide improvement leading to a culture that creates adequacy at best rather than the excellence we all aspire for.

Index